TO: Peter & Heidi:
God Bless You!

Best Wishes,
Jim Shaw
01/20/01

# Jack & Jill
# Why They Kill

## Saving Our Children, Saving Ourselves

§

James E. Shaw, Ph.D.

*Onjinjinkta* **P**ublishing

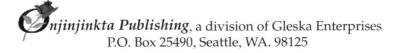*njinjinkta Publishing*, a division of Gleska Enterprises
P.O. Box 25490, Seattle, WA. 98125

Copyright © 2000 by James E. Shaw
Art & Cover design by Tom Eadie
© Onjinjinkta Publishing

ISBN: 1-892714-08-6

First Onjinjinkta Publishing hardcover printing April 2000

Gleska Enterprises.

10   9   8   7   6   5   4   3   2   1

Onjinjinkta is a registered trademark of Onjinjinkta Enterprises

Printed in the U.S.A.

This book is dedicated to all the victims of adolescentcide: children slain in acts of homicide committed by other children. The light of their lives so terribly extinguished, we are a poorer nation bereft of:

the leadership they might have provided;
the cures they might have discovered;
the books and music they might have written;
the poems they might have penned;
the voices they might have raised in song and oratory;
and the love they might have shared.

May they rest in peace, for we, the living, must not. Our work of saving our children has only begun.

# Acknowledgments

The road to the publication of this book was, in my case, a route lined with singularly important persons, each indispensable, all proffering their time and talents, guidance, generous expertise and other forms of support and assistance that were as abundant and well-placed as they were necessary. It was only among such a community of professionals, family, and friends that the countless hours of research and years expended in the writing and re-writing of "Jack and Jill, Why They Kill: Saving Our Children, Saving Ourselves" could have been thinkable or possible. Indeed, it was only because of them that the road to this book, on which I embarked in 1991, became a journey to success.

To these very special persons at Onjinjinkta Publishing: Tom Eadie, thank you for recognizing the urgent social need for this kind of book at this particular time in the nation's history. I very much appreciate your vision and solid support. To Peter Orullian, thank you for your great editorial instincts, your deft guiding hand, and always necessary suggestions. You believed in and championed this book from the start and have lived and breathed it for too long. To Betty J. Eadie, best-selling author and founder of Onjinjinkta Publishing, I thank you so very much for your courageous written works that have changed my life, and for your deep interest in and firm backing of this book.

I owe Carol Mann, president of the Carol Mann Literary Agency, New York, a debt of gratitude for taking the time to repeatedly converse with me, nearly a decade ago, about "adolescentcide," my word for the socially urgent, deadly phenomenon that would later explode into frightening proportions. Her relentless ear listening to my incubating idea to write a book and her oft-repeated advice—"Decide what kind of book you want it to be"—became my ten-word cantusfirmus, the recurrent theme that droned in my head and constantly brought me back to first-floor grounding. Ms. Mann was right: The kind of book it was, determined who would read it. The more I talked to children incarcerated in prison for committing homicide, the more I became persuaded that parents of children at home and not incarcerated, ought to be the readers for whom I should write.

My professors at the Claremont Graduate University were especially helpful, encouraging, and accessible. The members of my dissertation committee took a special interest in the subject of children killing children and supported my desire to enter the state's juvenile prisons and ask children incarcerated for homicide to tell me the stories of their lives. These professors set the compass and charted the course of research so I could successfully navigate it: Professors Mary Poplin, John Regan, Charles Kerchner, Lourdes Arguelles, Philip Dreyer, Doty Hale, Diane Schuster, and Joe Weeres. They were each brilliant, committed, and endowed with luminous wisdom and experience which they shared generously. David Drew and Ethel Rogers, directors of the Center for Educational Studies, I stand in awe of your commitment to educational leadership. Thank you for your unflagging efforts to help me succeed.

I am especially appreciative to Mr. Michael Doyle and the board of directors of the Mt. Baldy Chapter of Phi Delta Kappa for bestowing upon my dissertation the Peter Lincoln Spencer "Dissertation of the Year" award (1997).

To Jack Miles, former literary editor and member of the editorial board at the Los Angeles Times, and director of the Humanities Center at the Claremont Graduate University: Thank you for responding so quickly and making it possible for "Jack and Jill, Why They Kill..." to start getting read by key people, even while it was still only in the two chapters-and-an-outline stage.

The newspaper media have been especially kind to me, working on my behalf to provide me a wide readership for my written pieces. My deepest appreciation to the fine staff of the Los Angeles Times-Washington Post Media Group and, especially, editor Bob Berger. I am also very grateful to Randall Murray, editor of Florida's Boca Raton Times, and Gayden Wren, of the

New York Times Syndicate. They each went beyond the call of duty to familiarize others with my work.

Professor Marcel Soriano, of the California State University at Los Angeles, and Dr. Joseph Dear, of the California Commission for Teacher Credentialing, recognized early on the importance of my research and provided opportunities for me to present my findings at various forums convened to address the issue of adolescent violence in schools. The Commission for Teacher Credentialing saw a need to engage in specialized professional development and credentialing of new teachers for the urban public schools. Misters Soriano and Dear saw, in my research, highly relevant and critically important information to aid the credentialing endeavor.

To Bill Ybarra, Gus Frias, and Ms. Tracy Fried, of the Los Angeles County Office of Education's Safe Schools Center and "Gang Risk Intervention Program" (GRIP): Thank you for enthusiastically endorsing my research and sharing materials, information, and opportunities to collaborate on programs and projects to improve school safety. I was proud and honored to accept the invitation to become an editor of the "Los Angeles County Master Plan For School Safety."

A very special thanks to the California Association of Supervisors of Child Welfare and Attendance (CASCWA) for providing me with various leadership opportunities and for publicizing my research.

My sincerest thanks to Al Martinez, columnist for the Los Angeles Times, who saw my research as vital and wrote a column featuring me.

To the staff at Weller-Grossman, producers of the television program, "Save Our Streets," and especially to the show's narrator, actor Tim Reid ("Sister, Sister"; "Frank's Place"): Thank you for recognizing the importance of my research and filming and featuring me for the segment of "Save Our Streets," which was widely watched and constantly repeated because of viewer demand.

My sincerest thanks to Phil Kauble for his leadership and direction in the complex field of public school law, and to the rest of my colleagues at the Los Angeles County Office of Education, the Norwalk La Mirada Unified School District, the Norwalk Superior Court, the Los Angeles County Superior Court, the Downey Superior Court, and the Los Angeles County Office of the District Attorney.

It would have been impossible to begin, continue and complete my research without the cooperation and assistance of the professional staff at the California Youth Authority (CYA). I am deeply grateful to the following for giving generously of their time, providing me access to the adolescent participants in my survey sample, coordinating and formalizing interview dates and schedules, and ensuring the manageability and success of the entire research study: Mr. Richard Tillson, Deputy Director, Institutions and Camps Branch; Dr. Norman Skonovd, Chief of Research; Dr. Shirley Winter, Research Psychologist; Mr. Wayne Sparr, Automated Systems Division; Mr. James Frazier, former Superintendent (ret.); Ms. Felicia Bracey, former Assistant to the Superintendent; Ms. Dawn Watson, Administrative Assistant; Ms. Vivian Crawford, Assistant Deputy Director; Ms. Elverta Mock, Parole Agent III; Ms. Cynthia Brown, Program Administrator; Mr. Henry McGrath, Parole Agent II; Ms. Robin Hatter, Parole Agent I; Mr. James Grimball, Youth Counselor; Ms. Aurelia Ruvalcaba, Youth Counselor; Ms. Martha Vasquez-Shanahan, Senior Youth Counselor; Mr. Joe Kraics, Licensed Clinical Social Worker; and Ms. Joan Loucraft, Licensed Clinical Social Worker.

My bottomless gratitude and best wishes are extended to the scores of children I interviewed and, especially, the thirteen "voices" that are the connective tissue of this book and whose lives are framed in each chapter. All of them, for years, and of their own volition, adhered punctually to my interview schedules, patiently answering and re answering my questions, and telling me the unpretty stories of their incredible and desperate lives. To: Charity, Jonathan, Ruth, Jerry, Paul, Jeremy, Leonard, Kenny, Bobby, Lorraine, Josie, Pamela, and Marguerite: May you each experience only happiness, live only for peace, achieve your dreams, and share your love. I thank you from the bottom of my heart.

My deep appreciation to Drs. Alice and Sam Bessman, who repeatedly and graciously opened up their home and provided dinner feasts for not only the body but also nourishment for the mind; and to the towering other intellects and writers who gathered at Alice's and Sam's "Bessman Literary Circle" to listen as I read parts of the manuscript long before it became this book: Vilma and Bert Potter, and Dorrie and Wendell Miller. Thank you for your relentless ears, your hardy hearts, and your incisive minds.

Thank you, my friend and pastor, Reverend Dr. O.C. Smith, for your life-saving and life-transforming ministry.

To Sylvia Joycelyn Shaw, my wife and best friend: You are my love, my inspiration, my soul mate. You shared your enthusiasm, caring, understanding, and gave your support in innumerable other ways that lightened the load of writing this book which, because of its subject matter and social urgency, was anything but light. You enabled me to make it to the end of the road and complete this important work when at times I was not sure if I could. Thank you so very much!

And to my sons James Ernest (Jimmy), Lawrence Eli, and Aaron David: Thank you for always reminding me of who and what the real treasures in life are. I love you madly!

# Contents

# Publisher's Note

Our focus at Onjinjinkta Publishing is to publish books that teach and nurture love, respect, and understanding. These three principles are the building blocks for harmony and happiness. I chose to publish this book because the essence of Dr. James Shaw's message is creating and restoring harmony and happiness in the homes of our children.

Dr. Shaw is eminently qualified as both an author and educator to share sound methods for parenting. He has worked as a teacher in high-risk school districts; served as a public school law consultant with the Los Angeles County Office of Education; maintains associate membership status with the American Bar Association and National Council of Juvenile and Family Court Judges; and is the Director of Child Welfare and Attendance at the La Mirada Unified School District in Norwalk. His most striking qualification, I believe, is his desire to serve. That is a credential that cannot be earned at college or through professional career training. It is something that was learned and nurtured as a result of the unwavering love and support he received as a child in his own home.

James is a man of principle and diligence, of concern and caring. His commitment and love for our children is what drives him to work so steadfastly against the rising tide of teenage violence; and it is this same value for life and teaching peace-building and love-nurturing skills that makes *Jack & Jill* a perfect complement to Onjinjinkta's other titles.

I know you will find this book to be an invaluable resource to you as a parent or teacher. The methods and lessons within it are simple, effective, and necessary if we are to rise above the negative emotions of hate and anger, and embrace a more peaceful, loving tomorrow.

—Betty J. Eadie
President,
Onjinjinkta Publishing

# Author's Note

In 1991, I entered the doctorate program in the School of education at the University of Southern California. Alarmed by the rising national trend in juvenile crime, I was convinced that prolonged, rigorous study and training in research would afford me insight into and solutions for what I believed was a rapidly growing social cancer: Kids killing kids. The nation's juvenile courts were doing a standing-room-only business that year. Figures released by the National Center for Juvenile Justice showed that in the country's 75 largest counties, 370,424 juvenile defendants were formally processed through the juvenile courts; 22 percent of them were murder defendants, and 1,638 of these children were later prosecuted as adults, in criminal court. At that time (1991), in the country's 75 largest counties, 92 percent of the juveniles in criminal court were male. And 96 percent of them had been charged with murder.

That same year, I wrote a one-page letter to the California Department of the Youth Authority and requested permission to go inside juvenile prisons to interview the children incarcerated for murder and homicide. I had been a teacher among widely diverse student populations; at various times I had taught kids in juvenile court and probation camp schools, special education kids, and inner city kids in public schools. Despite their different locales and the varying years that spanned my teaching of them, these kids were "united" in one respect: They had a dominant preference for violent behavior.

Also in 1991, I advised the 53 (that's right!) students in my high school class not to come to school on a certain day because the air in the city was thick with rumors of an imminent gang retaliation for the death of a popular student who had been fatally shot in the back after hurdling the fence to his front yard. That was his last act in life: A desperate, gasping and failed effort to make it into the arms of his waiting mother. Frozen with panic, she stood on the front porch, with the door open, as the gangbangers screeched to a stop and opened fire from their car. The image of that kid collapsing and bleeding out his life in his mother's arms was burned into my brain and the brains of all my students. Understandably, for the next few days, it was their "curriculum" and all they could talk about. Educational theorists love to wax eloquent about exploiting "teachable moments" in the classroom curriculum. Tell me: *What are you supposed to do when real life intrudes?*

I began thinking that, as a teacher, I probably had overlooked some opportunities to intervene and make a difference in the lives of at-risk students. Troubled by this recurrent thought, I explained, in my letter to the California Department of the Youth Authority, that I wanted children incarcerated for murder and homicide to tell me where and when those opportunities—for all teachers— occurred. I wanted to do in-person/in-prison interviews with children so I could hear, in their own voices, the stories of their home and school lives, and the routes they took in their peculiar odysseys from life at home to life in prison. I received no word from the Department of the Youth Authority that year. But that year (1991), 68 percent of the children convicted nationwide in criminal court were sentenced to incarceration in a state prison.

So when I returned to USC in 1991, I felt an urgent and compelling personal responsibility to try to find sense and meaning, to finally make that belated "difference" and contribute some answers to why more school children seemed to be committing adult crimes, specifically homicide.

The following year, 1992, the National School Safety Center disclosed that more than 3 million incidents of crime are reported in American schools every year. And the National Education Association later reported that on a typical day, 100,000 students bring guns to school and 40 children are killed or wounded by gunshots.

In 1993, the California Department of the Youth Authority finally called me. That agency approved my request to enter its prisons and interview children sentenced for murder and homicide. It had taken the agency twenty-four months to evaluate my one-page proposal and respond to it. No explanation for the "delay" was offered; however, I was informed by the official who had called me that "You are probably the only researcher in the entire country who is being allowed to go inside the state juvenile prisons, put a microphone in the faces of kids who murdered some-body, and say, 'Tell me the story of your life.' " After the first several interviews, I noticed a common thread in the stories of *rich* kids and *poor* kids: The fount from which their stories flowed had similar "streams" (themes). Those themes, which you will read in this book, remained constant over the years (no matter which kinds of children I talked to) as their numbers increased the size of my research population.

But after finally getting approval from the state to enter the juvenile prisons, I faced a different hurdle: My doctoral adviser at USC was not at all enthusiastic about my doing this kind of research. A former school superintendent himself, he showed his disinclination to support my objectives with this oft-repeated query: "Why do you want to go into the youth prisons and interview kids who committed suicide?" My constant response was: "It's homicide, not suicide." This apparent disinterest seemed to me to be symptomatic of a larger more pressing concern. So I left USC and enrolled in the Claremont Graduate University. There, I found an immediate and enthusiastic response to my goal, and I began my research.

Two powerful themes emerged in the life stories of the incarcerated adolescents I interviewed. These two messages, and others, would continue to be uttered repeatedly, over the nearly four-year period in which I interviewed these children: (1) *The lack of parental love and* (2) *sexual and other abuse in the home.*

The various worlds from which my adolescent interviewees came were divided by ethnicity and economics. Yet *all* my participants were *united* in *how* they *responded* to *their victims*: Some of my interviewees had killed other kids their own age; some had killed their parents; some had killed a sibling or other family member; and one had killed her seven-week old infant. In this book, I share with you the stories of *some* of the incarcerated children I interviewed, not all of them. During my research, I coined the term *adolescentcide*—the phenomenon of children taking the lives of other children. My wife complained that this word was not easy to say. *That is precisely the point*!

The Columbine High School shootings in Littleton, Colorado, were the worst school shootings in this country's history and the latest in a series of incidents termed "new wave" by the media. This "new wave" refers to incidents of kids killing kids in which the perpetrator does not fit the stereotypical profile of a teenage killer, more specifically, "new wave" is the advent of adolescentcide in "white suburbia." This new wave has killed at least 14 people and wounded more than 40 at schools across the nation since October 1997. These deaths occurred in school districts in affluent, pristine regions of the nation. The areas in which these tragedies took place were further distinguished by their scarcity of ethnic minorities, and they were light-years away from the urban heat and sizzle of the inner cities.

As a nation, we have expended Herculean amounts of time, money and effort preparing to meet the twenty-first century by immunizing our ubiquitous computerized-technology systems against the notorious "Y2K Bug." However necessary that crusade might have been, the larger issue is: How much time, money and effort are we prepared to continue to pour into the real Y2K's—*Year 2000 Kids*—who possess the power to change the course of American history forever? In the words of William J. Bennett, who served under Presidents Bush and Reagan as former director of the Office of National Drug Control Policy and Secretary of Education, it is only young twenty-first century America that can legitimately be called "history's most violent 'civilized' nation."

The purpose of this book is to show you snapshots into the lives of some of the incarcerated children I interviewed, and through them provide you with information and techniques to determine if your own child is "at-risk" and how you may either address or prevent his involvement in violent behavior. The tattered fabric of the lives of these children I interviewed will undoubtedly be recognizable and clear for you to see. In their own voices and in their own words, they say what went wrong in their lives and what they needed to make them right. You will *see,* as they "speak," awful parallels to the lives of the new wave of kids killing kids today.

It is my fervent hope that the *reasons* children kill will be abundantly clear to you. *For those reasons have nothing to do with how those children look, what color they are, where they live, whether they are wealthy or not, or anything else you think you might see externally. Yet those "invisible" to-kill-for reasons are real. Horrifyingly so. They are as real as the abject hurt, loneliness, isolation, and sense of being abandoned and unloved that every kid who has ever killed felt.*

The hurt and loneliness are also real for the *parents* of children who kill. It must be noted that parents of kids who commit adolescentcide often live with their own brand of pain. I wish to acknowledge their suffering. Yet, it is also necessary that we look unflinchingly at the root causes of this violent behavioral trend, whatever they may be.

In making this kind of critical inquiry, I spent four years interviewing these 103 incarcerated youths, each a multitude of times. The acts of homicide committed by these children are so far outside our social and cultural reckoning that these vicious acts appear unreal and untrue. The lives of these children in this book also appear to be stranger than fiction. As you read this book, you may find yourself shaking your head, just as I did when I interviewed these kids. The fictional quality of the incredible stories they told me gave me pause each time I heard them. Sometimes their narratives grew eerily story-like. Thus, in some of the chapters that follow, I have conveyed the "commitment offenses" with the sort of narrative with which it was reported to me. But each is true and accurate as these heinous crimes were voiced from the mouths of babes, however unseemly they appear.

While we are not currently at war with any foreign power, our children *have* declared war on each other. The Children's Defense Fund reports that every day seven teenagers and 10 young adults are the victims of homicide; homicide is the third leading cause of death for elementary/middle school children, ages 5 to 14; and every day 10 teenagers and 13 young adults are killed by firearms. We need to join our hands, our hearts, our minds, and our souls together in what will be the greatest rescue effort in history to save the lives of our children. That is the only way we will save ourselves.

*The bell is tolling. And it tolls for us.*

—James E. Shaw

# Foreword

I met Dr. Shaw in January of this year after addressing a gathering of "Safe Streets 2000" in Ontario, California. My message largely dealt with parenting skills and keeping our children protected. My daughter, Kristin Townsend, also spoke that day. Lauren Townsend, my younger daughter, as well as twelve other incredible people had been brutally murdered at Columbine High School on April 20, 1999. Dr. Shaw approached me after the "Safe Streets" gathering and excitedly discussed his research into *adolesentcide*–as he termed it–why children kill children.

We kept in contact through e-mails and telephone messages, and it was in the midst of one correspondence that he asked me to write the foreword to this book. The manuscript was promptly mailed to me, and I began reading it the following day. Upon finishing, I found writing this foreword more difficult than I first imagined. I was hesitant because I have a great responsibility to the Columbine families, staff and students, as well as their loved ones who were injured or murdered. With Columbine under a microscope, and every TV, magazine and newspaper article covering this tragedy, I feel the kids are constantly being re-victimized. I am so proud of how this community and others have come together to support each other. I am so proud of the daily affirmations of positive change I see in the school.

As I read each chapter of the manuscript, I found myself nodding in agreement with statements regarding the needs and expectations that children have of their parents. Being a mother of four, a teacher since 1971, and a coach since 1985, let me say that other than the chilling accounts of children he interviewed in prison I felt that Dr. Shaw wasn't telling me things I didn't already know. I lived amongst youngsters. I learned to go beyond the words they were saying to understand the full extent of their communication—verbalization, inflection, as well as body language.

For decades I have heard children implore adults to give them limits, to be consistent in their expectations of them, and to—please, please—be their parents and positive role models. They hunger for us to be their parents first, and—if we're lucky—their friends as a consequence. What makes this so difficult for adults is that out of love for them we are often forced to say "No," when we know it may not be the popular answer.

What impressed me about this book is that Dr. Shaw had taken all those important pieces of knowledge and placed them in written form as a primer for parents and anyone dealing with youth. In all my years of education, I have not encountered a book which so encompasses my sincere belief that children CRAVE boundaries. They will accept consequences if they occur consistently when those lines are overstepped. Why? Because it proves to them time and time again that we love them so much, we will stick by them unconditionally, every step of the way. This book emphasizes by examples the importance of parents being parents.

Early reports said that Harris and Klebold had been the victims of bullying. However, in my discussions with investigators and Columbine High School students, I learned that Harris and Klebold enjoyed the role of "being victimized" by baiting peers into bullying them and sometimes playing the role of bullies themselves. Students told me of their attempts to befriend Harris and Klebold, only to be turned away so that the two could perpetuate the idea of being loners, unwanted and isolated. Unfortunately, those early accounts were created by reporters who, in their frenzy to produce articles attempting to explain the *whys* behind the massacre, were using each other as sources. In doing so, they may have participated in the children's game of "telephone," attempting to relay what they thought the one before them had said.

Are there bullies in Columbine High School? Of course there are, just as in any community. To deny this would be a lie. Could we all be a kinder, gentler population? Definitely. But to hint that the massacre could have been avoided if those at Columbine would have simply reached out more to these two, is equally false, and takes the blame away from those who earned it—Harris and Klebold.

The attack on the school and the bullets which hit three dozen people were not directed at a specific culture, race, athlete or gender. Yet they were directed at all of those. If Harris and Klebold were targeting athletes, they attacked at the wrong place and time, and they knew it. Many student-athletes leave the campus at lunchtime. Anyone specifically targeting them would have chosen to attack after school when open gyms and practices were in full swing, not in midday and in the library where most of the massacre occurred. Videotapes produced by Harris and Klebold of themselves show them vilifying nearly anything that breathed. They hated everything, including the very ideals to which they held themselves.

Dr. Shaw states in this book that bullies "cannot stand themselves." I cannot think of anything which more graphically illustrates this than the cold-blooded hatred and destruction these two murderers wreaked on their school as they laughed and degraded their victims before shooting them, and then turned the guns on themselves.

So, then, where does that leave us? How does each of us as individuals make a positive change in this world? Do we have to be "larger" than ourselves and save masses at a time? Or, can each of us, with one small act of kindness and accountability each day, make a positive impact on each other's lives, not unlike single patches of a quilt which when stitched together form an enormous blanket to warm us with love? I taught my children to love, respect and embrace the wonderment of uniqueness.

I watched Lauren daily as she reached out to help others expecting nothing in return but, perhaps, a smile and the joy of showing she cared. My heart swelled with pride as I overheard others talking about how Lauren had gone out of her way to do something for them. All of us lived under an umbrella of "do unto others" and felt we *could* make the world better by treating those around us with kindness and respect. My daughter loved life, animals and people. She was incredibly intelligent—a valedictorian—she was athletic, she was beautiful, she was caring, she was giving, and she was murdered by the very people who, if had they known her, would have found her to be their friend. She was murdered while sitting in the library, studying in the middle of the school day. She was doing exactly what she was supposed to be doing at that time. No one could imagine she was in harms way. Yet, it was here, under adult supervision that she was murdered. In the end, all the love and kindness she and others gave could not protect them. Does that frighten you to the core? It should. If we cannot protect our children while they are harmlessly going about their own ways, how can we protect them?

Lauren wrote that she felt something "huge" was going to happen to make us all stop in our tracks and re-evaluate our priorities. How prophetic that she would know this beforehand. I am so proud of Lauren for being a catalyst in that change, yet so incredibly sickened by the acute loss of her physical presence. If the horrific attack on our innocent children at Columbine High School and other schools across our nation isn't "huge," then, please, don't tell me what is.

Being a parent is the hardest and most rewarding thing we will ever do, if we do it well. It has nothing to do with birthing, and everything to do with being responsible for the most precious gifts we have been given. It is providing the most consistent and loving upbringing we can give our children. I would not want to be a passenger in a plane piloted by persons who did not do their homework and take their work seriously. Nor should anyone become a parent without accepting the awesome responsibility that comes with it. There is no "auto-pilot" for parenting. Only we can take the controls and fly this plane.

How do *you* as an individual accomplish this? You begin by picking up this book and reading it. Take it to heart. Listen to the stories these young people tell through Dr. Shaw. When you've finished reading it, read it again, and then share it with others. Do it for yourself. Do it for your children. Do it for me. Do it for Lauren.

But just do it—NOW!

—Dawn Anna
Teacher, coach and mother of four,
including Lauren Townsend, a beautiful
spirit who lost her life in the Columbine
High School Tragedy

*It is easier to build strong children than to repair broken men.*

—Frederick Douglass

# Adolescentcide: All Kids Are At Risk

*Since I really got involved in the counseling and chapel ministry program here in prison, I couldn't wait to see my mom and dad because I really wanted to reach out to them and apologize and ask for their forgiveness. Well, for starters, they didn't visit me for over two years. When they finally came, my mother stayed in the car. My dad came to see me, but he wouldn't let me hug him, touch him, nothing like that. And he would cough and change the subject whenever I brought up Monica's death. You see, I've faced the fact that I killed my sister, and that I did it on purpose. My parents may never forgive me. I'm just another terrible family secret they'll lock up in the attic of their minds. At the end of my dad's visit, I felt so terrible. Even with all the counseling, I felt like I couldn't go on. I didn't eat for a week.*—Charity

I sat at the rectangular table in the Day Room and waited for the parole agent to bring in Charity. My two tape recorders were all set up and ready. An unopened giant box of "AA" batteries was between them, ready to be thrown into service at the first sound of tape-warble. A new spiral notebook lay open beneath two sharpened pencils. Our interview was for 9:00 a.m., just as it always was. I looked at my watch; it was 9:15. Charity was not here, and nobody else had come to tell me whether our interview was on or off. As I waited, I begin

1

to reflect on the prison's highly efficient communications system.

I recalled first being required to make a "why-am-I-here-and-what-do-I-want-to-do" presentation to the parole agents and counseling staff at a special meeting called specifically for them to meet and question me. Despite my having received the state's blessings to enter the juvenile prison system and interview children serving time for homicide, my "approval letter" had advised me that each prison would have to make its own determination about whether to allow me in. I knew that my task lay in convincing professional prison staff that teachers, parents and others were desperately concerned about finding answers to why kids were killing kids. I described my years as a teacher and ended my presentation by saying that I was prepared to invest years in the study of children incarcerated for homicide in order to help others around the nation, "including youth prison officials," solve this socially-urgent problem.

My presentation to the prison staff merely qualified me to make another presentation, at a different time, to children (wards) en masse, who were rounded up and marshaled into the gigantic Day Room. Even after my telling them that it would be a "multi-year project," most of the wards agreed to participate. I was almost beside myself with delight. However, one ward told me bluntly: "If you come back here wearing a jacket and tie, I ain't gonna talk to you."

Whenever I arrived at the prison, my immediate responsibilities included picking up my "package"—the two memos listing my day's interviewees and my "Visitor" badge—from the security checkpoint. If the memos were not there, usually a parole agent handed them to me when he or she ushered the first interviewee into the day room. My final task, prior to interviewing a ward for the first time, was to go over with the ward the "informed consent" form I designed. It explained the purpose of the interviews—to provide information to significant adults and caregivers who work with children—and informed wards that they had the right to terminate interviews at any time, for any reason or for no reason. Their desire not to participate would not be held against them and was purely voluntary. However, they would receive no "points" or "credits." In other words, these interviews could not be used as "good behavior evidence" to show the parole board. Lastly, I stated my desire to interview them several times, over a number of years, to check, re-check, and verify information they gave me, and to get as accurate and complete a picture of their life as possible.

"Mr. Shaw?" The voice behind me sounded tentative. I turned around from the window through which I had been watching the rain hammering down. I had not heard any footsteps behind me, so engrossed was I in my thoughts and watching the downpour. "Good morning, Charity," I said. She smiled shyly. We shook hands. I gestured toward the table and we walked over to it. The parole agent gave me my "package" showing five more inter-views that day; then she left.

"I'm awful sorry I'm late," Charity began. "Uh, something happened, and they needed to question me. I mean, I'm not like in trouble or anything. They just needed to question me about some things." I told Charity that was okay, that I understood, that "things come up sometimes, just like the rain comes down." She glanced toward the window and we both laughed. She said, "I know we only have about a half hour." I told her we could still begin the interview, if she wanted to do so. She nodded her head enthusiastically. So, we began. The story I got from her persuaded me of the value in returning, time and again, to these children and repeatedly interviewing the same ones for better and more information. Charity, in our previous four interviews, was usually given to only a few words. Sometimes I had the impression she was there to put in the hour and be gone. Today, though, she gave me the story of her life.

"You overslept and missed breakfast *and* your medicine," Charity said with exasperation as she worked at the dishes. "Mom and Dad left for work hours ago."

"Watch your tone, please," Monica said. "You know I'm sick. Depression is sickness. *Most* people know that." The insult bur-rowed into Charity's patience. "Some sister you turned out to be."

"Listen, Monica—"

Just then, the doorbell rang. Charity dried her hands on her apron and went for the door.

"I'll get it!" announced Monica, who lunged at Charity and knocked her to one side.

"Are you sick or are you *sick*?!" Charity shouted.

Monica turned around, mid-stride, "Don't you *ever, ever* say that to me again. I've got enough people thinking I'm a head case. I don't need my sister joining the team. Do you hear me, slut?"

The doorbell rang again. Monica turned briskly toward the door.

The name Monica had called her echoed in her mind. *Slut? You're the slut, Monica. All these boys coming over all the time, and I never . . . If you were just dead.*

"Monica?" Charity called.

"What?!" Monica answered dismissively, continuing toward the door.

"Monica?" Charity called again, her voice softer, more calculated.

Monica, now just inches from the front door, turned toward Charity with impatience.

"Don't call me a slut . . . *ever*." Charity could feel the heat in her cheeks as she just barely controlled her rage.

"Well, sometimes you're not really into charity, either, despite your name," Monica said with annoyance.

*What a sick b\*\*\*\* you are, Monica. What kind of crap did you get into at that private school? Stuff that keeps you on medication. Stuff Mom and Dad won't talk about. I wonder if they'd miss you much.*

Charity returned to her sink full of dishes. Her eyes drifted to the knives atop the counter, which brought dark thoughts to her mind.

Moments later, Monica returned to the kitchen accompanied by one of her boyfriends, Brad. "Hi, Charity," Brad said. Charity did not return his greeting.

"I *think* Brad spoke to you." Monica said.

*Don't push it, Monica.*

"Just say 'hello,' Charity." Monica's voice rose, taking on

her demanding tone, which Monica knew always infuriated Charity

*Drop it. Don't push me right now.* Then something occurred to Charity. She turned around, her face beaming. "Hi Brad," she said with a lush, wanton voice.

"I said say hello, I didn't say flirt," Monica warned.

Charity watched as Brad appraised her from top to bottom. "Hey, I've got an idea," Brad said. "Let's go to the beach. The three of us, I mean." He spoke with expectation. "I could get my dad's car. We'd be back before your folks got home from work."

"I don't know. I've got lots of work to do. And I've got to keep my parents happy."

"Talk to *me*, Brad. It's *her* day to cook and clean. But it's *my* day off."

"I figured if we could all go . . . but whatever . . . we'll go alone." Brad smiled wide. "Two can have fun just as well as three." He and Monica drew close and looked ready to kiss.

Suddenly angry, Charity felt all the old pain crash in upon her. Monica always got what she wanted. From mom and dad, from whatever hormone-driven boy that showed up at the door. *If Monica just weren't around anymore*, Charity thought.

"Brad, you have to go," Charity said. "Monica is sick, and our folks don't like friends in the house when they're not here."

Brad turned to Monica. "You don't look sick to me. Matter of fact, you look very . . . healthy." His wit and charm reminded Charity of wax. But Monica glowed under his flattery.

*Get the hell out of here, Brad. Just be a good stud and get off on some other girl whose folks aren't so concerned about appearances.* "Brad, you have to go."

Suddenly, Monica was defensive. "He's *my* friend, and I say he stays!"

The command was strident in Monica's voice. It was always the same whenever she forgot to take her medicine. Charity felt her reserve slipping away. She had forgotten how long she had been looking after a crazy sister. *Now, you stupid flirt, why didn't you wake up, get a good breakfast and take your damn medicine so we could avoid scenes like this? I hate you.* Charity went to the china cabinet and took out a dessert plate. Then she took the bakery knife from its holder atop the counter. She cut a two-inch thick slice of lemon cake and placed it on the plate. Taking a cloth napkin from a wicker basket, she walked slowly to where Monica and Brad sat at the kitchen table.

"Monica, may I speak to you in the living room, please?" Charity's tone was polite, soft, resigned. She turned to Brad and gave him the slice of cake and the napkin.

"I'm not leaving this room!" Monica shouted. Her face became manic and accusatory. "Whatever you have to say to me can be said in front of my friends." She clasped Brad's arm just as he picked up the cake with it. Brad, seeming to feel trapped, looked searchingly from Monica to Charity.

Charity had seen this look in her sister's eyes many times. Her parents never said what it was, but it was there. *I'll bet you had some kind of problem with boys at that school. And because of all your mistakes you've messed things up for me. Mom and Dad won't talk about that school and won't let me go there. Everything for me is ruined because of you.* Suddenly, Charity's anger began to surface again.

"Okay. You know the rules. Mom and Dad . . ."

"Rules, fools!" Monica spat out. Then in a sing-song voice she repeated, "Rules are for fools, rules are for fools. That's why they rhyme all the time." Monica erupted in gales of laughter and collapsed against Brad. The piece of cake in his hand dropped onto the table, breaking in two. Charity knew each moment without her medication only pushed Monica deeper into this strange behavior.

"Monica, I will give you three choices: I call the police; I call Mom and Dad; or you tell Brad goodbye and he leaves."

"I don't like being threatened," Monica moaned, her voice assuming an eerie tone. "D-d-don't threaten m-me" Her words fell from stuttering lips and sounded like a two-year-old pleading for desert. "I good girl, you know that. I'm not a slut like you."

Charity froze, the insult searing her nerves. *You are definitely sick, talking baby talk, and you think I will just stand here and take your sh\*\*. Maybe if mom and dad won't get you some help, I ought to help you. 'Cause the dope you're on just ain't cuttin' it. And I won't put up with this anymore!*

Charity looked down at the knife in her hand.

Thinking of her parents, she screamed in her mind, *You're both cowards! You're miserable parents who keep your crazy daughter doped up like a dirty family secret and are too afraid to talk to your* sane *daughter and tell her what's going on, what life's all about. Why am I being punished for Monica's sorry life?! Yeah, you're rich, but that money won't bring Monica back.*

Charity raised the knife.

"Oh, my God! Charity, please!" Brad sprinted for the front door. Charity was only dimly aware of his exit. She heard his voice on the outside of the house, but it sounded so very far away. Why was he yelling 'Help, help!'

"P-please p-put the knife d-down. I be g-good for you."

Charity was a foot away from her sister. She held the bakery knife high in the air. She looked at her sister and barely recognized her. Monica looked years younger, and totally helpless. Her eyes pleaded. For the first time, Charity saw the deep and intense pain in them. Pain she never noticed before. But it was too late. Swiftly, in its deadly arc, the knife plunged downward.

Harsh statistics warn us that these are extraordinarily hard times for your child, my child and everybody else's child. There has never been another time in the country's history when children have been more at risk than they are today. While it comforts us that typhus and tuberculosis no longer pose fatal dangers to our children, as they did to a generation of children not so long ago, we can take no comfort in the fact that *adolescentcide*—kids killing kids—is the major cause of death for our children today.

The statistics on kids killing kids far surpass the mortality rates from even the nation's most feared pre-vaccine era virus. For example, in 1952 polio killed 3,152 adults and children. But just 40 years later, in 1992, a total of 5,326 children under the age of 19 were killed by guns. While advances in medical science spare our children from many of the diseases that once deformed, debilitated and denied them life, the *disease* of violence poisons them with death. Every 48 hours, the number of juvenile deaths from homicide—26—is equivalent to the population of the average classroom. *Kids killing kids is the nation's number one public health problem.*

The FBI's Violent Crimes Index indicates that between 1987 and 1991 the number of juvenile arrests increased by 50 percent—twice the increase for youth 18 years of age or older. As alarming as this statistic is, even more alarming is the fact that juvenile arrests for homicide during the same period increased by 85 percent. In 1982, 390 teenagers, 13 to 15 years of age, were arrested for homicide. By 1992, that figure had climbed to 740. *U.S. News & World Report* states that more than three million crimes a year are committed in or near the 85,000 public schools in the nation.

The U.S. Centers for Disease Control and Prevention reports that 1 in 20 students brings a gun to school at least once a month. The *National Education Goals Report* cites some 16 percent of the nation's twelfth-graders as admitting they had received violent threats and that half of those youths sustained injuries in school. Nationwide studies reveal that 1 in 12 high-schoolers is threatened or hurt with a weapon every year. Homicide is the nation's second leading cause of death for youth ages 10 to 19. *USA Today* reports that of the 65,000 students it polled in its *Weekend* survey, 55 percent of them, in grades 10 through 12, know that weapons are regularly brought to school.

While the instrument of Charity's commitment offense was a knife, and children do indeed make use of a wide array of weapons to demonstrate their anger, the most preferred weapon in youth aggression is the gun. An estimated 1.2 million elementary aged, latchkey children have access to guns in their homes. During the 1997-98 school year, nearly one million children grades 6 through 12 carried guns to school. In America, every two hours, a child is killed by a gun. To put this in perspective: If you were to finish reading this book in the next four to six hours, two or three children will have been killed by guns. But ponder this: If you finish tomorrow—24 hours from now—13 children will have been killed by guns. The point is, we are at the crisis in American history where death by gun violence is the rhythm beating out our children's lives. Time spent reading a book only peals the hours lost, tolls the lives forever gone.

Nationwide, children find modern life to be a constant grind, with mounting pressures. They are not alone. Their parents, too, find life to be tough with its stresses and constant challenges. The anxieties and pressures under which parents live are unlike any they've previously known. Most parents survived the distressing years of the battered 1990's economy with livable, if marginal, incomes; they cheered in the spring of 1999 when the news media announced a $1 trillion national economic surplus. Gradually, old fears about working all one's life only to die in the poor-house are giving way to renewed faith in the future and one's enhanced capabilities and opportunities to thrive in it. But as parents work harder to earn more in a robust economy, staring them in the face is the fact that the children—whose futures they are laboring to establish—are presently dying in ever-growing numbers at the hands of their peers.

Some of the underlying causes of adolescentcide attributable to their deaths lie in the "stories" in the statistics released by the U.S. Department of Health and Human Services. About 1 in every 10 children—as many as 6 million youngsters—may suffer from a serious emotional disturbance, such as severe depression, conduct disorder, anxiety disorder, or manic-depressive illness. For some reason, many of these kids traffic in weapons. In 1997-98, 6,000 kids were expelled from the nation's schools for gun possession. Unable to cope any longer with their anxiety and depression, these children simply dragged themselves off to school under the weight of their emotional turbulence, carrying a gun to solve their problems. In light of the nation's $1 trillion economic surplus, it might be said about this age, as Charles Dickens remarked in *A Tale of Two Cities*, that these are the best of times and the worst of times.

But more tragically than even the hapless children in Dickens' books, most of the 103 incarcerated children I interviewed—although they had been tried in court and sentenced to prison for committing homicide—were the victims of unseen and undocumented violence to their spirits as well as to their bodies. Ironically, this violence was largely inflicted by those entrusted with their care: their parents and other caregivers. Adults like you and me.

It is these children whose mostly-affirmative answers on the "Homicidally-at-Risk Adolescent Profile" (HARAP) assessment instrument I designed, regularly filled the boxes labeled "Abusive Parents," "Abused Mother," "Sexual Abuse," "Stress," "Drug and Alcohol Use," "Felt Victimized," and some thirty other descriptors. These children had run the torturous and terrorizing paths from life at home to life in prison. Despite their experiencing and describing a range of feelings in their lives—from anger to anxiety—there was one emotion whose absence was made the more evident by their complete failure to mention it: Love.

Sometimes openly, sometimes indirectly, the 103 children I talked to admitted to being deprived of consistent, continuous, and unconditional parental love. Without parental love to guide them, they became deeply lost, as proven by their ultimate acts, and could not find their way back to humanity. These children had been lost a long time. (Recall Charity's torrid thoughts, just before she knifed her sister, of constantly being the victim of her sister's behavior.) On nearly every occasion, most of the children spoke to me with a stark, unadulterated certainty and possessed an all-too-adult-like grasp of every seamy detail of their crimes and what led up to them. *No child should ever learn the awful things these children knew!* By the time they committed their acts of homicide, they were the shell-shocked, walking-wounded casualties of all they had daily seen or experienced.

As they talked about their shattered lives and shameful acts, most of these adolescents knew and admitted that they had committed unnatural and unlawful deeds. But this awareness had not been gained through loving parental guidance. They had eventually learned only through mandated counseling and therapy—without which their parole would be impossible—to admit and take responsibility for their crimes.

Children who kill come from poor *and* rich families. As a parole agent told me one day, "You've got a little bit of everybody—from Wall Street to Watts—in here." Whether blessed by fortune or cursed by fate, part of a racial majority or racial minority, children who kill are united by two elements:

10

- An *inner impoverishment of the spirit*—depression, insecurity, and low self-esteem—directly resulting from their being alienated and isolated from adults, especially parents who should have influence over them

- Feelings of being unloved, unlovable, rejected, and worthless which incites their anger and depression, and forges their distorted yet real view of the world as hostile and personally threatening.

It would be easy to say, of the 103 hapless children in my research pool, that because of the kinds of terrible home lives they endured, it was a foregone conclusion—a "slam dunk"—that they would end up in prison or dead. This presumption is perhaps understandable. They bore the physical and emotional scars of years of abuse. It might be expected that they would "share" their pain with others—and do so with a vengeance. Less understandable, however, are the children from Littleton, Colorado; Jonesboro, Arkansas; Springfield, Oregon and other affluent areas whose scars and hurts were not so readily visible, enabling them to maintain a façade of being "good kids," "straight arrows," "average," and "normal."

If there are such beings as children who are "born to kill," we might assume they exhibit telltale behaviors and warning signs. The assumption is only partly true, but the myth it spawns is potent and enduring: *Bad kids kill and you can identify them by what they look like, what color they are, what economic class they're in, what they wear, and where they live.* We have only recently turned our attention to, and looked on in horror at, the deaths and devastation wreaked by "good kids" from "good homes" who have suddenly and unexplainably detonated and "gone off." Of all the kids you could find in the country, *they* were born to take the reins of power, to lead, to win. Or so went the assumption. They came from homes that had affluence and influence. Yet, alienated and angry, these "good" children whose killings grabbed national headlines and gripped the nation by its collective throat, didn't seem to have an obvious "history" shadowing them, or terrifying and convoluted life-stories, as many of my adolescent interviewees had. Are we, then, to conclude that there were no signs or symptoms foretelling their future heinous acts? Surprisingly, there were; in fact, there were numerous witnesses to their early telltale signs. Unfortunately, being a witness does not necessarily make one an *alertist*—one with both desire and courage to report what danger or suspects he has seen.

An alertist might have deterred Kip Kinkel, the Springfield, Oregon teenager who shot and killed both his schoolteacher parents, and then went to school and laid waste the lives of so many others. Kip, according to news accounts, had read aloud in his literature class excerpts from his journal describing plans to "kill everybody." He also gave a talk in science class on how to build a bomb. But this affluent ninth-grader, was disregarded and ignored when he boldly wrote and spoke of his desire to take human life. How much more "believable" ought he to have been? A better question is, how much more *fearful* and *cautious* and *concerned* should his teachers and parents have been? By all accounts, he simply did not "look" the part of a killer. Be-spectacled and shy, he was a pimple-faced "nerd" whose appearance invited no suspicion as he orchestrated his plans to make everybody pay for his pain. But he escaped notice and was disregarded because he was an otherwise run-of-the-mill student.

Shortly after the tragic catastrophe that Kip Kinkel wrought at his high school, I spoke with his principal, Larry Bentz. Mr. Bentz told me that contrary to the media's description of Kip as a troubled, aimless youth, "he was a good kid" and a diligent student. Mr. Bentz particularly resented the "media trucks that invaded our town and took over, parking all around the back fence of our school property and really making a circus of it all. Their presence wasn't good for us; we all felt the heavy pressure. And all they wanted was to confirm their image of Kip as a disturbed, distraught young boy who finally snapped. But he wasn't that way at all. Both his parents were teachers—one taught Spanish and the other taught History. He was from a good home and good parents."

Do good kids from good homes write threatening essays rhapsodizing about dealing deadly violence? Of course not. Then why was everybody who knew Kip Kinkel locked into a common mindset about him, even when he became blatant in his expressed desire to kill? Perhaps we will never know the answer to that. Kip Kinkel was seen as a good kid with all the right trappings: A home in an affluent suburb, parents in the "right" professions, just the right dose of academic diligence at school. His brimming, overflowing anger was merely seen as live theater, nothing more. Was everybody—their guards down—fooled by Kip, or were they simply doing their duty, as a caring and nurturing community, to embrace him? Could it be that his essays warning of his murderous intentions were ignored because that community believed its unconditional love would change him? How were they to know that their benign disregard that greeted his ravings might insult him and fuel his final angry moments?

The ranting press coverage that followed the Springfield, Oregon disaster would have us believe that Kip Kinkel was no more a good kid than Charles Manson was a social worker. Journalists wondered why, when he expressed his dark desires, the head-in-the-sand response from adults who knew him was so universal. The day before he opened fire in his high school's cafeteria, he purportedly had been suspended from school for bringing a gun on campus.

Again, good kids do not kill. But viewing kids as either "good" or "bad" isn't enough. More helpful is to see students demonstrating or verbalizing anti-social behaviors and sentiments as "at-risk," "angry," "assaultive," "combative," exhibiting "violence-fantasy" or "violence-tendency," and the like to accurately portray the picture such students are showing of themselves? "Good" and "Bad" are terms that confuse more than they clarify. They are cliches that simply fail to accurately describe a person or situation.

Kids kill only when they feel alienated, abused, hurt, isolated, unloved, unlovable, helpless and of little worth. Teachers and administrators on campus should use some of these words and any others that accurately and succinctly describe chronic behaviors on campus that show a student is speaking or behaving dangerously. Harboring these negative feelings does not make kids bad. In Kip's case, he was mentally unhealthy. The response he chose to his negative feelings—to solve his problems with a loaded gun—was bad.

Kids can be viewed as "good" to the extent that they are enabled to use, and actually do use, conflict-reduction strategies, anger management strategies, and nonviolent communication strategies in solving their array of problems, and in making moral determinations about right and wrong. Good kids, like good drivers, occasionally get onto the wrong path, head in the wrong direction and need to be turned around and re-directed, especially when they are crying out for help, as was Kip Kinkel. His simple acts of reading aloud his plans for "killing everybody" and building a bomb were more than self-aggrandizing attention-getters: They were proofs of his inner torment and rage. He was calling attention to what his teachers, friends, and even parents could not see but which he painfully felt. So numbed with pain and inner suffering was he, apparently, that he just could not feel anything for the folks at home in his inner circle—his parents who dearly loved him—or the people at school in his outer circle. Totally ignored despite his radical tactics to gain attention, he was finally paid "attention" to after it was much too late.

Even though Kip seemed to want nothing more than to find audiences for his madcap verbal rhapsodizing about death and destruction, his teachers, and whoever else heard him, should have been apprehensive about him. Their heartbeats should have told them that good kids have a clear perspective and can control their interactions with and reactions to various social circumstances. Under everybody's noses, Kip, was a kid who was deconstructing—cracking up—and announcing it. Everybody who listened to him undoubtedly thought he was crying "wolf." Nobody wanted to rat on or confront a kid that, according to press accounts, everyone thought was too dumb and dorky to be dangerous. Nobody wanted to be ridiculed by peers for being too serious about Kip, everybody's favorite dork who, after all, was probably joking. None of Kip's teachers said or did anything about his verbal behavior. It should be noted that had he made his comments just *once* at any airport in his state, everybody within earshot would have been on instant alert and summoned the police. Kids who kill *always* tip their hand; their telltale behaviors have been visible and observed by *somebody* long before they picked up a gun and used it to kill people. Failing to take seriously the signs of their imminent destruction that these kids put out there, will only enable them to carry out their insane desires.

As a parent, you already know that children crave attention; they want to be in the limelight, on center stage, and want you to see them there, constantly bragging and lying about feats never accomplished and roles that may have belonged to someone else. All kids are sometimes inclined to brag and inflate their prominence. Bragging is good, old-fashioned fun and necessary to a child's development. It's a child's tool for telling his "story." Their involvement in the recounted events may range from only knowledge about them, to limited involvement of no importance, to full but undistinguished involvement. Hence, their need to give you their biased report.

Although your children's boasts may cause you to cringe and mildly or sternly admonish them to "tell the truth" or "don't brag so much," boasting, and the bravado that accompanies it, is usually a temporary phase of development. Most children go through a healthy "yarn-spinning" phase that helps them establish identity, become recognized, and bolster self-esteem. It also serves to inform the child that language is powerful, meaningful, and when used in certain ways—inventing stories— gets attention of grownups, at the least. At most, it frequently raises stature among peers.

However, excessive bragging is a warning signal that parents need to pay attention to. Incessant and prolonged bragging is a sign that a child feels inferior. If your child makes a habit of bragging (one parent told me, "she brags like she breaths") you must determine its source. What's happening in the home that makes a child feel that it is necessary to get attention? Are you paying too little attention to that child, whether you know it or not? Do all your children feel loved equally? Communication is of utmost importance. Listen to what is being told to you and how. Could your child be overshadowed by other kids or over- powered by their feats?

Charity told me: "Monica and I were very articulate, something we got from our parents. Through bragging, we put each other down; in addition to the achievements we boasted about, we competed with each other in the *language* we used to describe them."

Talk to your children about their school and other activities; really listen to *how* they describe those activities to you and *what* they say. Whenever possible, and as much as you can, watch your children as they play with other children. Their being overshadowed by other kids or overpowered by their feats, on the playground or at the park, might be your clue to why your children feel the need to brag. Incessant and prolonged bragging is a sign that a child feels inferior.

But let's look at a uniquely different language mechanism used by a fraction of the nation's total child population. Wanting attention but *craving* love, respect, and acceptance, their language is laden with not-so-subtle threats and desires to commit violent deeds. When they are among peers, instead of bragging about achievements, real or imagined, they engage in morbid revenge-speech: they talk violence, engage in hate-speech, and concoct death fantasies where vengeance is exacted. During a talk I gave to a parent group, I was asked if this kind of talk wasn't "as innocent as bragging and merely taking it to a different level." Absolutely not. As a parent, it is critical that you know the difference.

Children who engage in morbid revenge-speech are *braying* and *bellowing*. That means (in this narrow context) they are gloating, fantasizing, or rhapsodizing about violent and destructive events, their role in them—or their regret about not being involved. Some go so far as memorializing their plans in writing. Children who engage in normal bragging desire to *build up*; they imagine a future filled with attention, respect, and popularity. On the other hand, children who bray and bellow yearn to *destroy*. They (1) either desire no future at all, or (2) want a future in which they take the lives those they blame for making the present threatening, unbearable, and undesirable for them.

It is important to recognize that braying and bellowing are verbal telltale signs of feelings of worthlessness, hurt, rejection, frustration, bitterness, isolation, resentment and more. Charity told me that in addition to Monica calling her a "slut," "slave" and other derogatory words, Monica would rage with hatred. Charity said, "she threatened to kill me lots of times."

The following is a sampling of some of the *braying* and *bellowing* events that occurred in and around the nation, beginning in October 1998. Carefully observe *what* the brayer/ bellower says:

• A 14-year-old from Edinboro, Pennsylvania accused of murdering a science teacher during a school dance had earlier shown other students a handgun in his father's dresser and told them he *planned to kill nine people he hated.*

• The 13-year-old from Jonesboro, Arkansas accused of gunning down four girls and a teacher *told other students before hand* that he *"had some killing to do."*

• Two Pittsburgh seventh-graders were suspended for *distributing* a *"hit list"* of 10 teachers they wanted killed.

• In Miami, nine high school students were jailed for *distributing* an underground newspaper in which one writer speculated: "I have often wondered what would happen if I shot Dawson [the school principal] in the head and other teachers who have p***ed me off."

• A Wheaton, Illinois 15-year-old was jailed after *trying to recruit a friend* to help him gun down fellow students.

• In Macon County, Tennessee, two 13-year-olds were suspended *after a teacher found a note* titled "Death List" naming 15 students. A police investigation turned up a second list with 77 names.

• In three separate instances occurring the same week, officials in Fairfax County, Virginia suspended students for *posting* a "personal death list" of 17 names on a website, writing a note naming seven students the writer wanted to die, and threatening to put a bomb in a teacher's cabinet.

• A 15-year-old in Incline Village, Nevada was jailed for *writing a note* threatening to kill several classmates.

• In St. Charles, Missouri, police arrested three sixth-grade boys for *plotting to shoot* classmates on the last day of school.

• Police in Cheshire, Connecticut launched an investigation into a student underground newspaper for *printing a column* suggesting that a science teacher "needs a serious attitude adjustment, possibly a hollow-point .45 to the head."

• In Texas, gunpowder, crude bombs and computer disks with bomb-making information were found in the homes of three 14-year-old boys accused of plotting an assault at their junior high school. Before their arrests, they were targeting fellow students and teachers.

• Police in Littleton, Colorado discovered a year-long, *hand-written diary in which Eric Harris and Dylan Klebold wrote their "massacre plan,"* set specific dates and times for their assault, worked with a campus map, and even designed intricate hand signals to help ensure a high body count when they stormed the building. Their diary was laden with Nazi epithets and racial slurs.

Braying and bellowing do not always foreshadow violent acts, but they do indicate violent thoughts and even violent obsessions. Adults who work with children and teens—especially parents—must take this form of bragging as a warning and as a cry for help, and they must intervene. Prevention, however, is highly desirable over intervention and is the natural domain of good parenting.

Braying and bellowing need not define a child's life. But there is one universal fact that will forever continue to define the relationship between parents and their children. This fact can be neither overstated nor overlooked: Parents are their children's first teachers. Parents have control over their children long before they begin to socialize outside the family as school-age minors. Parents are the "captains" of the family "ship" and set the compass that determines *where* the family is going. Whether and how moral and spiritual training are instilled, what particular values and beliefs are necessary to hold the family together, and the kind and quality of education required for making a child a significant contributor to society, are all critical decisions that must be made by parents. Being a parent is a full-time job. Parental responsibilities cannot be fulfilled by people who have only a half-hearted commitment and, of course, are never fulfilled by those who abandon their responsibilities altogether.

*It would not be an exaggeration to say that the weight and fate of the world rests upon the shoulders of parents.*

# Teaching Moral Intelligence

*I'm a prisoner of war. The Statue of Liberty is a racist
bitch!* —Paul

Paul is a 20 year-old youth who heard through his parole
agent that I wanted to talk to children serving time in prison
for killing. The morning we met, he was dressed for the
occasion. His raven-colored hair was slicked back, his sneakers
were white and spotless, and his eyes shone with excitement.
Despite the heavy, blue-denim, standard-issue prison garb he
wore, he looked dapper. After we shook hands, I noticed the care
with which he sat down in the chair opposite me; he lifted back
the tail of his starched shirt, then flicked a finger at an imaginary
piece of lint on his razor-creased pant leg. For several seconds he
stared at me with an overly studious gaze. Then I realized he was
actually checking himself out in the lenses of my glasses—
vanity survives even in prison. His, though, was well-placed; he
had actor-quality good looks and a confident, relaxed demeanor.

Through dint of hard work, Paul had risen to become the
prison's computer networker, a position of considerable responsibility. Known throughout the institution for being a quick study
with a prodigious memory, he was both the pride of the huge
prison and its liaison to the various computer salespersons and
telephone representatives who regularly came calling. Despite

being a high school dropout, he was looking forward soon to receiving his Baccalaureate (B.S.) degree from a local university in whose branch program, inside the prison, he had enrolled some four years earlier.

His parole agent also told me that Paul had been "A-Phase" for about four years, and explained that this was a behavioral standard that was not only difficult to achieve but also rigorous to maintain. Paul, he said, after having had a rough couple of first years, had "finally got the message and really grabbed hold of the system and taken the best the prison had to offer." Yet the parole agent now confided to me that he felt something was wrong.

Paul had been overheard telling a group of other wards that he was a prisoner of war and a political prisoner. He said he was an avowed communist and that much of the wealth of the capitalist system came from imprisoning young men like himself. Armed with this useful advance information from his parole agent, I asked Paul to tell me about prison life and whether or not he felt he was successful. I was hardly prepared for his answer.

"My eyes have been opened to how the youth prison system sets up guys like me to fail," he said. "I want to get out on parole, yeah, but lots of times I get nervous thinking about it—there are traps out there for black people like me. Since my incarceration, I've been doing an extensive amount of reading, ranging any-where from Huey Newton, Bobby Seale, Elaine Brown and George Jackson (all members of the Black Panther Party), Shakespeare, Marcus Garvey, Malcolm X, Karl Marx, and Plato. It is essential for those of us who are colored to learn the truth of our roots, heritage and culture. It's all been damaged, lost, manipulated and distorted throughout time, by political castration. In fact, I've been writing about it." With that, he pulled out of his pocket a packet of carefully folded papers and handed them to me. I opened them and noted the careful, straight penmanship on each of the ten, or so, unlined pages. The first sentence on the first page declared: "Police who dedicate their lives to mass torture and murder have no reason to lock up convicted murderers."

Caught quite off guard by his brief tirade and what I held in my hand, I asked him to tell me a little bit about himself. He told me pretty much the same thing that his parole agent had told me earlier: that he was the prison's computer networker and had "learned all about computers inside [the prison] because [he] dropped out of high school and never even touched a computer." I asked Paul if he agreed that he was a beneficiary of the same capitalistic system he condemned. Further, I told him it appeared that prison had been a rewarding experience for him, that he was a standout, because of his academic achievements, among males his age, regardless of their race. "Would you have accomplished as much as you have, on the outside?" I asked him.

He sidestepped the question and said, "The system always has bones to throw you as prizes."

I told him that however he defined his achievements, it would be difficult for anybody to believe that the system had oppressed him. Further, I told him it appeared that the system had given him the tools for success and the opportunity to use them as a free, responsible person in a democratic society.

He looked at me for a long while before he spoke. "The Statue of Liberty is a racist bitch!" he spat out in a voice husky with anger. He then said he wanted to talk about his "commitment offense," the crime for which he had been sentenced. His parole agent had not mentioned it to me. Paul said he was serving time for "emptying a military carbine" into another youth's head, killing him instantly. According to Paul, the youth had "beaten [him] down on the quad at high school, in front of everybody," because Paul had been dating a girl of an ethnicity different than his own—but identical to the ethnicity of his attacker. Paul calmly recounted this particular high school experience, and explained precisely what he had done about it, in a well-modulated voice. "You're probably thinking that I'm middle class, come from a successful family—not one parent but two—and could have been my high school's valedictorian and off to college, right?"

This guy was one cool number, I thought. He had pegged me right. His observation was as insightful as any college-bound student I had taught. Even in his prison garb, he looked like Mr. Teenage Success.

"Well, you're right," he continued, interrupting and confirming my thoughts. "That's what my victim thought, too. And that's how I caught him off guard. Just 'cuz I had both parents at home and food on the table every day, I wasn't no pussy. My brother and me had guns hidden upstairs, in the attic. But lots of people don't know that. They look at me and think I'm some goody-two-shoes kid, some kind of geek. To get respect, you gotta be able to take somebody out. My victim did not survive the brain surgery I did on him [chuckle]. I took him *all the way out.*"

Paul is part of an alarming statistic. He joins the ranks of children and teenagers who are responsible for over 10 percent of the nation's homicides, many of them hate-motivated crimes driven by an intolerance for a person's race, ethnicity, gender, or lifestyle. At least part of what is lacking in these extreme acts of violence is a well-developed moral intelligence in the character of the perpetrators.

Today, as we bask in the corona of the New Millennium, hate-inspired violence committed by youth devoid of moral intelligence increasingly threatens the lives of our adolescents. Indeed, as the nation cries for "diversity" and "tolerance," we ought to engage in some national soul-searching: *Is our push toward multiculturalism moving us toward diversity or throwing us into division?*

Certain renowned, charismatic social-activists unfailingly blame the government in particular and society in general for producing a national environment where our youth become victims of virulent, relentless racial discrimination. But as any number of "youth-watch" organizations—from the Children's Defense Fund, to the U.S. Justice Department's Office of Juvenile Justice and Delinquency Prevention, to the Centers for Disease Prevention and Control—continue to report it is today's youth who are a hazardous, lethal threat to themselves. Their ruthless, homicidal violence, according to Dr. Deborah Prothrow-Stith of Harvard University's School of Public Health, is the number one public health problem faced by today's adolescents. In 1981, Dr. Prothrow-Stith documented what she saw, in her swelling caseload of severely wounded patients, as an alarming trend in youth-on-youth violence, viewing it as a galloping public health problem which would eventually dominate the nation's attention. *Adolescentcide is a national emergency that potentially affects every child in America.*

But contrary to the rhetoric of today's social-activist oppor-
tunists, it is America's families that need overhauling, not the
government. It is the thinking patterns of youth that must be
reversed. It is clear to me from my experience acting under the
auspices of the Los Angeles District Attorney's office to conduct
expulsion hearings on children that it is these children's violent
impulses that must be dropped, not the school-expulsion policy
nor the police-arrest charges they incur after inciting deadly brawls
at athletic events. If police officers are to be judged and made to
give an account for their alleged brutality and misuse of weapons,
then so must our children also be made to give an account about
the sources of their weapons' and why they have all but declared
what appears to be the Children's Civil War, or as one of my
parent education seminar attendees said the "Wee Wars."

Our society is populated with children representing perhaps
every nationality, culture and religion on the face of the earth. It
is vital that parents ensure that their own children grow up free of
the shackles of stereotyped ideas and prejudices—ideas that fuel
racism, sexism, religionism, alienation and social discomfort—
and learn to respect and interact with others, regardless of their
race, creed, religion, or lifestyle preference. Such respect is an
invaluable asset that, combined with other significant elements,
can only assure children's safety and success in our multiethnic,
polycultural society.

As your children make friends, encourage them to reach out
beyond their usual social circle to others who talk or look differently than they do. Of course, the best "modeler" of this is you,
that is, the range and diversity of your social behaviors. So invite
other families, representing different cultures, nationalities and
backgrounds, into your home. Interact socially with different
cultures outside your home. Participate in intercultural events and
encourage your children to do so, too. Thus, the gift you give
your children will be a natural sense and ability for working and
playing and getting along with others. You will engender moral
intelligence in them

And yet, tolerance and respect for diversity is only a part of
moral intelligence. The broader dimensions of moral intelligence
include the non-negotiable belief that life must be lived within a

moral frame of right and wrong, and the conviction that it is possible to know and deliberately choose moral standards to guide one's behavior.

Of the 103 incarcerated adolescents I interviewed, who were serving prison sentences for homicide, only three recalled being instructed in the principles of right and wrong. The remaining 100 told me that they received no formal or consistent instruction in moral behavior until they began serving their prison sentence and began attending mandated counseling and therapy sessions. During these sessions, they were explicitly told that they had committed a moral wrong and an act against society. With each group meeting, they learned successively more about right and wrong and the patterns of their own thinking that led them to commit their heinous capital crimes. Six of the adolescents I interviewed were incarcerated in prison for killing a member of their own family.

This phenomenon underscores a marked lack of moral intelligence and respect among the young citizens of a nation where adhering to moral principles and leading a virtuous life were once viewed as highly desirable and even, in some instances, divinely ordered; virtue and morality were taught as the source of spiritual and physical freedom and enlightenment.

The brilliant *Wall Street Journal* writer and researcher Daniel Goleman calls these vital human attributes "emotional intelligence," an especially apt phrase given that acts of violence are almost totally driven by the emotions, notwithstanding the cliché "cold-blooded murderer." Only you, as a parent, can ensure that your children know and understand that this great nation was built by people driven by their *perception of a high moral purpose.* If our country is to survive, today's children must also be taught to pursue high moral purposes; they must become enlightened by a moral intelligence and directed by a moral energy and inspiration.

Today, however, we seldom say the words "moral" and "education" in the same breath. Like fire and fuel, they inflame. Heated arguments about mixing church and state delude us into thinking that a free and united country is only achieved and guaranteed by the separation of church and state. So, moral education and guiding principles of right and wrong are largely abandoned by public school educators and left to the classrooms of the private schools. Right behaviors are kindness, honesty, and civility—the list goes on. Unfortunately, these behaviors are not taught but rather when they are breached, the child is punished—such as detention for cheating or fighting. This suppression technique is virtually ineffective in causing a change in the child's behavior. Telling a child not to cheat or fight is an admonition given without the appropriate exploration of why such behaviors are morally wrong. Teaching proper behavior in a directed, structured way is a vastly superior approach to punishing negative behavior, especially because the child may have no inclination that his behavior violated good moral conduct. The irony is perhaps most poignant in considering this simple truth: you can teach moral intelligence—observing right over wrong—without teaching religious doctrine. It is likely that some basic right/wrong instruction is observed in schools, but it is equally clear that it is a cursory and unstructured approach that leaves children bereft of the skills they need to make safe, conflict-reducing choices. My experience as both an educator and parent, not to mention the ever-rising child death tolls, makes this clear.

The following poem struck me powerfully in the way it speaks to this very issue:

Dear Teacher,

I am a survivor of a concentration camp. My eyes saw what no man should witness:

* Gas chambers built by learned engineers.
* Children poisoned by educated physicians.
* Infants killed by trained nurses.
* Women and babies shot and burned by high school and college graduates.

So I am suspicious of education.

My request is: Help your students become human. Your efforts must never produce learned monsters, skilled psychopaths, educated Eichmanns.

> Reading, writing, arithmetic are important only if they serve to make our child more human.
>
> —Anonymous

Neglecting to instill moral education in our public schools and moral thinking in the children who attend them has not united this nation but only divided it. Children, engaged in their own civil wars, are killing each other at ever-alarming rates—even in small communities long prized as preferential enclaves, affluent and far removed from the [common notion of the] heat and hate and sin and sizzle of the urban cities. Thinking we are guaranteeing religious and social freedoms by prohibiting moral principles from being taught in the public school, we thus turn our backs against the guiding and unerring light of moral instruction that ought to infuse education.

Our deliberate disregard for our moral obligation to our children has stranded and blinded them. Stumbling and struggling, they slay their peers and threaten us, causing us to fear. Today, when students are turning whole campuses upside down in murderous shooting sprees, public school educators who fail to see the need to inculcate moral intelligence in their students must prepare themselves for that sad day when their school yards are transformed into grave yards by some of those students.

If your children's schools flee from the word "moral" and simply refuse to teach right and wrong behavior, then perhaps you should insist that schools devote certain class periods to discussing the headlines and corresponding stories of children killed by other children on school campuses. In this way, those uncomfortable with the use of the word "moral" in school curriculum might be availed of the opportunity to, at the very least, show the dire consequences of certain actions. Children will thus have exposure to the immorality and pain of youth aggression.

Schools that are not teaching students what is right, wrong and morally acceptable, as well as peace-building and non-violent conflict-reduction skills, are failing in their total educational obligation to their students.

Whether you are a religious or non-religious person, the act of murder undoubtedly violates *whatever* beliefs you do hold. For whatever reason we hold our beliefs about murder—that it is wrong and is a moral crime—it is our obligation to pass on that reason and belief to our children. If we fail to do that, we will leave them deprived of the real blessings of living peacefully and nonviolently.

Certainly, there are a multitude of ways to engender peaceful, nonviolent living, many of which I will cover in this book. But it is neither naïve nor excessively rudimentary to begin with basic civility, such as courtesy and etiquette.

In this light, the state of Louisiana, on July 5, 1999, passed a law mandating that its public school children be taught to say "Thank you," "Excuse me," "Yes, sir," and "Yes, ma'am." Shocked by the horrifying national picture of adolescent homicide, the state's lawmakers are attempting to engender respect for others—a good start toward stemming the tide of adolescentcide Does your child's school have this program? Are you teaching these basic courtesies in your own home? And yet this is just a beginning. Concerned parents can go further and request that school districts build moral education curriculum components into *every* subject. Don't be put off by fuzzy arguments about "mixing church and state." Moral intelligence is not solely a "church" issue, it is an issue wherever violent and aggressive behavior causes harm to another individual. It may be that some of those who remain uncomfortable with moral education don't realize that being moral can be a separate thing from being religious. Be aware of those whose ignorance on this matter might quell positive curriculum changes because of their "comfort" level with a word—morality.

A month after Louisiana's "etiquette education" law, volunteers in McKee, Kentucky placed the Ten Commandments in every classroom in the eastern Kentucky school district. The Jackson County School Board and its superintendent made the decision as part of what Principal Betty Bond called "an effort to start having good morals in school." The school district's attorney stated that since the plaques in the district's five schools were paid for and posted by local volunteers, they are allowed by law.

Equally eager as Louisiana and Kentucky were to spark an ethical/moral awakening in their students, the Anaheim Union High School District, in Anaheim, California, voted to institute "moments of reflection" at each of its high school campuses. The view of the Anaheim board was that its students needed opportunities during the school day to privately, and without interruption or interference, think, ponder and reflect—and the confidence that it is okay to do so. That these quiet moments were sanctioned by the school district, should go far in persuading students that traditional school subjects are only part of the education they ought to be seeking.

Schools need not search very far to find examples of their on-campus courses grounded in the fundamentals of right and wrong behaviors. For example, Driver Training is taught from a framework of right and wrong vehicular behavior. Moreover, nobody—certainly not the teens who are obsessed about learning to drive—questions the moral framework within which the life-and-death fundamentals of Driver Training are taught. I've used this example before to demonstrate to parents how a moral frame-work can be used to educate children concerning behavior, and have had parents respond that it seems over-simplified and silly. In part, that is the very point. Driving, for a large number of people, is a necessary part of daily life. We operate what law enforcement agencies list as a deadly weapon—road vehicles—with ease and little thought, often performing other functions—reading, talking to passengers, chatting on cell phones—while we commute to our various destinations. Yet we all subscribe to a set of rules that, when followed, ensure our safety against potential injury and death. This training is mandatory in every state, and once it is learned, as automatic as breathing. How noticeably absent is it then, that schools do not devote specific courses to personal conduct—interpersonal skills, nonviolent communication, and social interaction—from the standpoint of right and wrong behavior? Our interrelations with one another ought to be as automatic as driving and guided by rules that ensure our safety, and it should be part of the education every child receives.

Even our schools athletic programs work from a framework of *right* and *wrong* behaviors. Not only does such positive instruction help to avoid or reduce personal injuries and the resultant financial liabilities, but such indoctrination also helps to win games. In football, "illegal procedure" and "clipping" are a couple of terms referees use to identify unnecessary, dangerous, and prohibited behaviors that, in the eyes of some, are nothing short of deliberate or reckless assault-and-battery.

The games of athletics develop numerous but fully-accepted burdensome regulations to ensure that our children-athletes play fair, remain eligible to play, and continue to qualify to be judged as "fit for the team" (physically *and* ethically). Today, a student athlete learns that he can be benched if he "clips" (potentially injurious hand-strike in the neck or back) an opponent, but might easily fail to learn that emptying a gun clip into another student he doesn't like is immoral and illegal. Such fundamental knowledge of right and wrong behavior might seem extremely obvious, and without specific need of being taught. But I can attest to the real and urgent need of exactly such training. Important knowledge, behavioral or otherwise, must be structurally verbalized as well as demonstrated.

Another way in which athletics maintains discipline over wrong behavior is through the wearing of uniforms. Studies continue to prove that the wearing of uniforms reduces violent behavior. Not only must you play and act unified, you must also *look* unified. President Clinton's 1998 visit to the Long Beach Unified School District (California), the nation's best-known uniform-driven public school, was a visit described by the press as "seen around the nation." The visit brought into sharp focus the need to take a page out of the gospel of athletics: Acknowledge, once and for all, that where the education of students is concerned, uniformity in dress produces conformity in behavior and establishes a common school spirit.

You owe your children more than an expectation that they go to school and succeed academically and make you proud. Today's child needs to know more than mathematics, science, history, social science and language arts. They must be versed in the subjects of social behavior, right and wrong, and conflict-resolution.

It is wise to have a keen awareness of your children's moral as well as academic GPA (grade point average). Ask yourself,

*"Do I really know how morally intelligent my child is, even though I know where he is academically?" "How often do I engage in moral problem-solving with my children?" "What are the indicators in their conversations that let me know they are engaged in moral contemplation or seeing and thinking through a moral frame?"* If your child's moral GPA, in your opinion, is less than it ought to be, do you know what to do to raise it? You should be as worried about your child's moral GPA as you are anxious about his/her academic GPA. Raising the moral grade is a process that requires teaching, listening, nurturing, understanding, debating, correcting, prompting, confronting, and expecting—all with love. It requires commitment, sacrifice, and time.

But according to a Newsweek poll conducted in spring 1999, 47 percent of Americans believe that very few parents really know what their teens are up to, and 90 percent of Americans say parents aren't spending enough time with their teens.

The lives of Paul, the ward in the California youth prison; Eric Harris, one half of the pair of shooters at Columbine High School; and Ted Kacynski share some disturbing similarities and will serve to illustrate the need to monitor your child's moral GPA. Though not blood brothers, they certainly appear to have been brothers-in-arms, comrades in spirit. More than this, all three clearly show a marked lack of moral training.

Paul came from a good home. Both parents were professionals and had careers. One of his brothers was employed by the school system in the city in which the family lived; and his other siblings were all doing well and had not been involved in law violations. Paul had ready access to a variety of weapons, as though prepared for war. During my third interview with him, he said that he and his friends merely "hopped the back fence to get into school and bypass the metal detectors, because we had guns in our backpacks."

Paul's rage was ignited by his feelings of having been pushed around, disrespected, and embarrassed in front of others at school. Although unable to exact vengeance right away, he nevertheless was eventually successful in achieving his goal of getting even. "My buddy and I passed this car on the street one day, about a month after the fight at school. I didn't see who was in it, but my buddy did and said, 'Hey, that's the guy that rolled you up at school, isn't it? Wanna take him out now?' " His buddy sped to Paul's home and Paul went inside and emerged from it with an M-16 carbine "wrapped in a jacket so the neighbors wouldn't think nothin.' "

The memory still vivid, Paul summarized the "execution" of his victim. "We drove back onto that street and the guy's car was still there. I said, 'Damn, is this my lucky day!' My buddy slowed down and crawled right up next to the car. The guy was still sitting inside, probably waiting for somebody, but not for me. He was on my side of the car. I had my hat on, so he didn't recognize me. I waved at him and he rolled the window down. Before he knew it, he was looking right into my carbine. Then I took off my hat. I saw his mouth drop open, and I filled his face with fire. My buddy gunned the car. I put on another clip and held the carbine out the window in case he had his crew backing him up and return-ing fire. But nobody did. I got my man by himself and he died alone."

Paul's parents never knew about the arsenal of weapons he stored in his upstairs bedroom. Trusting, doting parents, or, worse, seriously out of touch parents became the best "enablers" he could ever have.

In April 1999, Eric Harris and Dylan Klebold committed the worst school shooting in American history. The two teens went to the school cafeteria, began hurling pipe bombs and opening fire with their automatic weapons. Sheriff John Stone, of Littleton, said the cafeteria was laid waste in "entire carnage."

Eric Harris' parents seemed just as out of touch as were Paul's. Reportedly, Harris' garage and bedroom contained bombs, a sawed-off shotgun, and a diary filled with writings depicting his hatred for others. Harris bought an Internet website and used it to write death threats against schoolmates. His hate-filled prose stated: "I don't care if I live or die in the shootout, all I want to do is kill and injure as many of you pricks as I can." In another paragraph revealing his highly disturbed mental state, he wrote: "G** D*** it, DEAD PEOPLE DON'T ARGUE! G** D*** I AM P***ED!!" The graphic self-profile he proudly placed on the America Online Web site included the quote "Kill 'em AALLL!!!"

Though not everybody knew the "complete Harris," as it were, through his website, some people had heard Harris often boasting of making bombs. Supposedly, concerned neighbors spoke to Harris' mother and returned from the home saying she had merely cried. When alerted by neighbors about his son, Harris' father, a retired Air Force officer, purportedly disregarded their warnings and decided that his son hadn't meant what he had written. Eric's diary contained accounts of being been pushed around, demeaned and bullied at school by student-athletes and others. Among those with whom he felt he had scores to settle, he targeted student-athletes, gay students, and black students as his enemies who "must pay" for the misery he endured in high school.

A student in advanced-placement calculus, Harris was one of his school's well-known "geeks," a reputation he despised. He and his friend Dylan Klebold created a murderous video they showed in their film class at school. Neither their teacher nor the other students took it seriously. Harris had been infatuated with neo-Nazi groups. He attended meetings of Aryan supremacy groups, learned their lingo, dressed like them, and chose their same targeted groups—"the others"—on which to spew his hatred and vitriol. Both he and Klebold were the proud members of a group, the "Trenchcoat Mafia," that took every opportunity to flaunt their outsider status. The group even made their own group-portrait postcard, which included in its caption this in-your-face statement: *"Who says we're different! Insanity's healthy!"* Part of their sign-off was: *"Stay alive, stay different, stay crazy!"*

Dr. Ted Kacynski, the "Unabomber," was an outstanding student. On paper, he was exemplary. With graduate degrees, he possessed much more than the average tools for success. Ted Kacynski, however, was devoid of moral intelligence and a capacity for ethics. He spent his adult life building intricate letter-bombs and mailing them to people he hated all over the United States. The FBI believes his premeditated, heinous and murderous acts, spanning almost 20 years, were responsible for the killing of 17 people and maiming of countless others.

When a person grows and develops with an absence of moral intelligence and an ethical sensibility, that person has a huge void in the area of sensitivity, sympathy, and compassion for others. It is little wonder that they operate like Ted Kacynski at an almost animalistic level. While Paul, my interviewee in juvenile prison, Eric Harris of Columbine High School's "Trenchcoat Mafia," and Ted Kacynski, were exceptionally intelligent and articulate, lived at primitive and barbaric levels, morally because they were untutored in principles of right and wrong. They functioned as illiterates in their own moral wasteland, and became preoccupied with death and destruction, obsessed with exacting revenge for having suffered real or imagined insults, slights, and abuse.

As seen by these examples, "good" parents and children with high IQ's are poor predictors of social success in the real world. High intelligence and academic brilliance have absolutely nothing to do with moral intelligence. They are as different as airplanes and automobiles. Unless you nurture your children's moral intelligence and their ethical senses, and educate them in the fundamentals of moral behavior, they could well become dead, morally speaking, although radiating with life, intellectually speaking. As a parent, you simply cannot assume that providing your children a good education will lead to a good moral life. With disturbing frequency, we are seeing tragic examples that education and morality are not the allies they should be. Indeed, they are as aliens, each occupying separate worlds.

As a parent, you are your child's first teacher. And teach you must. Rearing and educating children is fraught with challenges and complexities like no other single endeavor. And, now, with more and more children taking up guns and hauling them to school in their backpacks as the "answer" to their personal suffering and interpersonal pains, it is vital that you teach your children how to survive what are, arguably, the most unsafe times (including the turn-of-the-century periods of "sweat-shop children" and "child coal miners") for all children in the entirety of the nation's history. Here are some basic steps you can take to train your child to be morally intelligent and reduce his risk for becoming a victim or perpetrator of violence, accidental or otherwise.

### 1. *Spend as much time with your children as you can*.

Your wholesome and positive influence will affect your children's thinking and behavior.

Impress upon them the importance of family life, versus "street life" in the malls, parks, or at parties or other events away from home.

Create fun, enjoyable, and educational activities for them at home, or combine these with friends and neighbors, so that your child bonds with others whose families have a positive, protective, and peaceful orientation.

Provide leadership roles for your child, to give him practice in designing and conducting family activities.

Provide as many outlets for creative and artistic expression as you possibly can. Music, Art, Storytelling, Creative Writing, and Dance can be tremendously positive influences for developing children.

Use the resources of your local library: check out books with activities, projects, and entertainment that can be carried out at home; and keep current with the library's bulletin board, which posts free community events and educational activities.

**2. *Take a good view of your own behavior and notice your own responses to the various stresses and challenges of raising a family.***

If you explode in anger, your children feel the shock of your temper and your words. Instead, maintain a calm demeanor, take deep breaths, and express yourself in a relaxed, controlled manner. This is also especially important when you're talking with another adult in the home. Remember: children will match your tone, words, and actions.

Don't threaten, belittle or bully your children. If they are the recipients of this kind of treatment at home, they will duplicate it in their interactions with others, because it has become so natural to them.

**3. *Openly discuss violent or tragic situations that occur locally or nationally.***

When your child hears of or knows about tragic events, he intuitively expects and trusts your views. So, express your views and candidly talk to your child about the causes and consequences of violence.

Be open to questions and different viewpoints from your child. These are indications of his desire for answers and guidance. Don't become insulted, become inspired. Always let him know that he and his viewpoints are very important.

Ask your child questions to get him thinking. Point out different aspects of an issue and ask him for solutions to the "problems" you pose or that are inherent in the issues themselves.

### 4. *Teach your children the difference between violence on television or in the movies and violence in real life.*

Explain to your children that the violence they see on television is not real, nor should it be imitated as a strategy for solving conflicts in real life. Emphasize that guns used in real life can kill or maim, and that real life is no movie.

Monitor what your children watch on television. A steady diet of violent TV fare, whether Saturday cartoons or "family hour" dramas, is unhealthy. Remember: children learn and mimic what they see.

### 5. *Take time daily with your children to discuss spiritual, philosophical, and moral issues of right and wrong.*

Think of these times as "mining the mind" and "coaching the conscience." Just as children learn their timestables by constantly practicing them, the moral intelligence of your child can be sparked through constant practice—discussions, questions, analysis, and problem-solving.

Be patient and loving with your child. Do not attack him with "You know better!" That may be true, but what is more important is your reaction. So, be proactive and use as many teachable moments with your child as you can. Coach him, coax him, cheer him, and counsel him.

### 6. *Develop ways and means for rewarding your children for their moral behavior.*

Design a behavior-reward plan. It need not be complicated. In fact, the simpler the better, since you will expect your child to remember it. For our household, I purchase a roll of tickets printed with $.25 on each ticket stub. Each child receives 60 tickets, the equivalent of $15. All of us discuss the behaviors my wife and I need to see from them in order for them not to have to pay "fines." For example, failing to get dressed for school on time costs two tickets, whereas fighting, rather than using words to solve sibling problems, costs five tickets. Further, they can earn extra tickets for doing extra chores, for completing additional academic work we obtain from an educational supplies store. My children look forward to the first day of each month when they trade their remaining tickets in for real cash—they call it "toy buying time." It is a reward program that they can design and re-design as they like. The point is, they respect and obey it and, overall, it seems to work well. It certainly keeps them thinking, which should be one of the primary goals of your behavior-reward program.

Other behavior rewards can range from hikes and picnics to all-day excursions at the zoo or amusement park. They can be as simple as "earning" books to check out at the local library. A friend's son earned an expensive bicycle by reading 50 books over the summer and typing a one-page report on each. In choosing rewards, observe what things and events excite your child. It is best for parents and children to design a behavior-reward plan together. You may wish to outline the program on paper and secure it to the refrigerator or the wall of your child's room. Some parents use large paper with grid lines for the placement of names, tasks, and "extra credit" activities, then use an assortment of colored stars or stickers to affix for "grading." Be open and negotiate with your child as you co-design the program. It is more his program than it is yours. It is important that he realize that life is negotiable and that a large amount of its control is in his hands. That lesson, as do all others, begins in his interaction and communication with you.

In helping your child design the behavior reward program, gently yet constantly spell out and reiterate the kind of behavior you're looking for and want to see demonstrated. Without being unduly negative, frankly state what behaviors are not good, safe, helpful, legitimate or in any other way desirable. Then spend considerable time stressing how happy you are when your child demonstrates wholesome, responsible, responsive, and positive behaviors. Cite examples. Let him know how very proud of him you are when you see that kind of behavior.

Tell your child the purpose of the behavior reward program is to help him keep up the good behavior. As his behavior improves (sometimes the weathervane for this will be the *ease* with which he earn toys or other rewards), set higher goals and make him "stretch" to achieve them. That way he won't get bored with the "same-ole-same-ole."

**7. Take stock of the kinds of toys you buy your children. Change your buying habits and patterns if necessary**.

How many kinds of guns, projectiles and attack toys are in their "arsenal?" How many "war heroes" make up their collection of toys?

Spurred by the release of a major children's movie, the giant fast-food corporations, eager to keep children thinking that fast food is fun, place toy replicas of the movie's "action heroes" inside their ever-popular "Kids Meals." These companies do not advocate or promote criminal or violent behavior by children. In fact, they donate millions of dollars annually to children's charities, foundations, and programs for youth across the country. Yet, many of the "Kids Meals" "heroes" are idolized by children expressly for the on-screen violence they enact.

What can you do? Encourage your children to select something other than the "Kids Meal." If they insist, perhaps allow them to have the meal without the toy, and reward them by taking them shopping at their favorite toy store. Teach them that you don't approve of bringing replicas of weapons or of violent screen heroes into your home. Then co-design with them a toy-reward program whereby they earn a trip to the toy store because they *purposely* chose a "hero" or "heroine" not associated with violence of any kind. Make certain their input—rather than simply your own—is prominently reflected in the rules for earning trips to the toy store. If there are sufficient other toy choices at the fast-food establishment, use the time there as a teaching moment to help your children discriminate between the action/violent hero and the toy figure known on-screen for being kind, benevolent, generous, and good.

**8. *Talk to your children about guns and violence. Explain that it is better and safer to use words to communicate, no matter how angry one becomes*.**

Show your children safe, healthy ways to express their disagreement and feelings of anger. Take time to notice when your children are using positive means for reducing or resolving conflicts, and praise them for their efforts. Let them know you care about their feelings and support all their nonviolent attempts to handle conflicts.

**9. *Do everything in your power to ensure that your children know guns are dangerous and are not to be touched, played with, or handled*.**

Don't think your children will automatically know what to do if they come upon a gun in somebody's home, inside a trash dumpster, or at the park beneath a tree. A child's shock and confusion of stumbling upon a weapon has led to many tragedies nationwide.

Teach your children to summon help immediately from a parent or other trusted adult if they find an unattended gun, or see another child with a gun. Emphasize that they are never to touch or handle the gun in such a circumstance but are to immediately leave the area and get help.

**10. *Keep guns away from your children*.**

Just as you keep your car keys and credit cards away from your children, you must also keep guns away from them. The best and easiest strategy is not to keep a gun in the home, period. If you feel you must keep a gun at home, take out all the ammunition. Put a trigger lock on the gun and store it away. Take the ammunition somewhere else and lock it up.

As a parent, never let your guard down concerning guns and your children. You already know that children often can mysteriously "unlock" cabinets, drawers, doors, chests, and closets. Children are driven by their insatiable curiosity. They can be extraordinarily resourceful and will often find a gun anywhere it's hidden in the house. A child's entire being can vibrate with the urge to discover. What's behind the locked door or cabine?. A mystery makes the "hunt" all the more fun and exciting. And that's what can make the "mystery" of a locked-away gun deadly.

As a parent, you need to know that having even an unloaded gun in the home at all increases risks for suicide, domestic homicide and accidents. A person intent on using a gun can buy or steal a box of bullets for it. If you make it a personal choice to have a gun in your home, make sure to take extreme measures and extraordinary precautions to teach your children gun safety— *and* still keep the weapon away from them entirely. There are any number of news reports of gun tragedies in homes where the very best efforts of parents to safeguard their children from the in-home gun the parents insisted on keeping, failed in a childish moment made fatal by curiosity and carelessness.

# Shaping a Non-Violent Boy

*I tied my dead victim by his legs and pulled him, dragged him, on the sidewalk 'til I got to the alley where my homeboys were. When they saw me, they went crazy—they got off on the fact that I was like a soldier dragging my prisoner of war in my own victory parade. Everybody was yelling my name and praising me. I got high, got drunk, found my girlfriend and stayed out all night 'cuz I had my reputation back.—Jerry*

Jerry was fifteen when I met and interviewed him. His life, as he recounted it, was spent in constant quests for power. As a "soldier" in a gang, he was always "jumpy (nervous) about new faces and cars going a little too fast on my street." Jerry says that he never took to people very well; they were all too willing to make even familiar and safe environments threatening for him. "One day me and my mama were going to church and I got jumped. They beat me up on the way to church, can you believe that? My mama was right there and they jacked me up anyway." With some cynicism he said, "I stopped going to church after that. Too dangerous. I got jacked up with my mama right there. See, that's no respect at all. Now, mama, she loves me, I guess. But she couldn't do nothing for me. You know, like, back me up. I mean, when you get jacked up going to church, what's the world coming to?"

Jerry, filled with aggression and anger, decided he had to get revenge. Word of his being "jacked up" had spread like wildfire and was destroying his reputation with every re-telling of his beating. "So I waited," he said, his eyes gleaming with the memory of his revenge. "I had to control myself and wait real long. What was so hard was I knew that everybody, at school and in the streets, thought I was a punk since I'd been jacked up. I got over it. You know, my bruises healed and everything. My pride took longer. But I got that back too." Jerry regained his pride, as he put it, by catching one of his assailants "slipping," that is, passing through Jerry's turf without his gun or partners or any other kinds of defense—utterly off guard. Jerry took this "slipping" behavior as a public insult. "He was drunk, I knew that, 'cuz he was *walking*. But still, I knew guys who could drink buckets of beer and they'd never be caught slipping. So, that told me he thought he could rub my face in it even when he was drunk. By the time I got my gun up in his neck, real close and so tight he couldn't talk good, I was real angry. I yelled my head off at him and told him how dare he come back into my neighborhood, drunk, and walk up and down my street. I told him he didn't have enough brains to live. Then I pulled the trigger and he fell right there at my feet. That's when I got the idea."

Jerry's "idea" was to use an impressive (to his peers) but extremely macabre stunt to publicly show off his coup. "You know that movie with Kirk Douglas, 'Spartacus' I think it was, where he leads a victory parade in the street and drags his enemies in a chariot? Well, that's just what I did. I tied my dead victim by his legs and pulled him, dragged him, on the sidewalk until I got to the alley where my homeboys were. When they saw me, they went crazy—they got off on the fact that I was like a soldier dragging my prisoner of war in my own victory parade. Everybody was yelling my name and praising me. I got high, got drunk, found my girlfriend and stayed out all night 'cuz I had my reputation back. I even had some new friends but I knew a lot more people were scared of me. They started treating me like I was the death angel or something. But I had to do what I did to get my reputation back and keep people from screwing with me."

Jerry had paid his dues and secured the reputation he craved. In his harsh, primitive world, reputation was everything: his protection as well as his prestige. In his dog-eat-dog world, the fatal shooting of his victim was a natural development in his cycle of aggression. Boys like Jerry respond to aggression with aggression. From then on, the perception that others had of him was that of an AGGRESSOR—and an especially brutal one.

Inside the constantly regulated and controlled prison environment, Jerry learned that reputation was everything, too. What his parole officer, psychologist, chaplain, and parole board thought of him and how they viewed him became more important than anything else to him. He was obsessed with "doing my program," which consisted, in part, of attending mandated counseling sessions, going to school, and working in the various prison pre-vocational programs such as upholstery, landscaping, dog grooming, and food services. Not only did Jerry want to consistently "do" his "program," he wanted to be recognized for doing it well above the minimum standards. Written evaluations by those who had custody over him was of paramount concern to him. Publicity, as you may recall from his aforementioned aggressor behavior, was a highly-valued commodity to him.

"I knew that whatever my parole officer thought about me, he would be writing it down. Everybody that had authority over me was always writing something down. I seen lots of guys bad-mouth their parole officers and try to jack them up, even. Fifteen- and sixteen-year-old guys. That's insane. I ain't never seen none of them win. Guys got sent to solitary confinement and got time added to their sentences. When they went to their parole hearing, they got denied because of the bad behavior crap in their record. Me, I stumbled in the beginning, because I thought I was a bad dude. But I ain't no dumb dude. I seen where the power was, and it wasn't with me no more. I left my power in the streets the second I killed my victim. Real quick, I decided I wasn't going to win here by fighting the system. So, I decided to do my program to the max, you know what I mean? Right now, I'm considered a model prisoner by everybody. And I got respect. So,

I got a better reputation—something that can do me some good and take me somewhere—than I had on the outside. And you want to know what the strange part of it is?" I nodded yes. How could I decline? "I didn't even have to *fight* for it—lay somebody down, jack somebody up, shoot back, make threats, or carry a weapon."

Jerry realizes that a positive reputation, built from constructive and nonviolent accomplishments, is socially more advantageous and produces more benefits. He admits that he often wishes he had "known all this before, how to get along with people, and stuff like that." I asked Jerry if he was happy and he said yes. When I asked him if he regretted killing his victim, he said, "For a long while after, I didn't. I felt he deserved it for what he did to me. But during my court trial, I spent days and weeks watching my victim's family staring at me. And he had a big family. His mother and sisters were always crying and that started getting to me. Nobody from my family came to court, not even my mother. I began thinking that I had taken the life of somebody special. And it seemed like I had taken part of their lives, too . . . you know, his whole family. I started feeling pains inside me, started getting rashes, and even had trouble eating and sleeping. I knew what I was feeling was guilt. I guess I learned that from church. That went on for a long time, until the trial was over. One day I couldn't even make it to court, I was so sick."

Jerry received a twelve-year sentence and would be forced to face his crime, its results, and its cause, in a variety of mandated therapy and encounter programs almost as soon as he was delivered to the prison in which he served his time. He explains: "In prison, I felt that guilt all over again, and even though I was no longer in that courtroom where I was tried, I began to see my victim's family and the faces of his mother and sisters. I thought I was going crazy. Everywhere I turned, there they were, in my mind. Nothing I did—go to sleep or not go to sleep—made them go away. I never felt so empty before, even when I was on the streets. Even when they jacked me up, I didn't feel hollow and empty and wanted to die."

The way boys are bred is what and who they become. How Jerry was treated by family members and peers had a dominant influence on the development of his character. *Children who kill are not born—they are made*. Jerry came from a family where hostility and ongoing tensions were the norm. His mother, though perhaps devoted to him, was nevertheless seen by Jerry as weak and non-supportive. When they were both confronted and Jerry was assaulted, he saw his mother as totally useless in defending him. He was witness both to his own victimization by others and his mother's inability to care for (help) him. Jerry's revenge-motive was also nurtured in him. His home and social backgrounds were defined by force and violence. While his mother may not have promoted violence in the home, Jerry felt she stood idly by and neither stopped it nor trained him in social etiquette and decent, civil behavior.

Jerry, having little other choice inside prison, determined that he was going to overcome his upbringing and change. He gave up the macho attitude that he must cultivate a reputation, accord himself prestige, or inspire fear in others in order to protect himself. Convinced that he couldn't fight the prison system, and that he was smarter than to let his life be ruined by his own behavior, his deportment changed, he progressed and became a model prisoner.

Juvenile prisons are filled with effective rehabilitation programs conducted by teams of dedicated and conscientious therapists, clinical case workers, parole agents, and others whose mission is to rehabilitate the person by addressing the root causes of his destructive behavior. But juvenile prison is not the best place for our sons to learn the costs of their own extreme, anti-social behaviors. Juvenile prison is likewise too late in the game for adopting the code of nonviolent, decent and polite behavior that serves as the foundation and salvation of a civil society. The route to or away from juvenile prison begins at home. It is there that we can ensure that "boys-will-be-boys" social behavior in our sons doesn't worsen and lead them to trouble. Committed and loving parents can guide their sons toward good, socially-acceptable behavior. As parents, we all want our sons to grow up to become good, kind, morally upright men whose contributions to society are eagerly anticipated. We can purposefully *unlearn* stereotypical thinking about boys by teaching our sons to be caring, loving, sensitive, nonviolent human beings whose prominent concern for others shows the force of love, not the love of force.

Every parent knows that boys, the much-heralded princes of society, can be extremely aggressive. "Boys will be boys," the saying goes. But the social costs of extreme male juvenile behavior, and the fact that most homicides are committed by males like Jerry, shows our societies failure to control aggression in our male youths. The year that I began my in-person/in-prison research on children incarcerated for killing, California's number of female adolescents incarcerated for killing was 55. So "small" was this number, that these females were all incarcerated inside one prison in southern California. In dramatic contrast, 1,835 male juveniles in the state had killed that same year. It was impossible to house such a huge number in one prison. These males were incarcerated throughout the state's sprawling juvenile prison network. For each girl in California who killed that year, 33 boys took someone's life. The national average of boys versus girls committing homicide is 9:1. In other words, boys tend to be nine times as homicidal as girls.

If boys are potentially menacing to society, as the statistics on juvenile homicide and the wave of school shootings in even all-white affluent areas clearly show, we need to confront the reasons for their aggression and hostile social behavior. We are at the point, socially, when we must save our boys in order to save ourselves. "Boys will be boys" is an old-fashioned, sappy, mindless notion that has stereotyped male adolescents and excused a wide range of their socially-unacceptable, illicit, illegal, violent, immoral and destructive behaviors. This maxim has operated as a "cultural cover" for harmful male behavior while we parents have been reduced to the role of spectators watching that behavior escalate beyond the "norm" and our wildest nightmares. If "boys will be boys"—and commit vandalism, date-rape, drive-by shootings, and homicide—then what becomes of the rest of us? As our boys go, so goes our society. To bring the point closer to home, as your sons go, so goes your family.

We endanger our sons with such myths as: "Males that are tough are leaders," "Males don't cry, it shows weakness," "Real males fight to settle scores," and "Males must be heroes." Our cultural lore says it's in the male blood and genes for males to make war, be arbitrary and confrontational, and that males must always protect the mystique of invincibility. These comprise the cult of the male, the myth of the hero. "Boys will be boys" is nothing but a convenient cover that mindlessly assigns aggressive male behavior to biological imperatives. Not only does contemporary research debunk that bit of folklore, but my own studies of male juveniles and their accounts of their life histories, also discredit this cultural belief.

Let's consider Paul from the previous chapter: As horrific as his act of homicide was—to deliberately empty a military carbine into somebody's head—as detestable as his description of it as "brain surgery" was, and as inexcusable as his "rehabilitation" into rhetoric- and hate-filled communism was, violence and murder were not in his genes nor even his background. But Paul was taught in the ways of violence and killing by others, he "practiced" what he had been taught, and he adopted the twisted ideas of others as his own, using them to condemn those he labeled as responsible for his current predicament of being imprisoned.

Our adolescent society will only become more dangerous if we don't change our views and thinking about its male members, and require a higher standard of behavior of them. If we fail in these requirements, the dangers from adolescent male aggression to the larger society will only increase—as will the male adult prison population. Why? Because "boys will be boys" is a myth with the power of a benediction. The power in this myth is the paralyzing effect it has had upon our society. We must face and put aside this *superstition* in order to regain control and assert our moral authority in the shaping, shepherding and civilizing of our male children. I use the word "moral" here because when boys kill, that's a moral crime, not just a violation of the penal code and social customs.

Attributing the behavior of boys to nature is pure misconception. It is true that, biologically speaking, testosterone is the hormone that contributes to a boy's behavior. But, as a parent, you need to know that testosterone does not play a dominant role in *determining* that behavior. Yes, boys love running, jumping, and climbing. Anything that requires action and activity, they seem to yearn and live for. Of course, this is fine and most boys' testosterone drives are satisfied with such healthy, vigorous kinds of activities. But many girls love these activities as well; if you have daughters or work with girls, you undoubtedly know this. However, when boys' behaviors cross the line and become risky or reckless, we seem to automatically apply the "boys will be boys" maxim to explain and excuse them. Boys, then, are pardoned for behaviors like daredevil running back and forth across the street in front of passing cars, pushing a playmate into a swimming pool, dropping water balloons from a balcony onto persons walking below, or throwing rocks from a bridge at cars traveling beneath.

The paradox of the myth is that when a boy's behavior changes from harmless fun to hostile force, the myth continues to reinforce both the harmful behavior and a social blindness to it by allowing us, like ostriches, to hide our heads in the sand. *What can we do about it? That's how boys are!* is the defense that instantly launches us into denial about what we have seen or known and what we *must* do about it. As a parent of three boys, I know that a boy's behavior can be nurtured, that his natural tendency toward active fun can be encouraged and satisfied. In this light, any impulses (stirred by peer pressure or whipped up by action/adventure television shows and movies) can be discouraged and diverted or trained into creative, healthy, and positive pursuits.

Honoring the traditional stereotype of boys liking only toys that shoot and blow things up, toy manufacturers annually produce such mock-combat toys in the millions. Toys with parts that can be swallowed, penetrate the eye, or become lodged in the ear are usually attached with a label warning that such events have been known to occur before. It gives one pause to consider whether the manufacturers of toys should likewise label combat toys with a cautionary label of: *"CAUTION: This toy may inspire your child to enact or re-create violence-through-play or an act of violence itself."*

Of course, toy manufacturers may never state such truth in advertising. Toy manufacturing is a big and serious business, even though its customers are tiny in stature and devoted to pleasure and play. Simply stated, sales of mock-combat toys and replicas of violent action-heroes make money. And toy manufacturers eagerly make contracts with the giant motion picture companies and fast-food conglomerates to produce after-market toy replicas of action/adventure movies' popular weaponry. Yes, it is true that most of these violence-laden movies have a protective Motion Picture Association of America (MPAA) rating code declaring that the movie is not for children under the age of 17, or that children must be accompanied by their parents. But children of any age have easy access to the mock-combat toy replicas of the weapons featured in popular action/adventure movies.

Eating to satisfy hunger is a biological necessity. By fast-food conglomerates featuring mock-combat toys with their meals for children, they subliminally encourage children to associate weapons with food. Children do not possess mature powers of discrimination; some may subconsciously perceive the need for weapons (in the guise of toys) to be as basic as, or even synonymous with, the need for food. Weapons achieve legitimacy and prestige since they are featured in children's meals—a prize to be valued. Thus the picture is complete: a meal, a hungry child ready to devour it, and a full and satisfied child playing war games with the toy weapon of the season.

You may be a parent who rejects any direct link between fast-food/mock-combat toys and teenage male violence, particularly gun violence. But consider the other subtle ways in which male violence is normalized and validated as a behavioral option. War games and mortal combat games are the captivating and controlling features of electronic toy games marketed to young males. No matter what the rules of the games are, or how complicated their plots, in order to win, you must "kill" your opponent or reduce, again by killing, the size of his group/team/battalion so that "you" and your "men" are the only ones left alive and standing. You win by remaining alive; you remain alive by doing the most killing.

Arcades in the malls feature intriguing games whose titles typically use words like 'annihilation.' These arcades spare no expense in outfitting their play spaces with the very latest, most colorful, electronic war and combat games. These games are preset by the manufacturer with high decibel levels and designed with special effects to create as much realism as possible, not the least of which is graphic, gory deaths for the enemies your child shoots. What realism they lack is more than compensated for by the imaginative, fertile minds of the young males who are infatuated by "zapping," "toasting," "crushing," "blasting," and "killing"—all synonyms in common use by male adolescents to mean the taking of somebody's life. I have deliberately omitted obscene expressions that are synonyms for the word "killing." Killing, itself, is the ultimate obscenity. War toys and violent games desensitize and confuse children about the dangers of gun accidents.

Children today are continuously invited to play with violence. The toy chests you might recall from your (or others') childhood have become war chests stockpiled with "action figures," toy guns and swords, war toys, laser guns, and other instruments of destruction. As you have certainly noticed, wherever you and your child go, you confront violent arcade games, video games, computer games and virtual-reality games. Look around you and you'll notice that your child and other children see violence on television, in the movies, and on video.

Neither your child nor anybody else's child was born violent. Research shows that violence is learned behavior. We are teaching younger and younger children to be violent. Military historian Lt. Col. Dave Grossman, who is the author of the book *On Killing*, observes that "the inflicting of pain and suffering has become a source of entertainment and vicarious pleasure rather than revulsion. We are learning to kill, and we are learning to like it." Violent or mock-violent toys are helping to reinforce this "lesson." And through their hands-on toys, our children are "graduating" highly proficient in the "science" of violence and the "art" of war.

Twenty-five thousand Americans are murdered each year—more people than were killed at the height of the Vietnam War. This upsurge in violence has been noted in schools, playgrounds and even churchyards. Children under eight have a difficult time distinguishing between fantasy and reality: they receive very mixed messages from a society that glorifies violence through toys, movies and other entertainment—and at the same time tells them that violence is "bad."

How do you, as a parent, keep your son from drowning in the sea of combat toys and war games all around him? That is not an easy question to answer. Navigating your son through the arcades, fast-food joints, toy stores, malls, carnivals, and amusement parks; and monitoring his friends, his movies, magazines and television shows takes will, energy, courage, patience, and a constant readiness to deliver fast, clear and complete answers that are believable—because you yourself believe them. It also requires that you have and keep a vision of your son as a human being who will grow into a man able to use positive communication skills, conflict-reduction skills, and nonviolent negotiation skills in his social interactions with others. Your vision should tell you that yours is a son who is capable of caring so much for life and respecting and appreciating other human beings so much, that striving to achieve positive outcomes through positive communication is his goal.

Of course, in all likelihood he may object and complain that you have reduced him to geek status and he will be the only one among his friends who doesn't have the latest mortal combat toy, or even know how to play the latest Armageddon war game. All my sons were given guns as birthday gifts by well-intentioned friends and relatives. For many people toy guns are easy, snap purchases because boys are stereotyped as loving guns as well as toys that blow up things. So, busy adults rushing through a crowded toy store in search of a gift do what comes easily—they buy a boy a gun toy. Over my sons' loud and strenuous objections, I sat them down, and carefully explained to them that "real guns kill, and I do not want you *practicing* killing with play guns." I told them that "Mommy and Daddy do not like guns and we don't have them in the house." But rather than simply taking the guns away, I gave them a choice: "It is your birthday and it's not your fault that you received a gun as a present. Since our family doesn't like or have guns, what kind of *different* toy would you like to trade this gun for?"

If your choice is to allow guns in your home—whether real or toys—it would be wise to make it a practice of having your son complete gun safety courses and training. Spend enough time talking with him about guns that he understands their destructive power. And with toy guns, articulate rules that will guide his play behavior: don't allow him to pretend to shoot someone while he is angry, and have him institute pretend gun safety as part of his play—holding the gun barrel decidedly up or down while walking or running, and thumbing the safety into the lock position when he is not playing.

As a parent, you have to make the decision as to how you want your son to grow up. The seeds for his development are sown at home. You can teach him and he will learn. For example, if you want him to be polite and well-mannered, give him opportunities to practice these skills. Tell him the polite expressions you want him to say, for which occasions they are appropriate, and give him exercises so that he can practice. "Thank you," "Excuse me," "I'm sorry" and other courteous expressions will come easily with practice. Pay close attention to your son's development and note his feeling about various ideas and events. How does he express his feelings? If he doesn't, encourage him to do so. Studies across the nation indicate that men are reluctant and often unable to express their feelings. Because the inability to express feelings is a cultural and gender patent—yes, women excel here—most boys are not encouraged to express their feelings. As a result, their hostile and negative feelings go undetected until they explode in uncontrollable rage.

Jerry's life was so filled with aggression and anger that he was a walking bomb. He "had to control" himself "and wait real long" for revenge. Unfortunately, the energy he used to control himself was merely stored up for the moment he would unleash his aggression on somebody else. Conversation and sharing his feelings were foreign concepts to him; controlling them was the deadly "tool" he used.

Encourage your son to tell you what is on his mind. Start by sharing what's on your mind. Use this as a framework for expressing your ideas but allowing him to achieve a level of comfort and ease in expressing his own feelings and views. When he sees how important your feelings are to you, he will develop a respect for his own feelings and any timidity will yield to confident expression. The sooner you engage in such sharing of feelings, the better. No age is too soon. It is better to be many years too soon than even one day too late. Again, Jerry comes to mind. That fact that he went to church with his mother shows some degree of positive control she had over him (of course, when he got jumped going to church, that changed).

Such times—when parents can still get their young boys to accompany them to specific places, events—are the right times for encouraging your son to share his feelings with you, just as he might become aware of his feelings in private moments of prayer (a different kind of "sharing") at church. Before you know it, your conversations will be seasoned with how you feel about a variety of things. Hearing what you have to say is one thing. His *feeling* what you say is far more important. The trust he places in the communication of his own feelings will grow to the point where he feels entirely comfortable telling the truth about how he feels. To the extent that your son can do this, without having to be urged and prompted, you will have more clues and trails to follow to the blueprint of his thinking.

Think of feelings as having size and shape, dimension and form. Knowing the kind and quality of your son's feelings on various issues will enable you to (1) determine whether and how much he is out of "synch" with your own parental ideas; (2) know how much information he is revealing; (3) spot where his "hot buttons" are; and (4) determine whether he is in control of his feelings or whether they are controlling him. Generally speaking, the bigger the feeling, the more power it exerts. Feelings unshared can grow like deeply planted seeds and blossom into strange behaviors. Most of the boys I interviewed in my study had no experience sharing their feelings until they attended mandated therapy and counseling sessions. Most were from "macho" backgrounds and grew up in a culture of "might makes right." Many of them told me that even when they killed their victims, they didn't feel any remorse until intensive counseling was well underway. Knowing your son's feelings will give you an edge; you'll have progressive insight into his behavior. Feelings are fed by thoughts. And his thoughts will only be known if you ask him for them.

Train your sons in the art of conversation. Start by reducing the number of hours the television is watched and increasing the discussions and conversations on a variety of issues. Conversation requires alertness and attention; television watching tends to zap both. According to the National PTA, by age 18, the average child has seen 200,000 acts of violence, including 40,000 murders, on television.

Since conversation requires effort, make sure your son gets a good workout. Talk to him, question him, ask him for his views, and share your own views. You will see a smarter boy emerge before your eyes. He won't think of making conversation as tiring but will grow to appreciate it. A good talk is good for the soul. And it will let you know just where your son's most soulful feelings are. The therapeutic effects of talking are enormous and can not be overestimated. That's why counseling therapy stresses talking and talking and talking. If more boys were encouraged to talk and get things off their chests, they wouldn't be so moved to put a bullet into somebody else's chest. To know the true boy, you must also know his feelings.

# Shaping a Non-Violent Girl

*My parents never knew how I felt. They never even asked, which means they never cared. You know what I mean? It was like I was some kind of pet for them to smile at, hug and feed. Stuff like that. They never even cared enough to get mad at me. When there were problems, all they did was keep me out of sight or in school. I used to lock myself in the bathroom and drink bleach. I wanted to die, man, just die. I've been wanting to die since I was seven.*—Ruth

When I interviewed her inside the cramped, tiny office the parole agent provided, Ruth was serving a twelve-year sentence for murder in the first degree. If she's lucky and gets released by her expected parole date in 2003, she will be 21 years old. Ruth was due to go to her "Anger Management" therapy session after our morning talk. Yet she didn't try to hide from me her consuming hatred for her "ex-boyfriend, Ralph, for abandoning [her]." I could see it in her eyes.

Although formerly a bright, "B+" student with college goals, it took Ruth three years to realize that she would never see or hear from Ralph again. "What a fool I was!" she spat out. "I can't believe, now, that I was actually in love with Ralph then. And I shot and killed a guy out jogging because he gave me the gun and told me I had to prove my love. I didn't even know the guy I

55

killed, and Ralph didn't, either. And strong, fearless Ralph? He fled to another state and left me holding the bag."

The sunlight streamed through the top row of windowpanes below the ceiling. However, Ruth's manner was anything but sunny as she remembered all too well the details of her life and times with her family and with Ralph, who was a forceful personality in her life. Clinging to Ralph was apparently a subconscious effort on her part to replace the dominant personality of the grandfather she idolized who had died years earlier. The story she told me holds lessons for parents whose child feels the parents have torn her away from or blocked her access to another beloved family member, and have thus denied her happiness. Indeed, each time I interviewed Ruth, one question kept repeating itself over in my mind: *What do you do when your child blames you?*

Ruth raised the huge, heavy gun and aimed. Her lips quivered; through chattering teeth she prayed.

*Holy Mary, Mother of God . . .*

She was thirteen and had just made her Confirmation. Only two weeks old, the rite at St. Augustine Catholic Church was fresh in her memory. Her family was so proud of her. Even her mother's first husband, her natural father, had come. Usually, he visited her once a month. But on that special day, he had taken almost two hours off of work to attend. He had parked his police car in the red "No Parking" zone next to the rectory in his haste to get inside. When Father Clement had seen her dad enter the church, he had looked at her and, with a twinkle in his eye, said, "Both the Lord and the law are here with us this blessed day."

As she flexed her arm against the gun's dead weight, her eighteen-year-old boyfriend, Ralph, stood beside her, stern and stoic, his eyes hard and demanding. Icy ripples of fear ran over Ruth's skin and through her body. Though the night was warm, she shuddered and her muscles grew rigid. She hoped her trigger finger wouldn't freeze up when her target came into view. Her heart was an anvil pounding in her ears. She began to perspire. It was hard to breathe.

*. . . pray for us sinners . . .*

The firearm—a stolen Smith & Wesson magnum—was Ralph's gift to her, commemorating her Confirmation. It was, he told her, "The best, baby. I love you and only want you to have the best." He had taken her into his arms from behind and helped her tear off the Scotch tape and Sunday comics pages cocooning the weapon. "See how I'm holding you in my arms right now? Well, this big machine will take care of you when my arms are nowhere near," he promised. Ralph was such a romantic, Ruth thought. She cradled his head in one hand and pressed her cheek up against his face. She loved his fierce protective concern for her. He thought of everything.

Ralph couldn't make her Confirmation ceremony because he had "work" to do. She told him she understood. She really didn't, but she didn't want to insult him. He could be very touchy about certain things; occasionally, he had slapped her around or called her names when he needed to make a point. "To make our love work in a world that's against us," was his romantic-warrior justification to her for his abuse and lifestyle. To her, his world seemed filled with only enemies. He even derided her for "coming from a good family," and told her he felt out of place in her home; so, she always met him elsewhere.

She accepted the reasons for his "work," which involved fights on campus, truancy, then dropping out of school; mugging tourists downtown; thefts; drive-by shootings at rival gangs; dealing and doing drugs; hiding out from the cops; and getting sent to a probation camp. Because of his activities, it seemed to her that they spent more time separated than together. She noticed a dramatic rise in his jealousy whenever he returned after a long separation. She once asked him why he spent more time questioning her than holding her. "You're my lady and I need to know what you've been doing while I'm gone," he had retorted. She started to remind him that he was the one who was always leaving, but stopped and, instead, said nothing.

"Now, Ruth! There he is! Get him! Show me you love me!" Holding the gun steady, but not yet seeing her human target, Ruth stole a glance at Ralph. "What the hell are you looking at me for?! He's in your sights! Look! Get him! Shoot him! Now!"

*. . . now, and at the hour of our death . . .*

Her heartbeat roared in her ears, and her head suddenly felt light. Ruth squeezed the trigger with all her waning strength. The magnum's report thundered in her ears. The world went silent except for the ringing that filled her head. Instantly, she became dizzy. The recoil threw her violenty backwards. She looked up from where she lay to see the hazy outline of Ralph standing over her. "Get up off the ground! Don't you see what you did? Half his head's gone. We gotta go before the cops get here. Let's go!"

Perhaps you are thinking that Ruth's is an extreme case, an aberration so rare as to be unreal, not to mention unimaginable, for most girls. But perhaps you, like most parents of adolescent girls, have also seen, heard, and felt the shock waves of the emotional juggernauts that have blasted your daughter into the heights of ecstasy and buried her beneath avalanches of melancholy. What did you do during those times? How did you involve effective communication in your efforts to support your daughter through the emotional upheaval of adolescence? Were you able to find available resources inside or outside the family to help you and your daughter get through the confusion and frustration successfully? What were *her* attitude, feelings, and behavior like during these times? What were *your* attitude, feelings, and behavior like during these times?

These are some questions to help you reflect on your role as a parent confronting your growing adolescent's ego and identity needs and the rocky emotional terrain you both travel. With this in mind, Ruth's case is not an aberration. Any adolescent, left alone, abandoned and adrift against the emotional blizzards battering her life, has the potential for engaging in self-destructive behavior and dangerous anti-social acts.

I tell parents that any child who has constantly been shunted aside, treated like a slave and ordered around, seldom heard "I/We love you" from parents or been seriously listened to, and whose emotions have been hurt and ignored, could indeed become so unhappy and emotionally numbed that, guided by her anger, hurt, and resentment, will make the decision—or have it forced upon them by another—to take somebody's life. Ruth's unconscious kettle was boiling over with scalding resentment, confusion, hurt, and anger. Her eyes held a distorted view of life, but her view grew out of definable actions taken by her parents in her home.

Ruth's parents thought the family "highway" they constructed for her was solid, safe, smooth, and would not only sustain her but also guarantee her success. Perhaps even to outsiders, the family unit looked perfect. However, when Ruth described her life within her family to me, it was apparent that her healthy, happy self had encountered more than her share of "potholes," which created great emotional unrest. The framework for her eventual commission of homicide was constructed nowhere else *but within her own family.*

From our first interview session and continuing until our last, some four years later, Ruth was constant and candid in telling me how her family had failed her and even betrayed her. She described her initial emotional pain as beginning with the onset of her grandfather's illness. He was her idol. He doted on her and she loved him more than anybody else in her family. She was terrified when his daily visits to see her were suddenly interrupted by his being stricken ill. She was only five when he first became ill, but it wasn't long before those visits from her grandfather were replaced by Ruth's stays with other relatives as the extended family took turns visiting the ailing man. "They never even told me why I had to stay with first this cousin, then next with this aunt, and back and forth. I would have understood if somebody had just told me. But no, they just came and took him away." Ruth saw the daily crusade of relatives to her grandfather's hospital room as "just a whole lot of people being with him and nobody letting me. And I loved him the most."

Not only was Ruth traumatized by her grandfather's sudden illness, but she also blamed her parents for keeping her in the dark. "Nobody told me anything. They just kept smiling and told me I wouldn't understand. It's like they didn't care how much my grandfather and I loved each other. We *understood* each other; of course, I would understand." Because her parents never took her to the hospital to see the dying man, she saw them as deliberately inflicting great misery and unhappiness upon her, and as not respecting her feelings.

On the day her grandfather died in the hospital, Ruth was not informed directly by her parents or anybody else in her family. She stated: "I knew something had happened because all the relatives stayed at my house late into the night. I was kept in the back or taken to the store or for a walk or something. Then it was time to go to bed. When nobody went to the hospital the next day, I knew. I went into the bathroom, locked the door, and drank bleach. I just wanted to die. The only person in my family that I really loved had died. I wanted to be with him, and I was so angry that I was being kept inside my house like a prisoner by the people—my own parents—who told me nothing about him for almost two years. That whole, long time was like slow death for me. I was seven when I started drinking bleach. I've been wanting to die ever since. I even began to hate my grandfather for abandoning me like everybody else."

Ruth did not succeed in committing suicide, although she became very sick. During her brief recovery period in the hospital, she was not at all grateful for the solicitous concern and attention her parents showered upon her, and she cynically dismissed their efforts. "Mom and Dad, they were both fakes. Even at seven years old, I could see right through them. Yeah, they came to see me in the hospital, but I still felt like an object, something to look at, push around, cover up. Even when I was sick, I never felt they took me into their hearts. I could see through their coolness and fake smiles that I was a burden. That's exactly how I felt when they'd always go see my grandfather but leave me behind."

Ruth told me that when she came home from the hospital, her hatred for her parents continued to grow. "I didn't want to be involved in anything that concerned them, so I would talk back to my mom. I would do what I wanted to do. I was my own person, and I just really bad-mouthed everybody."

Ruth felt her parents deserved her hostility and anti-social behavior for what they had done to her. She wanted to make them suffer like she felt they had made her suffer. She saw school as a convenient venue for leveling her anger at her parents. "I knew they wanted me to get good grades, so I wouldn't. I didn't care what kind of grades I got, so I let them drop." Her parents became especially concerned when Ruth was suspended from school. Her teachers called home to check on her and express their concerns to her parents. Her parents pondered the problem and announced the solution to Ruth. "They transferred me to another school. They thought maybe I'd change if I met new people." Ruth greeted her new school environment with the same hostile attitude. Her grades were still poor, though her parents never knew because she tore up her report cards.

Although her mother went to the school on several occasions to confer with her teachers, Ruth's grades remained poor, and her behavior worsened. "I started ditching school. I had it all scheduled out. You see, my mother worked during the day and my step-father would work nights. When he was sleeping, I'd be in my room or in the living room just watching TV. He never noticed." Ruth became attracted to other truant students and the activities in which they engaged. "When I decided to go to school, I'd go real early, like seven, seven-thirty in the morning, and go behind the gym and smoke cigarettes and sniff glue. I liked the company I was with; we all had something in common—some kind of pain to escape, or share, whatever. We'd hang out all day and never go to class. Sometimes we'd go to a friend's house for a ditching party. That's when I learned to drink, and I loved it. Sometimes I wouldn't even come home. I'd call my mom and tell her I was at a friend's house, somebody she liked and approved of. Then I'd use that friend to lie for me while I'd go spend the night with whoever I really wanted to be with. My grades went up and down. I could have done good all the time, but I really enjoyed drinking and smoking. I looked forward to it."

It was clear to Ruth that as long as she was doing good and bringing the family lots of flattering attention, they loved it. Her Confirmation was seen by her family as proof of their solidarity and success. Ruth saw herself "like being on Broadway. I was touched, hugged, and squeezed like an object. My family got more out of it than I did. And I hated them more for that."

It is clear that Ruth resented the power that she felt her family exercised over her. She delighted in circumventing their authority—lying to stay with friends—as well as establishing her own autonomy by making her own choices in the face of rules and regulations—ditching class and smoking and drinking as a minor. The trauma that Ruth's grandfather's illness caused was either unnoticed or disregarded by her family—the very group she felt suppressed by now pulled away from her. Their power came in their willingness and ability to ignore and neglect her. In her seven-year old mind, she deserved the most attention because she had loved her grandfather "the most," meaning more than anybody else. Perhaps she even subconsciously resented her natural father, whose monthly visits, due to their infrequency, represented a form of abandonment. Taking this reasoning further, it might then be concluded that Ruth's killing of the jogger was, in some manner, a retaliatory strike against higher authority— her parents and family, who repeatedly abandoned her at her most critical times.

Ruth's actions must also be understood in light of the difficulties commonly faced by adolescent girls. According to psychologist Mary Pipher, girls in early adolescence are forced to confront almost overwhelming changes. Their identity and sense of self list and heave like a capsizing ship and implode like a dynamited building. If you have daughters in early adolescence, you may notice that, among other "out-of-character" events, their test scores and grades crash—as did Ruth's—beneath the weight of their ego and identity struggles. And as they go through this difficult social-development stage, you may see a brooding pessimism in them that all but smothers the optimism so characteristic of their pre-adolescent years.

You may observe a marked decrease in their energy and curiosity, traits that once inspired you by their boundless abundance. Alas, you may also notice that their determinism and assertiveness, the hallmarks of their independent personalities, yield to all other social traffic. They quietly give up the right-of-way to everybody else, just as Ruth, ultimately, chose to take a life at the behest of another. Young girls are often unable to open up and tell you what's happening inside them; all you can see and know is that they are morbidly unhappy and highly critical of themselves and all that pertains to them, including their bodies. The radiant joy they once displayed becomes a mere memory. The pictures you now see are of girls whose personalities seem warped or in permanent idle.

Most adolescent girls survive these emotional onslaughts with egos intact with the guidance of trusted parents and adults. Their potential anti-social and destructive behaviors are diverted to saner, safer, and more productive pursuits. Ruth, however, did not survive. In fact, her psycho-emotional vacuum was filled by an obsessive and manipulative personality—Ralph—who saw in her a slave to fulfill his own emotional needs. Alienated from her own family, her already-weakened emotional walls crumbled when she agreed to let Ralph use her as his flunky to kill an innocent stranger.

Girls victimized by their erupting ego and identity needs, and thus made hostages to their emotional storms, live life under a dark cloud. They are often depressed, morbidly pessimistic, and devalue their worth. As parents we know this happens but are ill-informed about *why* it happens, and this compounds our ignorance. Lack of knowledge can tie our hands, rendering us helpless, and can threaten dramatic consequences for the whole family, indeed for society.

The lives of adolescent girls are fraught with so much emotional turbulence that it is only aware, conscientious, knowledgeable, and long-suffering parents who stand a chance of safely shepherding them through the precipitous climbs that mark their ascent toward adulthood.

Everything to an adolescent girl is significant and symbolic. Ruth, in prison, lashes out at everybody she blames for putting her there. In her mind, every move her family made, and every act they committed, symbolized their way of distancing themselves from and abandoning her. For years, she acted as though she was a stranger in her own home. A slave to her own emotional needs, she sought out the comfort and companionship of other kindred souls at school. More than being merely a retaliatory act against higher authority, her heinous crime can also be seen as her unconscious way of rallying her family around her, to be in control of them like they had long been in control of her.

As a parent, what guarantees do you have that your daughter will not turn out like Ruth? Put another way, what are the parenting practices you are using that will ensure your daughter will blossom into a happy, kind, caring, and loving human being with a healthy ego and identity? As one way of answering that, let's analyze the parenting practices of Ruth's parents. Ruth said, "My parents never knew how I felt. They never even asked, which means they never cared."

The fundamental first step in positive and effective parenting is to *listen* to your children—true for both female *and* male adolescents. This means you have to *ask* them how they feel. Their expression of their feelings is the "weather report" you need for determining their emotional climate. If you never ask for or allow them to express their own feelings, you won't have a clue as to the nature and severity of the silent storms raging inside them.

Instead of asking Ruth how she felt about being isolated from the grandfather whom she loved so much, they *told* Ruth how *they* wanted her to feel. No child would feel happy about first being separated from a family member whom she adores and then told, time after time: "That's the way it has to be, get used to it." The effect on the hapless child and the feelings she harbors about this state of affairs is that she is being treated cruelly. Her parents, of course, would stoutly deny this. Those same parents would probably also *reject or revise* the feelings expressed by the child about their situation. A big mistake.

Once your children express their true feelings to you, the second fundamental step of effective parenting is to not negate those feelings or try to change them. "Don't feel like that," "You don't know what you're saying," or "Oh, you don't mean that" are examples of the *rejection-by-negation* responses some parents are inclined to make. When a parent answers a child in these ways the child feels instantly discounted, controlled, and humiliated. From the child's point of view, she has risked expressing her true feelings and instead of being taken seriously, she is made to feel unacceptable, inappropriate, or even bad. When parents attempt to control how children express their feelings they insult their children. The clear message they send is: "I will not accept your true feelings and don't even want to hear them," or "When I want to hear your true feelings I will give them to you," or even "You are only allowed to feel that way when I tell you." This kind of parental attitude is arrogant, selfish, insensitive, and of course only further erodes what in many cases is an already faltering or fractured parent-daughter relationship.

Another common mistake many parents make is to *revise-by-rewording* their child's expression of feelings, which they really are not ready, or simply do not want, to hear. "No, what you are *really* feeling is . . ." or "You don't want to feel like *that*; try instead to feel . . ." or "C'mon, you don't feel like that and you know it. What's the matter with you?"

Children's feelings are not written essays presented to parents for editing. When your child comes to you and presents her own words to describe her feelings, it is both disrespectful and irresponsible for you to act as though she is working a cross-word puzzle and merely wants a synonym from you to replace her chosen vocabulary for her feelings. Children *know* what they feel; that's why they often tell it like it is. Your hearing every word they are saying and *how* they are saying it, is the grand prize they long for in such tense, turbulent, agonizing, and confusing times.

I know a mother who always defends her editing, evaluating, or invalidating responses to her daughter, by telling me, "Look, she may try that on other folks, but not on me, honey. I cut her off at the pass and tell her I've heard enough." It is a small wonder that this mother pays a small fortune in professional therapy bills. She even complains that her daughter has gotten worse. Unfortunately, this mother is blind to her direct causal role in making her daughter worse.

Cutting your child "off at the pass" and telling her you've "heard enough" is one of the worst things you can do. First, your child is only talking because you invited her to do so; she took you at your word and assumed you were operating on good faith. Second, you cheat yourself out of valuable information that may enlighten you as to the real source of her problems. And third, you may never know what role you are playing in creating her problems if you fail to give her the opportunity to identify you as a *part* of her problems—something that many parents secretly fear. Talking is a nonviolent way to jointly detect problems and agree to solutions. So, always use dialog as the route to the truth. No matter how painful it is to hear, truth is the only thing that will heal the relationship between you and your child. Do not compound the problem and risk the resentment and alienation of your child by putting up road blocks on the route to truth.

If you *reject-by-negation* or *revise-by-rewording* what your daughter wants to tell you, you are communicating that you do not want to listen to her and, worse, that you don't care. To you, you're only wishing she would express her feelings in a different, perhaps more positive, manner. To her, however, your interruptions in the expression of her true feelings are a wholesale negation of those feelings, and might be interpreted as an excessive use of power—not unlike the actions of Ruth's parents. Your daughter's *reactive feeling,* whether expressed or not, will be one of mistrust. Whether you agree with her feelings or not, they *are* real to her. And it is her point of view that you must accept, if you hope to establish or re-establish happy, pleasant, peaceful and healing communications. If you are going to earn and maintain her trust, you will have to accept how she wishes to express her true and honest feelings to you. Instead of trying to change the way your daughter expresses the *truth* (about her feelings) to you, it would be far better and wiser for you to carefully listen to her while she shares her feelings with you.

This kind of action presupposes that you, the parent, do indeed know best. But isn't it possible that Ruth's parents thought this very thing? Take a few moments and think about the ways in which you are different from them. What is it that you do and how is it that you interact with your daughter that sets you apart from Ruth's parents? What are some of the things you do *not* do that clearly defines where you and Ruth's parents part company? This mental survey will undoubtedly suggest several areas. Hopefully, one area will be in communication. Ruth's parents never gave her permission to express her feelings, or opportunities to do so. Therefore, her *voice* was never heard or heeded; she was never accorded a say-so in family affairs. Interestingly enough, when Ruth was an infant, they undoubtedly rushed to her crib whenever she needed to be fed or changed, or whenever she cried for any reason. Caring how she felt, then, and feeling her pain, they instantly and instinctively did what they knew would change and correct the situation to make her feel better. However, when she grew older, they made the same mistake many parents make: They decided they *knew* what was best for her and gave her no voice and no vote.

Although you as a parent indeed do know "best" about many things, you will best know and understand your daughter's feelings if you simply *ask* her to tell you how and what she feels. Female adolescents bond more closely to others, including their parents, who demonstrate care and concern for their feelings. Ruth's accusation that her parents didn't even care enough about her to become angry at her, need not be an accusation leveled by your daughter at you. Ask your daughter how she feels about a particular situation, and then change the situation so that by her verification and agreement it becomes *better* for her. This will help build a healthy, trusting, low-stress relationship between you and your daughter. Obviously, every situation cannot be changed, nor do all need to be changed. But clear, complete explanations about a particular situation are always helpful. As a parent, you should never fail to advise, inform, and explain circumstances which may bring distress and upheaval into a child's life.

Realize that while you are an adult with an increased ability to function during times of family duress. But the pain you are able to cope with may touch your children more adversely. Ruth's parents failed to recognize that she was undergoing the same painful crisis they were. The family suffering could have been greatly alleviated if they had sat down in the beginning and repeatedly thereafter for heart-to-heart talks and for sharing their pain and apprehensions about their beloved, stricken family member.

Similarly, Ruth's parents did not invite her to share her feelings later on when her behavior at school became increasingly self-destructive as she turned to booze and drugs. They resorted to their particular practice of "problem-solving." The strategy they used, however, would seem to indicate that they felt Ruth was their *problem*, their *embarrassment*. And instead of talking with her or obtaining professional counseling for her, they employed the face-saving gesture of moving her to another school. How much simpler and healthier it would have been to engage in an honest, loving dialog with Ruth.

The rules for loving and successful communication between parent and child that Ruth's parents might have utilized are few but powerful: (1) Come to your children right away and regularly and express your desire to talk to them, to help them. Say so lovingly and tell them how much you love them and how much they mean to you. (2) Never, ever discount, evaluate, judge, or invalidate what they say. Give them the same respect you would give your most valued friend. (3) Do not interrupt unless or until your child asks you for specific information, advice, details, or direction. (4) Be alert, do not doze, yawn, stretch or otherwise communicate your tiredness or boredom. If you are tired, simply say, "Honey, I forgot how fast the time goes. Could we catch up on this tomorrow? We'll both be rested and feel much better. Thanks." (5) The next time you talk, begin by thanking your children for sharing the information from the last time you talked. Ask them how they feel about what you both discussed—this should be a regular question, as feelings often drive behavior. (6) Ask them what insights they have, what answers they might suggest to anyone else undergoing something similar, or in what ways they are now able to better handle the problem. (7) Ask them if there are other ways or persons you can enlist to help them. (8) Communicate your continual caring and love to them. Let them know they have your constant support. (9) Do not be afraid to give corrective advice. Be gentle but be firm. Try to verbalize some benefits of whatever corrective advice you give. In this way, you "sell" or persuade them rather than appear to sound as though you're *telling* them for the thousandth time. Think of corrective advice as something to be gift-wrapped. If it is packaged properly, your children wouldn't dream of resisting or ignoring it.

Ruth's parents failed to see the devastation occurring right before their very eyes. Ruth had been emotionally traumatized, and everything her parents did only increased her pain. Should your daughter experience emotional pain, whatever the degree, stay in constant touch with her about it. Stifle the impulse to *tell* her what emotions to feel and, instead, *ask* her *how* and *what* she feels. Consult her opinion about ways to solve or correct her problems. Avoid the urge to get on with "business"—whatever it is—and leave the problem, or any part of it, unaddressed. Though *you* may be free of the weight of the problem, she may feel more and more trapped by it. Your daughter needs you. Be there for her. Your emotional presence in her life is just as important as is your physical presence—and in certain ways, more important. Ruth's parents filled only half this requirement, and the consequences were infinitely tragic.

# Raising a Well-Balanced Child

*I finally completed the Victim Impact Program and, uh,
now I, uh, can take responsibility for shooting and killing my
stepbrother and, uh, for sending my mother to the emergency
ward with a bullet in her neck. I mean, like, I don't think I
would do anything like that again, but, uh, you never know,
right?*—Jonathan

Jonathan sat across from me in the huge day room and stared.
For a few seconds we did not say anything. When the parole
agent had escorted him over, I noticed the scowl on his face.
He was cordial enough; we shook hands, he sat down and the
parole agent left. I checked the package the parole agent gave me
to make sure Jonathan was scheduled and not a last-minute,
unwilling replacement for some other ward. He was indeed
scheduled. So why was he scowling? I did not have a clue but
figured the reason might come out later in the morning as we
talked. And it did. Jonathan told me: "I've been angry for days,
because I blew my parole hearing. The parole board thinks I'm
just learning about responsibility and wants me to spend more
time in here." Despite the loud, rumbling air conditioning system
in the day room, the stream of visitors, and the occasional

interruption from the public address system, Jonathan talked and I listened to what he told me about his life.

"Jonathan, where are you? Jo-o-n-a-a-a-th-a-a-a-n?"

*Damn*! Jonathan thought as he yanked his marijuana pipe out of his mouth. *It's getting harder and harder to score some bud in this house. What is it NOW?* Jonathan casually laid his full pipe on his bed, next to the sandwich bag bulging with marijuana, and went downstairs. "Hi, Mom, what's up?" he asked.

She looked at him and beamed. "You'll never believe what I have to tell you," she exclaimed. "I can't believe it myself." Her breath came out in short bursts.

Jonathan stared at her. *Must have won the lottery or something,* he thought. Stoically, he waited.

"Well, don't look so excited," she said sarcastically.

"Well, what is it, Mom?" Jonathan answered.

"Raul Amoretto can take me today, like right now."

Jonathan frowned. "Take you? Now? Where?" he asked.

Jonathan hated his mother's constant bubbling, babbling delight in things she barely explained. She simply assumed everybody figured out all her omitted details by themselves. The few times she *was* home, Jonathan found communicating with her to be a perpetual puzzle, fruitless and frustrating.

"Where?" she mimicked. "Come on, silly." She playfully slapped his forearm. "Raul Amoretto or, rather, THE Raul Amoretto is only the best hairstylist to be found anywhere. And I do mean anywhere. Even *you* should know that."

Jonathan also hated her slings at his intelligence, and her growing habit of slapping him, pinching his ear lobe, or gently pushing on him whenever she thought *he* was the one missing a twist here, or a turn there, in the broken trails of her aimless conversations.

"So that's it?" he asked.

"What's it?" she answered.

"The good news you called me about is, you're going to some beauty parlor?" He sounded incredulous.

Her eyes flashed and her once-beaming face turned stony. "You heard me, Jonathan," she said evenly. "I am going to the hairstylist, Raul Amoretto. And it's called a salon, *never* beauty parlor. S-a-l-o-n." She spelled it and drawled out each letter as though she was teaching him the alphabet. *Get lost, b\*\*\*\**, he thought. "Now be a good little guy while I'm gone, okay? Don't play so much Nintendo. I was just reading somewhere—I forget where—but kids like you, who play Nintendo all the time, have trouble remembering things."

*Where the hell does she get that crap? And what makes her think she knows what I do when she's only here every day for about as long as the mail lady*, Jonathan thought. *I haven't played Nintendo since my freshman year.*

"What's for dinner?" he asked as he opened the refrigerator.

She had already started down the long hall toward the front door. Her back to him, she said, "Now, don't make me late with *all* your questions, Jonathan. You're 16 years old. You can fry an egg, go shopping or do whatever you like. If you and Pam are still seeing each other, maybe she'll cook you something." She stopped mid-stride, seeming to remember something, and turned toward him. Her smile of anticipation only slightly crimped with irritation. "Here," she said, as she opened her handbag and fished around for some loose dollars. "There's enough here for MacDonald's, Burger King, and Carl's Jr., all combined."

He walked toward her slowly. A too-bright smile on her face as she waited, arm outstretched, her fist filled with money. He could feel his anger rising. *God, what's beneath the cool front she always puts on? Why does she do this to me?* he thought. *First, it's 'be a good little guy.' Then it's 'you're 16 years old and can do whatever you like.'* You're *the only one who gets all she wants out of life. I mean, once in a while, Mom, if it's not too much to ask, not too much of an intrusion into your own life, would you, like,* pretend *to be my mother? Quit being so damn happy?*

Jonathan crammed the money into his pocket and ran upstairs to his neglected marijuana pipe. Soon, the frustrating conversation he had just had with his mother was light years away.

"My God, what's happening here? No, no, no-o-o-o-o-o!" Harvey, Jonathan's stepfather, stopped and stared at the still bodies lying in the pool of blood on the floor, between the large kitchen and huge family room. He clasped his hands to his head and fell, prostrate, onto the floor next to where his semi-conscious wife and very dead son lay.

"Jonathan? Jonathan? Hey! Jonathan! Are you all right? Where are you?" Harvey ran from room to room, in the large, rambling two-story house, calling his stepson. Finally he stopped long enough to dial emergency.

"This is the 9-1-1 operator."

"Hello, hello," Harvey whimpered. "I just got home from work and my wife and son are lying in their own blood on the kitchen floor. Somebody's been inside my home and shot them. My wife's breathing, but my son . . . oh, my God. It's awful. Please send an ambulance quick to. . . ."

From the other side of the bullet-proof glass that separated them in the jail, Jonathan stared glumly back at his stepfather, Harvey.

"Jonathan, please, I'm begging you. Tell me what did I do to you to make you hate your own mother and brother? God, if I only knew." Harvey squirmed with anger and frustration as he gripped the telephone receiver hard against his ear. That ear began to throb, and he switched the phone to the other one. Jonathan wanted to drop the telephone and tell the trustee to take him back to his cell. But he couldn't do that to Harvey. Harvey had been—or tried to be—a real friend. He was naturally cool. But as cool as he was, he just couldn't fill Jonathan's need for a father. Jonathan simply stared.

"What the hell are you staring at me for, you G** d*** murderer? Answer me. You owe me an explanation!"

Jonathan snapped out of his reverie. "I, uh, Harvey, none of this was personal. I mean, uh . . ."

"Personal? Why, you arrogant little punk. That is one word you should never, ever use again for the rest of your whole miserable life! Do you realize that you half-killed your own mother and murdered my only son? If you had anything against me, for hell's sake, you could have told me. Why, Jonathan?!"

Jonathan inhaled deeply, but his effort only got him the stale air in the jail. He missed his bud pipe. He could sure use some hits on it just now. *Damn Harvey, coming unglued and freaking out like this. It's so embarrassing. You're losing it, man. You're falling apart in front of my eyes.*

"Harvey, like I said, it wasn't personal. I mean I never had anything against you. You were always pretty cool. I mean you never got in my way. Sometimes I needed you, sometimes I didn't, you know? It's like my needs didn't count in that house, you know what I mean?"

"Jonathan, are you really trying to tell me you had a motive for what you did?" Harvey asked in near-disbelief. "How could you even suggest that? You know I broke my a\*\* every day selling stocks and mutual funds so you, your mother, and Bradley could have the best of everything—private schools, clothes, tennis and golf lessons, vacations, cars, boats, trust funds in your names. You name it, you got it. And whatever your other needs were, buddy, I sure never knew about them. If you're making all this up, you're sure doing a good job, because anybody half-blind could see you lived like a prince. And here, I thought I knew you. I loved you." Harvey's throat filled with emotion. "You were my stepson but I loved you like you were my own blood."

Jonathan was speechless. *This guy's out there*, he thought. *I mean, like, nobody ever has a reason to kill anybody, but there are times and situations and people that mess you up and push you over the edge. Things build up for a long time, people don't know about it, parents are too busy to care. And you and Mom never believed I had a problem or a need. Even if I'd worn a neon sign saying so, you'd have missed it. So screw you, cool Harvey. My super cool family was doing me in, dude. Something you'd never understand in a million years. To you, I was a prince. Yeah, right. I was dying a slow princely death inside that very large, very cold house. If the judge asks me, and I know he's going to, I did what I did because Mom and Bradley were screwin' with me, messing with my mind, dissin' me, ignoring me, and all kinds of sh\*\*. And not just once but many times. It was like the whole family was a conspiracy against me. Even you, Harvey. You cool, uninvolved rich bast\*\*\*! I'm your Frankenstein, your home-grown poison!*

CRASH! The telephone receiver flew from Harvey's hand into the heavy glass. Surprised, though far from being hurt, Jonathan involuntarily fell back. Instantly, two burly bailiffs grabbed Harvey and dragged him to his feet.

"You ungrateful murderer. Why, Jonathan, why? Answer me, you dope fiend!" Tears poured down Harvey's face, and he sank against the bailiffs' arms.

Jonathan watched, stunned. *Dope fiend? Is* that *what his lips said?* Jonathan pondered for a moment. *So he* did *know! But he was so cool, he never gave a damn . . . until now.*

It is vital for you, as a parent, to know what is going on with your child—natural child, stepchild, or foster child—all the time. Not some of the time, not most of the time, but ALL the time. Without a doubt you need to be as much aware of his problems, pressures, wants and needs as you are of the day's weather or your family's grocery and clothing needs. In today's fast-paced, complex and ever-dangerous school environment, you simply cannot afford to miss a beat in the complicated rhythms of your child's life. Take the reins early in his life and hold onto them. You know more about life and living than he does. So, exercise your leadership, tell your child what's right and wrong. Don't be afraid to say "no" when it is necessary. Hold your child accountable for his behavior, and reward him for his right decisions and actions. Let him know that you trust him to make the right decisions. Tell him it is important that he maintain that trust. Teach him precisely how to do so.

Take time to be with your child, ask him questions and find out as much as you can about the happenings in his life. Your interest will make you his natural ally. You want him to confide in you, especially when the external social forces upon him become stronger and the pressures more demanding. Those are the times in his life when he needs you the most. Your being "there" for him must not be by accident. You can earn that position by virtue of your diligent work in parenting: pointing out right and wrong, asserting your leadership, rallying to his defense and support, educating him, being nosy—asking lots of questions—talking heart to heart, inviting and including him in family decision-making, nurturing him, and getting whatever additional or appropriate resources he needs. You will never be sorry for the investment in time, effort, resources and emotion it takes to really know your child. On the other hand, if you don't really know your child, the regret brought by your ignorance may be almost unbearable.

In this vein, the two students who turned the Columbine High schoolyard into a graveyard were virtually unknown by their peers on that campus. They kept to themselves and didn't share their thoughts or feelings. In the wake of their vicious assault on the school, the questions that keeps reverberating around the country are: "Who were Eric Harris and Dylan Klebold and what made them turn into cold-blooded killers? And why couldn't their behavior be predicted by earlier warning signs?" Even Klebold's mother purportedly claimed to be as "surprised as anyone else" about her son's unexpected, explosive, deadly-violent act. She described him as "sweet and happy," especially after attending the high school prom the weekend before the massacre he helped to unleash. "There's no way I could've known this would happen," she said. A friend described her as being stunned and as eager for answers as the teachers, students and police investigators who still search for clues. Mrs. Klebold is perplexed and especially sad because she will never be able to ask Dylan, himself.

Whatever value might be gained from asking an adolescent, after the fact, why he committed a violent and deadly attack in the first place, would be eclipsed by the value of knowing the entire picture of a child's life—his hopes, dreams, problems, challenges, accomplishments, disappointments, social skills, hurts, and all his high and low points. If a parent misses important, disturbing, unusual and dangerous behavioral cues, the result of such a lapse in attention might well be a tragedy of shocking proportions, as Susan Klebold's remarks clearly show. Parental ignorance was the one "cover" that allowed Klebold and Harris to operate in a clandestine, unhindered manner, as though they were home alone—permanently. Reports from neighbors of "constant strange noises of breaking glass and metal in the garage"—recalled, unfortunately, after the massacre—show how totally clueless the parents were. The Klebolds would learn about their son's bloody rampage and about his death only when the rest of the world did—from the paralyzing news reports that began almost immediately.

Susan and Thomas Klebold are like many parents who are aware of their children almost strictly in terms of material wants—Dylan was given a black BMW. The evident danger in this is failing to see obvious clues, like propane tanks, bomb-making materials, and guns.

But are children like Dylan such grand actors—smiling, cooperative, dutiful, well-mannered—that parents never have a single clue about their diabolical plans? Is there absolutely nothing unnatural in their behavior that tips them off? The answer is simply, no. Parents need to exercise enough curiosity to search their children's rooms, cars, and other areas of the home. Don't be put off by privacy arguments. You must move forward under the assumption that you are the first and best person to discover and address your child's problems. As such, you will need to exercise a degree of authority. Part of your approach must be to sit your potential actor down and talk to him, ask him pointed questions, find our what is happening with him. Certainly some kids can be great chameleons, and kids like Dylan Klebold may well have been one, but you can persist in discovering his "faces" and prevent potential problems. In doing so, you may save others, your child, and yourself from becoming victims.

Parents can be victimized and placed at-risk by the quality of the relationship with their children. Jonathan frequently told me how distant and uninvolved his parents were. He continually described them as "afraid to be grownups." When I asked him what he meant, he said, "Well, just to give you one example, I'm sure my mom knew I was doing weed, you know, marijuana? I mean, I kept my pipe right on top of the TV in my room. And the sandwich baggies next to it sure weren't filled with smelly socks. But she never asked me what it was, never accused me of smoking weed, whatever. She never showed any interest at all, even though she was in my room every day. Maybe she thought the pipe was the TV remote, I don't know. Both she and my step dad were so cool, I used to think they must have been doing drugs, too."

"Isn't the kind of freedom you're describing the perfect home situation most kids would die for?" I asked him. I wasn't prepared for his rather coarse response.

"Screw you, dude!" he spat out. "Oh, excuse me, sir. I forgot. I didn't mean that. I'm sorry. Really, okay."

"It's okay, but what *did* you mean?" I asked him.

"Well, it's just that, I don't know . . ." his voice trailed off and he looked up at the light fixture in the ceiling. "It's like they weren't plugged in. You know how an electric guitar's got to be plugged in so you can even hear it?" I nodded my head. "Well, my folks—my mom and stepdad—were just not plugged in to being parents. They were just too cool and into their own things. No matter what me and my stepbrother did—and we did a hell of a lot, believe me. Well, their aloofness started really getting to me. I mean, it started eating me up. It got to the point where I really wanted to feel they cared, especially my mom. I really loved her, but I never felt she was, well, like I said, plugged into me. Like I loved her more than she loved me. I had friends whose parents were really plugged in, had their noses in everything my friends were into. My friends would get all ticked off if their parents asked them questions—I mean if you got loaded and smashed in the front of your dad's Jaguar, you gotta expect questions, you know what I mean? Funny thing, I found myself getting jealous of my friends because their parents were all over them and showed they cared. At least in my opinion. I'd go home and would walk right into two icebergs. I don't know what it was about me that made them scared, but I think they were afraid to be grownups and take charge."

I asked Jonathan what he meant by "take charge."

"I didn't know what the hell I was doing. I had my weed pipe out in the open because I *wanted* my mom to find it . . . bust me, you know? Be a real parent and yell at me and tell me what to do and what not to do. Throw her weight around. I mean, if she didn't know how, all she had to do was listen to how other parents in the grocery store talked to their kids and bossed them around. But she didn't have one clue.

"My mom only got concerned and began to throw her weight around when she cussed at me after I shot my brother. He was right there on the floor, bleeding heavy and losing life fast. She ran down the hall and pushed me out of her way and threw herself down on him and started crying, moaning and sh**. Then she looked up at me, and to this day I get chill bumps remembering the look she gave me. I had never seen that look in her eyes before. She started shrieking, 'You animal. Get the hell out of here. I will see that you go to prison or put you in the grave myself. Look what you've done to your brother.' I looked down at him and saw that he was really wasted. He was already dead and his skin was changing color and starting to get rubbery-looking. There was a huge dent in his chest where the bullet had gone. I looked at my mom, looked at my gun, pointed it at her and said, 'Well, you finally showed me you cared, but not for me.' And you know what she told me?" I shook my head, no. "Well, this is what she said: 'You are so right, you bast***. I don't give one f*** about you.' I already had the gun pointed at her, so I shot her. That look never changed in her eyes, either.

"You know, when they lock you up for murder, they want you to face what you did right away. I couldn't deal with it for weeks. That look kept coming up in my sessions, and I would freak out big time. I swear I could see her right there in front of me. They said I was delusional and kept medicating me. I finally completed the Victim Impact Program and, uh, now I, uh, can take responsibility for sending my mother to the emergency ward with a bullet in her neck and for shooting and killing my stepbrother. I mean, I don't think I would do anything like that again, but, uh, you never know, right?"

Jonathan's account shows an adolescent who knew his drug use was not right. Moreover, he *wanted* his mother to reprimand ("bust") him for it. Perhaps he felt that her demonstrated interest in his life-with-drugs and any well deserved chewing out she might have given him would be the pathway they could take to uncover and resolve the personal problems that started his drug use in the first place. How much more explicit with a parent can you get than by setting your own trap—leaving your drug paraphernalia out in the open for her to see? Jonathan knew his personal life was flawed and out of control. The ineffectual parenting he was getting only angered him. Every time he visited the homes of his friends and saw the kind of parenting they were receiving, he was only reminded how inadequate and deficient his own parents were. In his case, he equated the lack of parental concern and involvement with lack of interest in and denial of love for him. His parents were so very removed—indeed, disconnected—from him and his stepbrother, that Jonathan had absolutely no confidence in their ability to help resolve the final conflict between he and his brother. *Only an adolescent who feels abandoned, excluded, unloved, unaccomplished, uninvolved, hopeless or helpless will ever pick up a gun and kill somebody to "solve" his problems.*

In spite of the bloodbaths unleashed on their campuses by emotionally-wounded, angry, and alienated students like Dylan Klebold, Eric Harris, Kip Kinkel, and other children around the nation, there are some things you and other parents can and must do so that your child never need become a victim at all. Because of my doctoral dissertation work among children who kill, my Urban Teacher Corps field studies of troubled adolescents, and my ongoing work in public school law and child welfare, I am viewed as having a certain expertise. But I must emphasize that you, too, are an expert in spotting the telltale signs of impending violence in children. It starts by knowing your child like you know yourself. You must know when he's safe and when he's dangerous. I am not an alarmist telling parents they are currently caring for a potential killer in their home. I am simply saying that we have reached a crisis point in our nation and its time to wake up. U.S. trauma centers report that gunshot fatalities among children and teens represent 11 percent of all pediatric gun injuries. This is the highest death rate for any mechanism of injury, according to The National Pediatric Trauma Registry at Tufts/New England Medical Center. Going to school has become hazardous duty for the nation's school children. At this time, like no other in our national history, it is to your advantage as a parent to thoroughly and completely know your own kids and to expect other parents to do the same.

There is no parent today who can afford to ignore the heart-rending and gut-wrenching tragedies which armed school children are bringing to their campuses. School killings, when they occur, dominate the news headlines. The names of permanently scarred towns like Springfield, Oregon; Edinboro, Pennsylvania; Jonesboro, Arkansas; Pearl, Mississippi; and Littleton, Colorado are seared into our memory.

With each radio, television and newspaper report of a campus shooting, school safety seems to be a myth. With each passing day, going to school is becoming more of a health hazard whose "warning label" is our own kids. The number one fear among school-age youth is fear for their own physical safety and survival. Ask your own children. Some of the nation's eighth-graders, for example, are so frightened that, according to a University of Michigan study, 9 percent of these 13 year-olds carry a gun, knife, or club to school at least once a month. In all, 270,000 guns go to school with their 8th-grade "owners" every day. In a 1998 *Newsweek* poll, 63 percent of Americans polled consider it "very or somewhat likely" that a shooting incident could happen at their local school.

School safety, in terms of student-anxiety level, ranks right up there with passing the S.A.T., Driver Training, graduating on time, or winning the league athletic title. However, it is the morbid quality of this anxiety that differentiates it from other "routine" school concerns. As more schoolyards become grave-yards, the nation's middle-schoolers—your own children among them—are worrying: *Will I make it home from school safely for dinner? Will I live to make it to high school?* High-schoolers, just as worried, are pondering: *Will I make it out of high school alive? What is the best weapon to protect myself with today as I go from class to class or hang out during lunch?*

Yet, despite the finger-pointing and blame hurled at the nation's public schools, in general, public school is the safest place for your children—other than home—during the day. School safety is the problem and responsibility of public school, but only to a certain degree. In spite of increased safety demands made on them by a frightened and unforgiving public, there are limits to what schools can do. As a parent, try not to fall into the trap of holding your child's school fully and forever responsible for his total safety and security. As a parent, you need to accept that *schools are only as safe as the homes and families they serve.* The more danger there is at home, the more danger there will be at school. Indeed, it is frighteningly mathematical: *Unsafe homes = unsafe schools*. What so frightens our kids at school are other "unsafe" kids who arrive there burdened with unresolved personal, emotional, and family problems. School is merely the source of a child's education. Home is the source of his *emotion*. A child's personal and psychological growth is tempered in the home by a multitude of family dynamics for good or ill. Troubles unresolved at home can grow and develop at school, aggravated by a variety of social situations until they find an outlet in public displays of violence. And home is usually the "culture" in which personal troubles begin, ripen, and putrify like toxic bacteria. Not unlike air-borne spores, they often lay dormant and therefore undetectable. Fully potent, they also remain "ready" to infect the environment and inflict damage. A 14-year-old uses a .32-caliber semi-automatic pistol to shoot and wound two at his high school in Richmond, Virginia. A 16-year-old kills two and wounds seven with a hunting rifle at his Pearl, Mississippi high school. At his high school in Paducah, Kentucky, a 14-year-old uses two .22-caliber rifles, two shotguns, and one .22-caliber handgun to kill three and would five.

Like most parents, you probably feel that I'm "preaching to the choir." Chances are that you are a superb parent who may agree with one of my workshop participants when she exclaimed: "I hear what you're saying, but I know my daughter so well that I know she'd just never do anything like what those kids did to Columbine High School. And that's the bottom line!"

I hope you will not turn a deaf ear, as she apparently did. For what I have to say to you could save your child's, and other children's, educational, emotional, spiritual, and physical lives.

**The Ten-Piece "Survival Toolkit" Your Child Needs**
**1. *To Know He is Loved***
Self-love and self-esteem are the most powerful emotions as well as vital skills. The instinct for protecting oneself, before everything else, is part of our nature. A child who lacks the capacity to cherish his own life can never feel deeply alive or fulfill his own potential. He cannot reach for the stars if his days are darkened by thoughts of inadequacy or self-hate. An infant

instinctively learns self-love by the way he is treated by the first people who care for him. But the limitless, eternal love we feel for our own children does not automatically give them a sense of self-love. Sometimes the way we were reared by our own parents gets in the way. "You parent the way you were parented" is an old maxim that is often true. To break a cycle of faulty parenting, we must be aware of our behavior and try to chance. Effective ways of changing parenting behavior include taking parent education classes, buying or reading books on parenting, or consulting a licensed family counselor.

The main objective is to incorporate and practice more positive and effective parenting methods. Constantly be aware of the times you slip into the automatic mode of parenting, behaviors of which might include shouting or storming, criticizing, demeaning, ridiculing, frequent irritability, demanding, indifference, and hitting or threatening. These leave a child feeling criticized, humiliated, oppressed, unliked and unloved, and unlovable. These feelings, reinforced over time, will inevitably turn into resentment, depression, brooding anger, and an obsession for revenge. Jonathan, who described his parents as being "afraid to be grownups," felt and deeply resented the harsh "iceberg" (his word) of his parent's cool and constant indifference. His bizarre reaction should speak volumes to parents who think that being overcritical and emotionally abusive to a child are the *only* parental behaviors that cause depression, resentment, lack of self-esteem, and thoughts of homicide. Jonathan's attempt to kill his mother dramatically underscores how deeply hurt and angry he was by her emotional negligence and estrangement.

Often, we can't help a child love himself until we reevaluate our own attitudes created by burdens we've been hauling around every day of our lives. But surely no effort is more noble than to heal ourselves in order to better parent a child. Once a child feels cherished and protected, he can begin to feel compassion for others. One of the earliest experiences can be loving a pet. A child who has been cared for lovingly and tenderly is able to hold a dog or cat gently, or even summon your parental interference if somebody else is mistreating a hapless animal. Any four-year-old who can, without thinking, exclaim to an injured puppy, "Oh, you itty, bitty thing. We'll make you feel good again!" has learned one of the most essential skills for changing the quality of life at not only his school but by extension the entire community—and yes, perhaps an entire nation!

### 2. *To Know Others and Himself by Behavior*

A child enters school and is thrown into a whole, new world. Though he is brave and feels well-loved at home, and knows how to love and respect others, he can still get off on the wrong foot, accidentally, if he doesn't know how to buzz through the beehive of behavior. Behavior, like road conditions, must be "read." Your child needs to know how to interpret the behavior of others as well as his own. His concentration on the teacher or on school work may be broken if students around him are off task and fooling around. Or if his first-period teacher gets annoyed with him, he might feel so humiliated or angry that his concentration in the rest of his classes remains broken for the rest of the day.

Teach your child about moods and behavior. Mood—how one feels and the quality or intensity of that emotion—controls one's behavior. Tell your child that human beings make mistakes, and that the biggest mistakes are sometimes accidental, and caused by stress, anxiety, or worry. Maybe his teacher received some bad news earlier that morning, or got into an argument at home and, without thinking, responded to your child angrily. Tell your child that even grownups' responses will not always match his attitude. While he shows confidence, friendliness, respect and humor, others—depending on what's on their minds—may respond differently. The students in class who play or waste time instead of paying attention or doing their work, may be scared to show they can't do the work because they don't understand it or may be too shy to ask the teacher for help. Tell your child that each new day brings new changes and challenges. "Things will get better, you'll see," or "Something was probably on Mrs. Bell's mind," are just a couple of ways you can let him know not to judge others too harshly or have his feelings hurt by them. Such coaching will enable him to instinctively give other people the benefit of the doubt and not get caught in their emotional net.

This kind of strategy can also create much needed latitude for parents. For example, if Ruth's parents had been forthright and candid with her about her grandfather's illness and admitted to the effect it had on them, she would have seen she was not alone and certainly not the only family member depressed and suffering. Instead of feeling in the dark, alone and driven to drink bleach, she would have felt enlightened and grown-up and more a part of the family. And although she still might not have been able to visit her terminally-ill grandfather in the hospital (some rules are outside of a family's control), she might have at least seen and understood the big picture and given her parents a break for all the blurry details in the "picture" they just did not explain.

As you guide your child in and around the "social traffic" confronting him at school, emphasize that reading the behavior of others is important, but interpreting his own feelings and behavior is equally important. My son doesn't like fluffy cereal made from rice or light grains. At eight years old, he knows what "soggy" means and uses that word whenever he is inadvertently served this kind of cereal. "You *know* I don't like soggy cereal, you're always serving me something I don't like. Take it back, because I'm not going to eat it!" is a demand that arrests everybody's attention at the kitchen table on a busy work- and school-day morning. If he refuses to eat it, despite told "we've run out of your favorite flakes," and decides to pout and play "cereal victim," he may, later on in school, regret his behavior and be so full of shame that he can't pay attention to the teacher. Or he may analyze why he erupted in anger and blame and immediately apologize. This latter response affords him the opportunity to forget about the incident while he's in school. With his mind thus free of anger and blame, he has the mental and emotional energy to stay on task and absorb what his teacher is saying.

### 3. *To Know How to Win With Words*

As your child becomes wiser about the true significance of his behavior, he will need skill in showing other people what he feels so that they can understand him correctly. If a girl says to her track coach, "I froze up at the last minute because high-jumping scares me," the coach will realize that fear-of-flying overtakes high-jumping novices and that she will only overcome it by encouragement and reassurance. The coach will lower the bar and praise her–even at heights she could have walked over. The keys are *connection, creation, and confidence. Connect* where she is, psychologically, and reduce her fear, and then *create* the situation that will inspire *confidence.* Winners are not born, they are *made* by others who guide them lovingly. If a child can tell his parent, "I jump and start shaking whenever you shout," it's a safe bet that Dad will strive to be calmer. He will hear in his child's words this message: *"Be calm when you talk to me; I feel better and safer that way."* Any four or five year-old who can confidently and immediately express his feelings by saying, "I'm scared of loud sounds," "I love you forever, Mommy," or "My tummy shakes inside when you take me to swim lessons, so maybe I'm not ready yet," has the tools he needs for learning, thinking, exploring, and, most of all, letting others know what he's feeling and why. Jonathan thought that simply leaving his marijuana pipe out in the open, so his mother could "bust" him, was an obvious sign to her of his desperate need to talk and open his heart to her. His own *words* would have been far better than the mute pipe for bridging the emotional distance between his mother and himself. Their mutual inability to talk led to tragic consequences.

### 4. *To Know the Power of Thought on Action*
This is a life-process skill (a skill that shapes life experiences) that if established early, say, before your child is seven, can reinforce and magnify his ability to concentrate in school. Justin, for example, may be looking out the window and daydreaming about acting in a Disney movie while his second-grade teacher explains simple addition and subtraction. The problem may not be his disinterest in his teacher or his interest in the movie, but his immersion, despite himself, in his personal problems. He concentrates on the movie to suppress memories of his parent's furious bickering; his mother shouting, "I'm leaving you! I'm getting a divorce!" These painful thoughts create painful feelings, which Justin may believe are "bad" feelings. Therefore, he escapes into a fantasy world and misses important instruction

from his teacher rather than express them. If Justin knew that expressing his feelings would free his mind, he might say to his teacher, "I hate my parents. They always fight, they're so selfish and they never think about me and how I feel. What do I need them for, anyway?! I wish they were dead." This would allow the energy Justin is using to suppress and avoid his feelings to be profitably devoted to other endeavors—including the astounding possibilities of arithmetic. Without a doubt, he needs assistance in surviving, emotionally, his very real crisis at home. However, he should be taught that it's natural and okay to have scary feelings when you hurt, when you are anxious and worried, when your world's dark and painful, and when life has thrown you a curve ball. When a child is drowning in feelings that he thinks are dangerous and bad, it is impossible for him to pay attention or think clearly. Ruth tried to drown her feelings of abandonment, loneliness, and estrangement with bleach and, later, with booze binges. Though once a good student, with demonstrated academic achievement, the drinking and truancy she engaged in eventually weakened her school performance and whittled her grade point average.

### 5. *To Know the Wonder of Why*

As a parent, you are often so overwhelmed by the need to keep up with the red tape and academic requirements that makes up your child's schooling that the teaching of good social skills, based on a moral framework of behavior, is either incomplete or ignored completely. There's more to life than schooling. Horses are schooled. Children, though, have to be educated in the life skills of getting along with others, treating others as they would want to be treated themselves, knowing right from wrong and doing it, and the value in respecting and protecting life. You will recall Paul, who in an earlier chapter saw life through the blurred lenses and embittered life-is-cheap writings of Marxist world revolutionaries. He accepted their stark views and, thus brainwashed, "graduated" to believe in the love of force—rather than the force of love—as the great equalizer.

One way to train your child in social and moral ethics is to listen to your child's marvelous and abundant questions, and weave moral and ethical issues into the fabric of your answers. "Why do leaves change color?" is a favorite question of children. As you tell your child the "scientific" answer, think of ways to make it morally relevant to his life. "Changing colors is part of being good little leaves. Their trees tell them to change, like the traffic signal tells us when to stop and go with red and green lights." Be creative and build life-teaching into your responses; your regular dialogue with your child will generously afford you abundant opportunities for doing so. "What makes grass grow?" can have a scientific answer and your life-teaching extension to it: "Grass grows right when it is fed and watered right, just like we can grow and act right only when we are told the right things to do." Other "wonder-of-why" questions can also be extended into moral and ethical dimensions: "Why do I grow taller? . . . What does being dead mean? . . . How does a grocery store get its food? . . . What makes this right, what makes this wrong?"

Children have a natural instinct for wondering and asking why. Encourage this instinct and purposefully shine the bright lights of your child's curiosity into the life-teaching areas. If you do this enough, you won't have to worry about having a "bright brute" on your hands. Instead, you'll have a thoughtful, sensitive, caring, loving, generous, civilized and considerate human being. You'll see this fantastic human being in the making and the effects of your teaching as he interacts with others. If you feed a child a fish, his hunger will be satisfied only temporarily. But if you *teach* your child to fish—by building a moral and ethical framework into their "curiosity center"—they will be able to fish for life.

By sharing in his natural curiosity and guiding him to the right answers, you expand a child's thinking beyond the mere need to acquire or know "stuff" and lay the groundwork for moral intelligence and a passion to think, behave, and live *right*. Ruth let her amoral boyfriend, Ralph, persuade her to kill a stranger to prove her love for him. Despite her religious upbringing, it was only when she entered prison that she began to truly understand why there has to be a moral framework within which to conduct one's life and to protect one from being "used" (her word) by those who lack a moral perspective of life.

### 6. *To Know That Every Question May Not Have a Quick Answer*

Today's "Y2K"—Year-2000 Kid—will be confronting complex issues and questions. There simply are no easy solutions to the problems of dysfunctional/nonfunctional families, a direction-less national leadership, environmental pollution, a constantly-growing population, cultural clashes, the prevalence of weapons that can wipe out human life, and adolescentcide. Beginning from when they are toddlers, children need to start understanding that there are no quick fixes to some of life's dilemmas. But you will have to continuously teach your child to plumb the depths and dig and dig until solutions emerge. This means that our Y2K's will need to learn to work considerably harder and with patient expectation. But what does this mean at home and on the playground? This is a critical question because these locales—a place called "home" and a place called "school"—are the sites of present-time problems that grow into the colossal social diseases left for future generations (your child) to cure. If Harry pushes Kaitlin in the sandbox, Kaitlin's quick-fix response should not be: "I'm going to shoot you, Harry." Billy should not write a list of "All the People I Hate and Must Kill," sparked by star-athlete Max's daily taunts of "Nerdy Billy" and Max's popularity with all the girls. Our social emphasis on revenge and getting even has been passed on to children generation after generation, and has only caused their lives to be infected with danger, hopelessness, and a yearning for vengeance. Paul's declaration: "To get respect, you gotta be able to take somebody out" is a credo our Y2K's must be taught to reject and prove false. Y2K's must be taught to understand that there is no victory or virtue in murder as a way to make trouble disappear.

Train your child to rely patiently on your help, intervention, and suggestions for resolving social disputes, or those of other trusted adults. "Well, Kaitlin, pushing and fighting aren't good. So say, 'Harry, that's not okay and I don't like that,' then go tell Harry's teacher," or "Billy, killing is not right. We were created to learn to live and work with each other peacefully. Killing never solves problems. Let's make an appointment with your principal and counselor and Max's parents, too. We've all got to talk about

Max's constantly bullying you and ask his parents to tell him to stop. Then, you and I really need to talk about your feelings and explore other responses to make, ones that are better and safer than writing a hate list." Yes, this takes time and effort on your part, but remember there are no quick answers to some problems, even for parents. "Well, Kaitlin, boys will be boys," or "Billy, don't you just feel better after making that hate list and getting your feelings onto paper? Now, tear it up and let's go out for a pizza," are short-cut parenting at best.

### 7. *To Know Why It's Best to Aim High*

Set your own high expectations for behavior and clearly communicate them to your child. Studies show that when parents *expect* their standards to be followed, children follow them more often than not. Standards are present everywhere in life and in nature, and your child needs to know that his behavior, too, must follow standards. Of course, this means you must constantly guide and coach your child on the aspects of right and wrong behavior. In so doing, you will be teaching him analytical, problem-solving, critical-thinking, and ethical skills. By possessing the tools to think better, he will be in a position to make better (right) responses. Informing him of your expectations and then helping him "get there" will eventually lead to his functioning at continually high levels. If you teach him to aim high, he'll hit the expected target more than he'll miss it. If you fail to teach him high standards based on your expectations, his targets will invariably be low. He will hit the target every time with his low-grade or negative behavior.

Paul's view of himself as a "prisoner of war" and the Statue of Liberty as "a racist bitch" is a bulls-eye score on the target of negative behavior. Despite his being considered a model prisoner, his observant parole agent sensed a definite negative shift in Paul's attitude. Observant parents, too, can become instantly informed whenever their children's attitudes and behaviors shift from positive to negative. Paul was later transferred to another prison in Northern California following the death of a female parole agent whose body was found in one of the prison's dumpsters.

As a parent your high standards must be a non-negotiable requirements. Right is right and wrong is wrong. If you allow your child to resist the standard, you are inviting confusion and trouble. Unlike Paul, Ruth came from a family with the trappings or appearances of high standards; her father was a deputy sheriff, and she attended church regularly and was well-regarded by the parish priest. Yet, she repeatedly failed to meet the standard, her behavior worsening until complete unconscious rejection of the standard caused her to take another's life. If Paul's case represents resistance to or domination over a standard, then Ruth's represents a rejection of standards. The outcomes of both are identical: *dangerous behaviors driven by lack of direction.* Who would argue that the consequences are dire and tragic when we set children adrift on life's high seas without standards as beacon lights?

Teach your children to view themselves as responsible members of the family, valuable resources for their school, and important contributors to the community. High standards are vital because your expectations will burrow deep into your child's subconscious and become the foundation of his self-concept. As he branches out socially, his short- and long-term decision-making and behavior will be affected by your (and, eventually, his) expectations. Your standards and expectations fulfill his need to belong and exert control over his own life. Children who behave without standards and expectations are unhappy and confused. They want the loving, guiding hand of a trusted adult, and want to experience success through achievement of standards. When they have none of these, they feel cheated and unfulfilled, fragmented and lost. Children who kill are dramatically displaying their need to get the attention they were deprived o, as a result of having no self-concept rooted in expectations of right and wrong behavior. Their brandishing a gun and desperate eleventh-hour how-do-you-like-me-now behavior is their last gasp for help and their public confession of self-hate.

### 8. *To Know How to Confide in Adults and Why*
The people who can do the most for children, and do it best, are adults. Paradoxically, it is once-trusted adults who have often

brought more physical hurt and emotional pain into the child's fragile life than anybody else he knows. If a foreign power brought such physical hurt and emotional pain to our children, we would consider it unpardonable and regard such treatment as an act of war. When children are guided only by their emotional suffering and bottomless sense of betrayal, they resort to weapons to make *somebody* pay for their pain. Children driven to kill have been made victims on the emotional battlefields of home. Whether or not we as a society like or admit it, children who grow up in loving, caring, emotionally healthy, nonviolent households, where their voices are respected and their views solicited by adults, can no more kill a human being than can a car traveling forward suddenly, and without warning, start rocketing backwards.

The director of research for the California Youth Authority ordered me not to ask my incarcerated interview participants any questions about being sexually abused in their homes. "If this is known," he said, "We would have to do a large investigation. It could get ugly and lots of family members could get hurt, since there are no statutory limitations on sexual abuse." I did not have to open this taboo subject myself, most of the children I talked to had, in fact, been sexually and physically abused and could not wait to tell me about it! They simply volunteered it shortly after we met and began talking. It's difficult for a child to trust people who lie, threaten, physically or verbally abuse him, repeatedly disappoint, and just are too unreliable and can't be counted on to "be there." The emotional toll on children and the heavy price we pay, due to their behavior, demands that we tell children the truth, ask for their understanding, treat them as friends, not enemies, understand their feelings, and tell them constantly how much we love them.

Some of the most untrustworthy adults are the most consistent, and some of the most inconsistent adults are the most trustworthy. So, in the eyes of the child, it is not consistency only that spells trustworthiness in adults. Rather, it is the degree and quality of communication between parent and child that informs the child whether to trust the parent or not. If a parent has a difficult work schedule that constantly changes at the last minute, thus torpedoing family plans, a child whose trust is important to the parent needs to be told by the parent the reason for the sudden schedule change *when* it occurs, not after the fact. A child can forgive the frequency of interruptions and will come to rely on the parent's consistent communications about them as valued care. So, be consistent where it is important: in your honest communications with your child, in your attempts to explain your inconsistencies as best you can, and in your apologies for those times when they don't make sense.

Most of your child's experiences with adults can be good, even as he begins to understand that not all people are loving and kind. Counsel your child that most people are good people and that it's important to know and believe that. However, be willing to hear your child out and share his feelings about people. Be diplomatic yet frank in saying such things as, "Yes, you're right. Aunt Sheila said her house isn't made for children and that was not a kind thing to say," or "Yes, I see what you mean. Mr. Pepper always takes Johnny's side whenever you and Johnny have an argument," or "Your teacher really shouldn't yell at you. She could tell you everything in a nice, polite way." This kind of sharing communicates to your child that you are an ally, that you listen, and that what he feels is confirmed by you as being legitimate. From such a foundation trust grows.

It is important that your child have adults in his world whom he can trust and consider allies. A child's feelings—just like his physical makeup—are fragile. It is your support and under-standing that will brace the child up and keep him from feeling "sandbagged" by and alone with his feelings. Never fear that you'll destroy your child's faith in people if you acknowledge their foibles and imperfections. Such faithlessness and distrust would occur only if the acknowledgement were never made at all. Consider using the resources of "Big Brother" and "Big Sister" programs to find mentors for your child. Mentoring is widely regarded for its wholesome leadership benefits. Ideal benefits from being a "mentee" are your child's increased confidence and social ease, acquisition of good habits such as time and goal management, and having a trusted friend whose lifestyle and behavior are exemplary. Other organizations, such as the YMCA, YWCA, and United Way, can, with a phone call, provide you information about mentorship programs. In addition, churches and community-based organizations may have this information readily available for you.

As essential and obvious are the benefits of good mentoring, so are glaringly evident the extreme effects of the absence of mentoring. One of the queries on the questionnaire instrument I designed and used for interviewing my incarcerated subjects asked: "Have you ever had a teacher or other adult in your life to lean on?" Sadly, only one respondent recalled having had such a person in her life. The rest of my interviewees claimed not to have had any mentor at all. It is tragically ironic that, bereft of mentoring, most of my research participants committed "adult" crimes that robbed them of their innocence and stole their childhood.

Some parents may contend that their own children do not trust them and, therefore, my putting such emphasis on mentoring is unrealistic. I appreciate this sentiment, as there are, indeed, parents who are experiencing their own children's chilling mistrust. Not being trusted by your own child hurts deeply, whether it is the current in-vogue fashion of his social set or something darker, deeper, and closer to home. In spite of the fact that your child may not trust you now, there *are* other adults—even if it is just *one*—whom he does trust. Find that person, and engage them in your child's life. Work together to bring your child back to a foundation of trusting again in you.

As an experiment and a mirror into the quality of communication between you and your child, ask him: *"Do you trust me some of the time, most of the time, or all of the time?" "Why do you trust me?" "Why don't you trust me?" "Have you ever trusted me?"* and *"Have you ever not trusted me?"* Have conversations around these questions. Listen closely and carefully to your child's answers. You may find them very revealing and they will tell you which of the questions may or may not apply. Do not become defensive. These are tough questions for any child to answer. If your child answers, he is risking that you are asking in good faith and really want to know the truth. Reward his faith in you and listen. And listen. And listen. You may find the experience a treasure-trove of "news" you might never have gathered or known otherwise.

### 9. *To Know the Power of an Independent Mind*

When a child says "No," he is really identifying himself. He means, "I am." His developing self-image is leading him to separate himself from the easy and expected response and asserts his independence by responding in the negative. Be happy when this occurs, rather than insulted, outraged, or flabbergasted. In short, don't take it personally. Your child's sense of being unique and having personal choice over his destiny will be a powerful social tool, particularly when peer pressure—in the service of the "in-crowd"—threatens to sacrifice personal choice on the altar of "group-think." If every child who carried a gun to school last year had instead made a decision *not* to follow the gun-toting crowd but, instead, to be unique and independent, far fewer guns would have taken far fewer lives. Instead, more students would have taken personal responsibility to solve their interpersonal difficulties in other ways.

As a parent, you can ensure that your child thinks for himself. Encourage him to be unique; tell him that the power of personal choice is the greatest power known to human beings. Despite his sounding aggressively independent, Paul's admission to being an "avowed communist," his surrounding himself with the writings of a community of notable revolutionaries, and even the coincidence of his friend fingering his past foe for him to kill, are all powerfully suggestive of a lack of personal control and a willingness to submit to and be dependent upon the thinking of others and the "choices" they made for him.

You want your child to be strong intellectually and spiritually, to make sound judgments based on well developed inner convictions. Don't wait until he is almost grown before you wonder if or when he will "acquire" these; he won't. So, begin very early and give him experiences in making choices, exercising his personal prerogatives, and voicing his own opinions. This powerful principle is already at work when you say, "Lawrence, now that you're five, I think *you* should decide what month we take the training wheels off your bicycle," or "I'm going to the store to get the food for our camping trip. Anybody who goes with me gets a chance to pick out something special for themselves," or "No, Joseph, I won't tell Mr. Jones that I don't like him because, actually, I do. But you have a right to your own feelings and opinions."

By providing your children with abundant opportunities to exercise their personality, share their views, voice their likes and dislikes, you prepare them for circumstances in which spontaneous, independent decisions will be necessary—such as whether to join a bunch of students in a "ditching party" at a vacant home, or whether to accept drugs from a student who promises the outcome will be instant popularity. Obviously, every "No!" is not necessarily good, such as when your child insists on walking against the traffic light and into a busy intersection. But when you think you can't take hearing another "No" from your three-year-old, remember that every "No" gets you closer to the day when you will shout, "Yes!" because, in response to negative peer pressure, he says "No!" and walks independently away from risky behavior. Conviction, judgment, and courage get better with practice.

### 10. *To Know When to Summon the "Cavalry"*

By the time your child enters kindergarten, he should have a firm sense that there are many circumstances that he cannot take care of by himself. As he gets older, gently remind him that there are social circumstances—gangs, teenage drug pushers, kids with weapons, strange-behaving teachers, adult predators loitering around campus—that are too threatening and overwhelming and for which he will need the "cavalry"—adult assistance. He needs to know that it is okay to call on trusted adults for guidance and intervention. Unless you tell him about the road ahead and the kinds of persons who travel it, he will not know otherwise. That's why many children are caught up in situations so overwhelming that their senses, save for the sense of fear, are completely overridden. Getting out of such situations can be extremely difficult. Ruth was fatally trapped by her situation. Buried so deep beneath Ralph's control, it was impossible for Ruth to dig herself out and escape to safety. Having turned completely away from her family, she had nobody to support her when Ralph betrayed her love and trust in him and then dumped her after she did precisely what he demanded.

Your child needs to hear you say that your are his friend as well as his parent. That you can help him without hassling or holding him. That, above everything else, you *understand* and will come running if he needs your help. Children have a right to have an adult protector. And if you're a parent, you're *It*. Get other human resources if you need to do so. But know that your child trusts you and it is that trust that becomes the "bridge" through which you can provide whatever is needed to help solve his problem or correct his situation.

Promise yourself to help your child achieve mastery in these ten skill areas. The bonus is that he will find school to be more pleasure than pain, and learning to be a labor of love. Of special benefit to you, is to know that your child, well-versed as he will be in these ten areas, will simply have little desire to be habitually antagonistic toward or abusive of others. Working in these ten areas allows you to plumb the depths of human values with your child. You can bequeath these valvues to your children and, their attention thus focused, they will become part of a new generation of visionary and loving human beings, who will have the capability to be change-agents and transform the world into a safe, sane, and better place for themselves and everyone else.

# Bullies: Campus Stalkers

*It was either me or them. Lots of times, I didn't have noth-ing to eat. I got used to no breakfast, but when I seen they had lunch or money, I figured they had already had breakfast and I wasn't really hurting them. So I picked out the ones I knew wouldn't give me no trouble and I went after them…. Naw, I ain't never jacked up no girl for no money. I'd have to be a punk to do that and I ain't no punk. I ain't never jacked up no girl for no money. That ain't right, that ain't me. I killed the guy at the store 'cuz he wouldn't give me the money.*—Jerome

Jerome was fifteen years old when I first met him. He was hardly conversational, and I presumed he would decide to drop out of the interviews at any time. But there we sat in the day room—it was strangely quiet for once—for our fifth interview. And I had to note: His ability to answer questions and express himself had improved significantly with each interview. Jerome was serving time for killing another youth who was working behind the counter of a convenience store when Jerome robbed the store. Jerome described his life as a constant struggle to "try to outsmart everybody." This urge began in junior high school where he discovered he could "punk other kids and make them give up their money." Never knowing which day his mother would prepare breakfast or lunch—he was one of eight children—Jerome decided it was "easier to take another kid's lunch or take their money and buy lunch." Jerome proudly stated that "nobody ain't never punked me." I asked him what the word "punk" meant. "That's when somebody can push you around, beat you up, or take something from you because you are like a girl, weak, and harmless," he answered. I asked him if he had ever taken a girl's lunch or her lunch money. He looked at me in anger for a moment. "I'd have to be a punk to do that, man. And I ain't no punk. Naw, I ain't never hit no girl up for no money. That ain't right, that ain't me."

According to Jerome, he "punked up" about 25 other kids on campus who had to pay him a few times a week, in money or lunch, to keep him from beating them up. I asked him what was so smart about that, since he claimed his life was spent out-smarting others. "Well," he began, "It was either me or them. Lots of times, I didn't have nothing to eat. I got used to no breakfast, but when I seen they had lunch or money, I figured they had already had breakfast and I wasn't really hurting them. So I picked out the ones I knew wouldn't give me no trouble." As a parent, listen carefully to what Jerome just said: ". . . I picked out the ones I knew wouldn't give me no trouble." Once he was certain his soon-to-be-victims would not resist, he "punked" them—accosted them and extorted their money. They soon became his "regular punks," weaklings who paid up on demand.

Jerome said he didn't consider himself "a mean person" and that he became angry only when somebody "wouldn't do what I wanted them to." I asked him if that was the reason he killed the teenager in the convenience store. "Well, if he had just given me the money—I could see it in his cash drawer—I wouldn't have got angry. I knew I was being taped (videotaped), there was other people in the store. Man, all that was making me tense, and I couldn't handle nobody not doing what I had told them." Jerome, the classic bully, became angry when he sensed himself losing control of the situation. And in true sociopathic style, his view of the robbery and killing for which he is serving time was that the unfortunate teen working behind the counter made him angry.

99

Ever the bully, Jerome tried to get his way by using brute and, this time, lethal force.

Jerome represents the kind of bully who rejects the rules of acceptable social custom and behavior and openly harasses others to fill his needs. To recoup the superiority and security he felt himself losing, he needed to declare his "authority" and "power." Having a gun conveniently allowed him to do so " 'cuz I really wasn't going to kill him. I went into the store for some money, like I used to go up to kids at school for some money." In Jerome's bullying mentality, he was merely doing what came naturally and, based on his experience with the school children he had "punked," robbing a convenience store should not have posed any problems.

Bullying is a word that is weighed down with various meanings. It sometimes involves hitting, pushing, kicking, and simply physically assaulting somebody. However, it can also include some very frightening behaviors. These behaviors are what makes bullying so very intimidating, and include such *non-physical* tactics as verbal threats, stalking, teasing, taunting, ridiculing, and name-calling. Particularly damaging, these non-physical tactics are a form of psychological terrorism that can reduce a student to being a fear-ridden, ashamed, depressed, suicidal, and helpless victim. A bullied child feels intense fear; never underestimate this. Bullying strips away self-esteem, confidence, and trust like nothing else can. Sometimes it is an individual student who is doing the bullying; sometimes it is a group that bullies. All bullies have an exaggerated need for power. Because of this, bullying often takes the form of excluding some-body from "the group" for whatever reasons the power-mad group devises.

It should perhaps come as no surprise that most bullies were themselves victims of bullying. The bully on the schoolyard today was once weak and helpless against some other strong, taunting, and physically intimidating bully. Although some might see bullying as part of the "natural" social fabric that touches everyone once in a while, it is not a pleasant experience for the victim. An "everybody-does-it-or-goes-through-it" attitude places bullying alongside the jungle protocol that Darwin defined as survival of the fittest. If we make the mistake of honoring bullying as a human form of primitive law that just *has* to be, then we only encourage our children to see and respond to life as an eat-or-be-eaten experience. Such a cynical view is *one* of the reasons our youth and adult prison populations are overflowing. On the other hand, if we can control, reduce, and wipe out bullying on our school campuses, we will have taken one of the most important steps in providing for all students safe, secure, and peaceful schools. School *can* be a place where students are proud to practice the humane and ethical arts of civility, respect, courteousness, kindness, altruism, generosity, charity, and decency.

Bullying survives and thrives in a culture or environment that *tolerates* it. That doesn't mean it necessarily *defines* or *controls* the environment in which it "resides." Like a large broken and drafty window in an otherwise complete house, it can be an ignored and tolerated nuisance. But because it is tolerated, it can thrive and threaten. School athletics is one example. Embarrassed though we may be, as a culture, to admit it, athletics *is* sometimes a haven for bullies. The campus bully is occasionally a student athlete.

Among all student organizations, school athletics teams have perhaps the most visibility and potential to put their unique stamp on the "life and times" at junior and senior high school campuses. The influence of an athletic team pervades much of what goes on: from the naming of the yearbook, to selecting the school mascot, to drumming the team "fight song" into the student body at pep rallies. In general, athletics is a positive pursuit designed to build an array of life-process skills: teamwork, loyalty, persistence, goal-setting, sportsmanship, accomplishment, and self-reliance. Star student athletes—or "jocks" as they are known—are often accorded excessive attention and given favors and benefits denied the majority of non-athlete students. Some of these athletes abuse their popularity and prestige. On the playing field they exhibit high skills in the areas of communication, coordination, and concentration. However, off the playing field they often demonstrate crude interpersonal skills and coarse anti-social behaviors—exact opposites of the class and sportsmanship on which their legends rest.

Other students, unable to defend themselves, often find themselves the object of pranks and taunts hurled their way by some of their school's popular athletes. Increasingly, non-athlete students throughout the country are harassed, assaulted, and victimized in other ways by their schools' athletic stars. Their emotional pain and suffering are intensified when bully athletes are not disciplined, warned, counseled, or sanctioned in any other way. If a deferential hands-off treatment is accorded, it sends and reinforces an obvious message to the entire student body on campus: star athletes are untouchable and their bullying is permitted.

Many schools have a united football team, for example, whose players check their egos and put aside personality differences in order to cooperate and function like well-oiled machinery. Often, however, their reckless, destructive, and harmful behaviors off the playing field hurt other students and *divide* the campus.

Eric Harris and Dylan Klebold, the two teenage killers from Columbine High School, had been increasingly losing their "place" in the world for some time before their shootout. Various reports have stated that they had been so constantly harassed by the school's athletes for being "different," "nerdy," or otherwise odd, that they joined the Trenchcoat Mafia, known for wearing long, black, oil-skin leather cloaks popular on Colorado ranches, and that the name of that group had been bestowed by the athletes who made fun of Harris and Klebold. These same reports suggest that Harris and Klebold would keep their heads down so as not to meet a jock face-to-face and get slammed repeatedly into lockers and called "fags." Harris so hated jocks that on the "kill list" he meticulously maintained, jocks were at the top. So shamed and battered was his life on campus that he was reportedly taking the antidepressant Luvox. Literally at his wit's end, the reports said, that in order to express the emotional storms inside himself, he even developed his own Internet web site and wrote on it that he hoped to kill as many jocks as he could in his planned shootout. In a shocking exhibition of their feelings about their constant victimization by jocks, the two boys even made a tape for a video production class in which they pretended to shoot all the jocks. In the video, they brandished a real rifle.

Other, more recent, reports suggest that Harris and Klebold deliberately played the victim in order to solicit the taunts and attacks from peers, savoring the social position of the loner. It has even been reported that Harris and Klebold did their share of bullying, and that some of the Columbine students reached out to them.

These seemingly contradictory behaviors are not uncommon in bullies. I stated earlier in this chapter that bullies have often been the victims of bullying, so is it also true that the same student can be both. Bullying is an effort to exercises control and power, and is usually done from a position of superior strength and/or status. Thus, a child may be in a position to be bullied by some children, while capable of bullying other children. But what of the child who deliberately invites a bully's threats and violence as some suggest Harris and Klebold did? These children are still exercising a certain kind of control. They chose to be physically or verbally attacked, putting themselves in situations that increase the likelihood of bullying, in order to feel the empowerment of control, as though they are *choosing,* and to fulfill a sometimes morbid identification with antisocial behaviors. I will discuss such behaviors in future chapters on depression.

Whatever their position in the social pecking order, Harris and Klebold became the negative inspiration and encouragement to hundreds of students nationwide. In a kind of post-mortem salute to Klebold and Harris, an Internet web site was launched and soon filled with the venom- and hate-laced ramblings of self-described geeks and nerds from all over the country proclaiming the "Week of the Geek." Hundreds of messages from senders, who sometimes identified themselves, praised the two teenagers. The writers confessed that they, too, had been harassed and victimized repeatedly and viciously by popular jocks at their schools. In the wake of Littleton, schools throughout the nation were on full alert for copycat acts. Across the nation, an entire population of emboldened yet desperate students suddenly sprang up and gave schools plenty to watch out for. Hundreds of threats were reported to police agencies, and several bombs and guns were found. Here is just a sampling:

- One state reported more than 100 minor threats state-wide.

- A letter calling Littleton "the tip of the iceberg" shut down a school.

- Five honor students were overheard planning a June graduation bombing.

- One city's entire school district was closed after a bomb threat.

- Two boys were suspended for wearing dark trench coats two days after Littleton.

- A boy shot a girl in the face after he shot at and missed a boy with whom he had fought.

- Five junior high students were charged with con spiracy to kill other students and teachers.

- A home-made chemical bomb exploded in a locker and injured a teacher.

- A Georgia teenager wounded six classmates in a shooting rampage.

Geeks and nerds and anybody else who had ever been taunted, assaulted, or victimized at school suddenly had a "presence," a fearsome reputation. Wicked, gruesome, and frightening though this presence was it was preferable to them to being known and harassed and humiliated as weak, puny oddball nobodies. Harris' and Klebold's acts and their deaths by their own hands were seen as sacrifices to advance the greater cause and deliver a bigger, more frightening message: that weak, isolated, and "loner" students who had heretofore been easy to pick on, bully, and beat up, would respond by declaring war and even, if need be, laying down their own lives—which had been so brutalized and devalued by others.

In a bizarre and tragic act of self-sacrifice to pay tribute to Klebold and Harris, a Los Angeles student wrote a note describing the endless days of harassment, humiliation, and torment he endured at the hands of jocks at his high school. He stated that the events at Columbine opened afresh old, painful wounds. After he finished his graphic and emotional essay, he folded it carefully and placed it in an envelope. Then he picked up a gun and shot and killed himself.

The pressure a child feels at school can be, as the foregoing shows, extreme and intense. The emotional stakes for your own child can be quite high. As a concerned and involved parent, one of the many things you will need to find out, as you interface with your child's teachers and participate in school programs and on committees, is whether your child is being bullied.

Bullying, whether by athletes or non-athletes, can mean a variety of things and assume many forms. To find out if your child has yet faced bullying, start by asking him what bullying means to him. He might describe it in one of the following ways: being called names, being teased, being pushed or pulled on, being hit or attacked, having his backpack or other possessions taken and thrown around, having lies and stories spread about him, being ignored and left out of activities, being forced to give over money or other things, or being attacked because of race or religion.

Hearing your child describe bullying in this manner and admit to having been the victim of bullying may be frightening or infuriating for you. Bullying represents the worst abuse of power in peer-adolescent relationships. So, your child's response to your question, although potentially troubling, will nonetheless give you one powerful indicator of how school life is affecting him and what precisely is wrong. If he has been bullied, he has been victimized. And although its effects are not always obvious to you, bullying hurts. It makes your child scared and upset. Particularly tragic, is that bullying can make your child feel that he is not as good as others, that there is something wrong with him. Many children take personal responsibility for being bullied;

they feel that it is their fault. Other children worry so much that they can't work well at school. But realize that bullies unleash their power everywhere. Your child may encounter bullies on the school playground, in class, or in the bathroom. But he may also be stopped by them on the way to and from school, or on the bus, or in the park.

The most recent studies indicate that about one in 10 children experience bullying on a regular basis. Parents and others do not always know about these incidents, and as a result, bullied children often feel helpless and afraid. Feeling isolated and alone, they may suffer from hyper-anxiety, low self-esteem, and chronic depression as the school year drags on. Moreover, research studies continue to show that bullies themselves are at risk for engaging in crimes and serious anti-social behavior as they age with the school year. Jerome did not limit his bullying to his school campus. Instead, he "branched out" and committed his final and *fatal* act of bullying in his attempt to rob the convenience store.

Bullies do not feel the pain they cause because they learn how to disconnect from that pain. Why is that? Bullies are often victims of bullying themselves—by a family member or another adolescent who is bigger, stronger, more threatening than they. The goal of a bully is to rise to a level of skill and power to match their attacker. Once they do, however, they usually turn their attention on bullying those weaker than themselves. This partially explains why most adult male prisoners were bullies in their prior lives; assault and battery incidents are often prominent features of their arrest records.

Take a moment to look at your child. Do you think he is, or will be, a victim of bullying exclusively because of his physical appearance? Actually, physical appearance has very little to do with the bully's selection of a victim. Rather, bullies select their victims based on their "reading" of them as insecure, shy, or lacking in confidence. In other words, there is something about the way a child carries himself that "tells" a bully whether or not he will be a "good" victim. Most bullies lack the physical skill or temperament for a prolonged fight. As a result, they usually pass over children whom they think will confront them, fight back, or otherwise resist.

106

The bully-athlete may not be in obvious emotional pain, although many athletes privately suffer from feelings of inadequacy brought on by treatment and conditions at home. One reason they produce spectacular results on the field is that athletics is their last, best hope for physical and psychological success: self-esteem. Failing in his attempts to earn praise and receive encouragement at home, the bully-athlete's head indeed becomes swollen by all the external adulation and attention he receives. Unable emotionally to show gratitude to his adoring fans, he turns their idolization into power-perversion and seeks out victims. Most researchers agree that by the time a potential bully-child is eight years old, his expression of aggressive habits has become so crystallized that change and rehabilitation becomes extremely difficult. As we have seen, Jerome, always triumphant in his bullying, *never* changed—indeed, he never seemed to have reason to do so— until he was arrested and sentenced to prison for homicide.

Bullies often use the cover of teasing. "I'm only joking" is perhaps their most used cliché, and serves to shield them from serious discipline or verbal berating. Yet, their heart's intent is to hurt, not to share a harmless laugh with their victim. As you watch children, including your own, for signs of bullying, pay close attention to their intent in all its masquerades. What you will see is a picture of bullying that ranges from mild to severe and includes physical and verbal aggression. It may also include a kind of social eviction: the victim, in the process of bullying, is evicted from the group and denied social protection. This victimization and its resultant power imbalance is at the heart of all bullying and spells the most damaging hurt for victims of bullying. Bullying is primitive behavior and parallels a master-slave or kidnapper-hostage relationship. The victim is diminished by the fact that the bully has power over him to demean and dehumanize.

As a parent you need to know whether your child is, or has been, a bully. Before you ask him, however, or make plans to observe him from afar, ask yourself questions about the atmosphere and conditions in your home. Is your child thriving or merely surviving? Don't make excuses; simply assess the home front as it truly is. What is the quality of communication at home. Analyze whether you criticize, berate, taunt, needle, or threaten your child. In your analysis, try to get a picture of your body language as you converse with your child. Try to determine whether your body language is taut, tense, raging, threatening, or if it is relaxed, comfortable *and* comforting.

"Do you think I'm too toxic in my words and actions with my son?" a worried mom asked me during a seminar I was conducting. What an interesting question and choice of words. Toxic? Her question alludes to an important fact. All of us are creatures who express in words and actions what we think, believe, and want. The very power to express ourselves affects others, especially children. Negative thoughts and actions are indeed *toxic* and can have a polluting effect on a child. So, check yourself for the toxicity levels in your words and actions. Then assess the toxicity levels emitted from the communication of everybody in your home. If you find unhealthy levels of toxicity, take immediate steps to change the communication at home.

After working to rid your home environment of toxic words and actions, work with your child by showing him positive ways to satisfy any apparent urges for power. Give him opportunities to achieve and feel the power that real accomplishment—versus anti-social behavior—brings. Praise him consistently and constantly. Tune his ear to praise rather than pain. Coach him on the behaviors that are good and those that are not, those that are playful and those that hurt others.

### What If Your Child Is the Bully or Is Being Bullied?
### Thirteen Tips

#### Being Bullied:

1. Keep your cool, don't lose it. Relax and survey your options. Determine if the problem is severe enough to call school personnel and other parents.

2. Sit down with your child and listen to him. Don't forget he has been victimized. Don't compound his pain and shame with angry, anxious, or accusatory responses. Let your child tell you how he feels. He has to "unload" and this act in itself is therapeutic.

Don't judge him with, "Why didn't you just face him, fight back, tell him off?"

3.   Tell your child what makes people act like bullies. Stress to your child that he is not to blame in any way, that it is the bully who has the problem. Explain that the bully is the most unhappy kid at school, despite what he does or the social power he seems to exercise.

4.   Sort and sift options with your child. Responding in kind should not be considered an option. Victims of bullying are usually timid and shy; they are unable to respond in kind. Besides, trying to fight back puts your child at risk. Role-play with them this strategy: Look the bully in the eye and say, "What you're doing is not okay. Stop it." Then walk away and ignore further taunts.

5.   Advise your child to develop friendships with others. By doing so, he won't get stuck with the bully in the neighborhood. Discourage gang membership, however, as an antidote to bully-ing. Do encourage your child to invite other children to your home on a regular basis.

6.   Bullying wears heavily on your child's self-esteem. Praise him for confronting his fears. The mere act of going to school is a brave feat in itself, if that's where the bully is. So, develop your child's self-confidence by praising his courage. Find appropriate activities in which your child can develop expertise and excel. It is not necessary to try to turn your child into a super-athlete simply because there is a bully athlete on campus. Allow your child to seek his own particular talents.

**Being the Bully:**

7.   If your child is the bully, don't minimize the problem. Take it seriously. Having a child-bully in the family is no reason to be proud. Young bullies in the family are at high risk for social problems as they grow older.

8.   If your child is the bully, search for hidden problems that may be triggering this behavior. Child bullies are angry and frustrated. Perhaps your child-bully is experiencing bullying from another child at school, so he "passes the baton" to the next

victim. This "relay-race" behavior is often observed in children who are the brunt of bullying behavior by parents, siblings, and other children.

9. If your child is the bully, monitor your child's behavior closely. Purposefully plan to increase his participation in supervised activities and team sports or youth associations. Make it a practice to be on hand whenever your child is playing with others.

10. If your child is the bully, communicate your dislike for bullying to your child and stress to him that others have rights. As you watch television, note those news or other stories where there is an identified victim. Ask your child how he thinks the victim is feeling. Ask for his ideas on what might make the victim feel better. The goal is to coach him into thinking about the welfare of others. Ask him to analyze his own feelings for how he would feel as a victim of bullying.

11. If your child is the bully, respond to incidents of bullying with definite consequences. Do not, however, react with force, violence, shouting, or criticism. Simply remove and reduce the time your child is allowed with others; a desired, expected activity; social interactions or events; or play time. Bullying children do not like to be isolated or separated. They can't stand themselves and need others to feel alive. So, correct their behavior by removing them from others.

12. If your child is the bully, demonstrate different approaches to interacting with others. Bullies need options for positive communication. Teach them that force is not the answer. Coach them on negotiating skills and respecting the rights of others. If you need materials, talk to your principal, faculty heads, and parent-teacher group representatives for materials on non-violent communication and conflict-reduction strategies.

13. If your child is the bully, be always on the lookout for fair play and positive negotiation-in-action. Praise it, reward it, and let your child know that he ranks high in your estimation. Encourage him to reach for these and other positive attributes. Thus, he will be encouraged to outgrow his bullying behavior. Soon, it will not be fun to linger in its depths for too long. Your consistent, patient reminders and regular rewards for taking the

"high road" of behavior will convince him that this is also the road to happiness.

The U.S. Justice Department, in its monthly adolescent assault countdown, estimates that by April 2000, one out of every four kids will be abused by another youth. Compared to other kids who bring guns and other weapons on school campuses, a bully and his behavior may seem like "small potatoes"—rather like an annoying mosquito buzzing around. Don't be fooled, though. Bullying is often disregarded and treated as part of growing up. As a parent you need to take a different point of view and know that it is an early form of aggression that precedes violent behavior. The U.S. Justice Department expects that one in four children who bully will have a criminal record before they reach age 30. Don't ignore the problems that bullies cause, even though other parents and teachers might be inclined to do so. Bus-stop teasing, extortion, pushing, name-calling, verbal threats—it's all open season to a bully. The fear and stress bullies engender in others can cause some children to ditch school, carry a weapon in their backpacks for protection, or be motivated to commit acts of violence themselves—almost always at school.

More and more schools are adopting "zero tolerance" policies for on-campus violence. As we have seen, through media and other accounts, even the youngest adolescents can grow up feeling isolated and alienated and yearning for revenge. Many of Eric Harris' profane ramblings in his diary express pain and anger about being bullied. *Bullying is a form of child molestation.* As a parent, you ought to view it that way and stop it, or order others to do so, before it becomes entrenched and its deadly seeds are sown. *Today's bullied child could be tomorrow's killer-bomber.*

# Depression: Symptoms & Why You Must See Them

*They've done all kinds of psych tests on me in here. My dad used to beat the crap out of me. My shrink says because of that, I burglarized and stole the money and jewels from a man I knew, the guy I used to deliver newspapers to. In other words, I purposely picked somebody I knew and it had to be a man. My shrink also says I set fire to his body after I shot him, when he sicked his dog on me, because I had a real deep hatred toward my dad and saw setting fire to the man I knew and killed as symbolically burning up my dad and purging out the depression he caused in me, and all the bad feelings and pain that represented his presence in my life. I cried when my shrink said that, because nobody's ever understood me. And it was, like, he told me the whole story of my life. Funny thing is, the real prison was when I was outside, free, and walking around depressed and hating myself. Now, I understand myself and I like myself, but I'm locked up.—Leonard*

By my third interview with Leonard, he admitted to liking his role in helping me with my research on kids who kill. He had arrived a few minutes early for his interview, and stood conversing with his parole agent while another ward and I finished talking. When he sat down inside the tiny office, which the administration had selected that day for me to use, Leonard watched me change the batteries in my two tape recorders. Obviously wanting to make conversation, he began noting that, in our previous interviews, I had been questioning him "pretty much just like [his] shrinks" but that I did not try to "sweat" him (pin him down) for answers. But, he observed, "You do come back later on, and get your answers every time." Pleased with what he told me, I asked, "Well, have I gotten everything so far?" He beamed broadly. "Yep. So far." I returned his gaze. "Is there more?" I asked. His eyes seemed to dance with mischief. "Yep. There's more. Always."

As soon as he entered the house, fourteen-year-old Leonard tripped, knocking over a potted plant at the side of the door. *Damn!* he thought. *If somebody's home, I'm outta here.* He made sure to leave the back door, through which he had entered, open just in case. He remembered seeing that tactic once in a movie. He crept along and listened for sounds of any other movement in the large house. *I know he's got money*, he thought. *Anybody whose got a fancy Chinese dog like that, and walks in the park everyday with lots of jewelry on, has got money.*

As his eyes became accustomed to the semi-darkened room, he saw the grand piano, the china cabinet, the overstuffed sofa and chairs. His gaze wandered upward. Quickly, he bounded up the stairs toward the landing. He sprang from it and faced the large master bedroom at the end of the hall. His large, hurried strides ate up yardage but when he was only a few feet away, he began to tiptoe. He reached the closed double-doors, stopped and listened, straining to hear even the slightest sound; he heard nothing and opened the door into the room. *Yeah, this is it,* he thought, viewing a large screen TV dominating the opposite wall. *I could play all kinds of video games in this place. I wish I lived here.*

Leonard quickly covered the bedroom and looked in every dresser drawer and cabinet. *Nothing! I know that old guy's got money. Where is it?* He swung open the door to a clothes closet. *The guy's got his own clothing store in here,* he thought as he surveyed the clothes rack from end to end. *But where is the money?* He dropped his head and butted his way through the clothes to the other side of the clothes rack. He fell clumsily against the wall, feeling something move when he hit it. Alternating with his open palm, then with his closed fist, he tapped the wall, hammered it, and slapped it. Finally, he was rewarded. A full sized door cut into the wall, a door that could hardly be detected, opened silently and slowly. He peered cautiously inside the opening, unsure what to expect as he continued to push the secret panel open.

The door stopped moving as suddenly as it had begun. Leonard's eyes widened as he stared at the 4-foot high floor safe before him. He walked toward it and into a small room. He found a light and switched it on. He immediately saw two gun cabinets. *Oh, sh\*\*! This guy's a probably a cop.* Leonard went quickly to the safe and bent down. He grabbed the handle and pulled. To his surprise, it opened! The contents were too good to be true. Stacks of neatly wrapped bills and a jewelry case filled with expensive looking items. *Jackpot!* Leonard went to work immediately. In moments, he had filled the pockets of his baggy pants and large jacket. Leaving the safe and jewelry case open, he went to the gun cabinets. There were so many cool guns that it was hard to choose. So, he closed his eyes and reached inside, pulling out a .45 caliber. Cradling it in his hands, he checked to see if it was loaded. It was. He placed it carefully inside his hip pocket.

The broad and smug smile on Leonard's fat, boyish face suddenly froze. He had not heard the dog. And yet there it was: A huge, black mastiff crouching rigid on its hind legs, ready to lunge. Its curiously dull eyes smoldered with fury. Leonard got the message. The dog was daring him to make a move. While waiting for Leonard to decide, the dog alternately yawned and lolled its huge red tongue back and forth over its lips. Its very sharp teeth glistened like rows of lights against its black body.

"Good boy, Jeeves, well done. When I saw the bicycle in the driveway, loaded with newspapers, I figured he was still inside." Leonard looked from the dog, Jeeves, to the man speaking. "Yes, you know me, son," the man said. "You ought to; you throw me my newspaper every afternoon."

Leonard was dumbfounded. *I hadn't planned on him returning so soon*, he thought.

"Speak, boy!" The man before him was suddenly angry. "Cat got your tongue? Ever heard of a dog getting your tongue? Well, Jeeves can do that and more. Can't you Jeeves?" The dog erupted in a spasm of wild and furious barking. "Okay, okay, Jeeves. You can have him. Go get him, boy." The man issued the command and crossed the room toward the stair. Leonard figured he was going to call the police.

Jeeves screamed in mid-air. Leonard just had time to raise the gun and squeeze the trigger once. He saw the fire from the barrel of the gun before he heard the awful explosion. The dog's head snapped to one side as though its neck had been broken by the force of the bullet. Jeeves was dead when he landed with a thud at Leonard's feet. The man paused and turned around. "Why you awful juvenile delinquent!" he screamed at the top of his lungs. "When I get my hands on you . . ." Once again, the huge gun exploded. The man's eyes widened at the shock of fire that spat from the gun, which was followed by another impossibly loud report. The bullet flew straight from Leonard's hand into the man's throat, tearing away his Adam's apple. He fell heavily on his back, his face turned upward, his lips twisted in an indignant frown, still struggling to form a last question. His blood flowed in a single, straight line down his neck.

In the aftermath of the Columbine shooting, an "open," "tell-all-share-your-feelings" writing assignment was spontaneously given by a teacher to a classroom full of students. It is the kind of project used to ferret out which particular student—among the numerous angry, depressed, suffering students countless schools have—is likely to explode in rage. Directly after this assignment was given, I received the following communication:

> *Dr. Shaw, we're detaining a student in the principal's office until his parents come to pick him up. Something about an essay he wrote. His Composition teacher asked her 10th grade class to express their feelings about Columbine. It was an "open assignment" and the teacher told the students they could write anything they wanted, anything they felt. She wanted their honest*

*feelings and the only restriction on the students was that they had to limit their thoughts and feelings to no more than 350 words. The student we're holding wrote that he agreed with what Klebold and Harris did but not their strategy. He wrote that they should have hit the front office first, where the administrators were, then gone to the classrooms and gotten the teachers, and left the students for last. He then wrote full-blown descriptions of weapons, bombs, grenades, like some war historian. When the teacher collected the assignment, well, she panicked and marched him to the principal's office. On the referral form, she wrote, "Making written threats to kill." She's pressing for him to be expelled because she thinks he's going to turn the school into something like Columbine. What do we do?*

I would suggest that it is illegal and unethical to *invite* students to openly share their feelings in writing about a horrific event and then decide, after the fact, that one of them is to be punished for what he wrote. What about the teacher's ethical commitment to honor the *implied* promise in an "open assignment" of immunity from sanction or censure? We should not violate the freedom of speech protections afforded by the First Amendment. It is not best for a teacher to invite students to candidly share their feelings about a tragedy, then turn around and yank away that freedom to speak openly.

The student who wrote this outrageous essay should not be expelled from his school. In fact, the school principal should have disagreed with the teacher and viewed what the student wrote as being symptomatic of some unresolved emotional and social problems. As shocking as his sentiments might have been, the student did not use the language of threats or terrorism. Yet he was signaling his need for attention and, possibly, help. Such signaling should have been his "ticket" to the counseling office, not the principal's office.

This student's immediate exploitation of this writing assignment was a kind of self-created "billboard." Through it, he cried out his urgent need to be on center stage receiving the full attention of adult counselors and school psychologists whose *demonstrated* interest and concern might relieve his obvious distress. Instead, he got caught in the clutches of a teacher who forgot that it was she who had asked her students to write freely about their thoughts concerning Columbine. She feared his thoughts, and to rid herself of her fears, she sought to rid herself of *him*. Leonard, our earlier case, shows that this kind of reaction—tantamount to *eviction*—is far less effective than counseling and other kinds of support for such angry students. Indeed, Leonard had been punished and *evicted* in various ways at home, including beatings by his dad. He committed the kind of violent act, in real life, that our offending student rhapsodized about on paper. Denied wholesome and healthy attention at home, he finally made it to "center stage" and received vital insight and understanding from his "shrink." According to him, this was precisely what he needed in his life, despite the irony of receiving such help in a prison cell.

The student writer who rhapsodized about the tragedy in Columbine might have come from a home much like Leonard's. He and his teacher reacted similarly: He, with *intellectual violence*, she, with a *hands-on violence to the spirit*—a "you're-danger-ous-get-out-of-here-I-don't-ever-want-you-in-my-class-again" attitude. The student's thoughts got him into trouble because his teacher felt threatened by them. Blinded by her own fear and anger, she failed to see the opportunity she was throwing away: To teach him better ways of thinking.

Anger is the chameleon of our emotions. It can express itself in many ways. Its ultimate power often lies in its lack of expression. When it does express itself, it may cause shock or peril to those who misinterpret it and are unprepared for the guise in which it expresses itself. There are no real evaluative standards for determining (diagnosing) whether your son or any other school-age minor is exhibiting the symptoms of depression in his anti-social behaviors, if he is merely "being bad," or if he is simply and chronically angry. Boys tend to express—act out—their depression in a variety of ways. But underlying all these expressions is a simmering and potentially volatile anger. As a parent, you need to be able to determine whether your son is suffering from depression. You can do so by being on the lookout for these signs in the following "Symptoms Index:"

- **Heating up and chilling out.**

The angrier a boy becomes, the more he tends to disengage from relationships. Family and friends may note an iciness in his attitude, a pulling away. He may show an unsympathetic side to things and events that others are sensitive about. This "misemotion" may not be appreciated by those around him; moreover, their response may only further antagonize and alienate him, causing him to retreat and keep to himself. At home he may answer questions with terse one word responses, guttural sounds, and with "attitude." He may hole up in his room to avoid verbal and physical contact with his family. When he's at school he may limit himself to mere slight or surface contacts with other students and teachers. His interactions are likely to be forced and reluctant. Often he will simply sit in the corner of the classroom or in the very back. No matter how loud and entertaining other students are during recess, snack and lunch times, he will segregate himself and sit quietly alone, disinterested. Often, he will "cut" classes or become truant altogether. If he were asked if he has friends, he might likely say that nobody is his friend. His me-against-the-world demeanor is troubling to all who know him. Sometimes his attitude threatens and baits other students who read him as having a chip on his shoulder. Leonard admitted to "using" his "friends," in behaviors that included lying to them or otherwise taking advantage of them. He said it did not bother him that he knew them; indeed, "that made it easier to manipulate them." We have already seen—in his act of homicide—the lengths to which Leonard "used" people he knew.

- **Immobile or impulsive mood.**

Picture a boy who acts totally bored and disinterested, and seems drained of energy. He may even neglect hobbies and pursuits he once seemed to live for, and respond with irritation when questioned about the sudden change. It isn't so much that his tastes have changed; indeed, you may think that he has no tastes—he seems to have zero zest for life. If he was animated in conversation before and highly sociable, you may see a boy increasingly glum, almost mute most of the time, and a virtual recluse. Alternately, he may act suddenly or rashly, and may make hints to you about his vague fears and forebodings. Leonard, in blaming his father for most of the pain in his childhood, appeared to be sending a message to all parents: *How parents treat their children can make them into free and loving persons or turn them into Frankensteins.*

- **Recency and frequency of episodic anger**.

You may notice that his episodes of anger have increased (frequency) and the length of time between them has decreased (recency). It seems that almost anything "ticks" him off. Whether the problem is trivial or tragic, he responds equally and goes into full storm. These are the times when he can become physically and verbally abusive toward others. His bad moods may instantly reveal these "ranges of rage:" periodic outbursts of raw anger, rather than mere annoyance; temper tantrums; the sulking and wounded warrior; or extreme and constant irritability. The rebel-without-a-cause anger, also called "staying mad," is a main route boys often take to express other feelings indirectly, such as grief (over loss), hopelessness (against the odds), and disappointment (with the results of his efforts). However, when a boy "stays mad" or seems to be turning into a real grouch, that's when you should look for something deeper. For what you're seeing is probably not anger; more than likely, it's depression. Age usually influences the kind of anger boys express. As a parent you may have seen your son express a certain kind of anger at one age but a different kind of response at another age. Depression, however, spans all ages for boys. Leonard told me that his teachers "were always writing some note on my report cards about my moods." All of them apparently saw, in Leonard, a very troubled student.

- **The pain game**.

It goes something like this: "Jason, I know Uncle Theo's death/ Dad's and my divorce/your flunking out of AP Calculus/my problems with alcohol caused you great pain that followed you

119

everywhere and really affected your life…." Jason: "Look, Mom, it's okay. Don't make such a big deal out of it. I'll live, all right? I'm not life's poor wounded traveler and you're not the Good Samaritan. So, would you quit bugging me, please? Why is everybody treating me like some victim?" Despite his utterances, behind the verbal barbed wire lives and hides a boy who is desperately afraid. He's hurt and wounded and perhaps confused. If, in spite of his denials, he mopes, slinks, sulks, and responds to everything with an attitude of hopelessness, then he undoubtedly is depressed. Leonard's mother might well have been a female version of Leonard because (according to him), "She did what my father told her to do, said what he said, thought like him, the whole nine yards." Leonard actually despised her because "she was all talk and no help at all."

- **Independence and escape**.

A real tug-of-war, this phase may mark the time when you and your son "cross swords," for it's here where a boy may begin to openly give orders to his parents. "Leave me alone." "Go away." "It's my room, I live here, right? So what if I decide to stay inside here all my life!" These are just a few of the many responses symptomatic of a boy's demand for independence and solitude. As one of my workshop participants once put it: "Whatever happened to the attitude of gratitude? Why is it replaced so quickly with the attitude of solitude?" It's called growing up. And your son may resist the authority that you, his closest adult, wield. His resistance may spill over into his school life as well. Younger boys, desiring to show the world their independence, may engage in exhibitionist outbursts in the classroom. If you have an older son, he may start coming home later, take his bicycle or his car, and go out for long solo excursions. Seemingly deliberate may be his avoidance of family-time activities or conformance to family rules. You need to know that it's normal for boys to show a rebellious streak as they work through the process of ego identity, called individuation. However, all boys are not rebelling this way; many segregate themselves to cope with their depression. Research continues to validate the finding that depressed boys often become delinquent boys. Their delinquency, when it follows depression, is part of the group of behaviors known as "conduct disorders." In 1990, two researchers from the University of Washington School of Medicine, Jeff Mitchell and Christopher Varley, found that 25 percent of preadolescent boys who were depressed had bouts of minor delinquency. Conduct disorder spans a wide spectrum; boys who engage in it are often nice, thoughtful, caring persons who, because of their depression, experience this irregular behavioral problem. If you are a parent of a boy who is, or has been, depressed, you need to know that boys who are depressed are neither dumb nor bad—they are laboring under a cloud that controls their mood and consumes their energy and attention. Leonard, as a result of his mandated counseling and psychotherapy, identified many of his depression-driven behaviors, from holing up in his room at home, to bullying other students at school, to shoplifting from stores in the mall, to his final act of robbing and killing his newspaper customer.

- **Physical signs and symptoms**.

It's perhaps not surprising to know that the boy suffering depression often finds no rest in sleep. He may sleep fitfully, wake up for a while, stir around, then return to sleep, only to awaken too early in the morning. As a result, he may be very tired and irritable during the day. Without sufficient sleep, his concentration is often fragmented and he may be assessed for a learning problem, such as Attention Deficit Disorder. By the same token he may consume a good deal of his waking hours sleeping off his chronic tiredness. His body weight may fluctuate and he may experience physical symptoms such as pains in his head and stomach. These, as well as erratic eating patterns, are some of the physical symptoms associated with depression and may occur in boys of any age. If you see these symptoms in your son, sit him down and talk about it. Listen to him and let him tell you what's going on with him. Accept, don't alter or dismiss, what he tells you. If he's suffering depression, he knows his own feelings only too well. Let these be your guide. Leonard stated that he had problems sleeping. Unlike some other students, who ditch school and hang out in the streets, he attended school regularly. However, he holed up "in a corner of the classroom" and slept a good deal of the time. He took his newspaper job more seriously than school because, as he put it, "I had a lot of customers and got paid every two weeks."

- **Ice-water veins.**

If what you see in your son are the confirming symptoms of depression, you may also notice that he appears strangely stoic, heroic even. Yet, that's odd; young boys simply don't have the wisdom and experience to be stoic. So, you're right to wonder why he's not crying from that sprained ankle, or why an emotionally wrenching experience, such as death or other emergency, only makes his stoicism seem more stolid. "Cold-blooded" is an expression that may fit his seeming absence of emotion and sensitivity. And what you may be observing is "shut down:" he may be trying to block out or conceal signs of his depression. His Herculean yet strength-draining attempts to remain strong and silent are themselves symptoms of his depression. Leonard told me that "cold-blooded" was often the term used in describing his crime. "The judge and the prosecutor—the guy arguing against me—kept saying it, over and over. They had a real hard time liking me because I shot and killed a man *and* his dog."

- **Twin symptoms of self-criticism.**

Your son may seem less confident and sure. This is the "bout-with-doubts" stage. You may hear him call himself names or otherwise refer to himself in less than flattering terms: "I can't do anything right," "I'm just stupid," "Crap like that always happens to me," "I'm just a no-good dork," and worse. His refusal to cry is now replaced with his crying the blues about himself. He may even take the blame for things in which he had no role. When praise comes his way, he may debate the one praising him, try to convince the person that they're wrong, and devalue and dismiss the flattery. The downpour from the woe-is-me cloud above his head drenches his responses to just about anything. His low opinion of himself can be both the cause and consequence of depression. Although you would certainly be correct in trying to boost your son's self-esteem by encouraging and supporting him, add to your efforts a heightened curiosity to find out whether his low self-esteem is tied to or caused by doubt and sadness about other things. Low self-confidence, symptomatic of depression, can occur in depressed boys as young as eight years of age. Likewise, depression, symptomatic of low self-esteem, can occur in boys at such a young age. When I asked Leonard how he remembered feeling most of the time, he replied: "Bad. I always felt bad. It seemed like nobody was happy to see me at home. They were always getting on my case. Even when I managed to get a 'thank you' from them, for a birthday present or Christmas gift I gave, it was like they forced it out, and I didn't believe them."

- **Cool about school**.

Depression in boys often clouds their entire life routine, so don't expect your depressed son's home life to be one thing and his life at school to be quite another. If he's showing symptoms of depression at home, chances are he's not so enthusiastic about school, either. The general listlessness, unproductiveness, sadness, and irritability you may notice at home is also his "scene" at school. At grade report time, you may see poor marks in both his grades and his conduct. Observe him carefully, talk to him but listen more, and you may note that his problems at school may be driven by both his feelings of doubt and inferiority and the pull of his general sadness upon him. He's like a sailboat being pulled over by a strong wind. He simply doesn't feel like doing his schoolwork; that is, he lacks the level of inner joy that would propel him forward. He is no different than the co-workers or other adults you may know whose depression renders them unable to really focus on their job responsibilities. Depression renders boys unable to concentrate on what is given to or required of them. Thus, homework assignments are returned with what you might view as silly mistakes; a new sloppiness may be occurring in his penmanship; and work turned in may be incomplete and smudged with dirt. The boy turning in this work may himself be tired and wan-looking. His appearance may be sullied and soiled as though he slept the night in the park. What you're looking at is a boy who is withdrawn or propelled backward by his depression. He is literally *pressed down* or *pressed back*. Leonard said that some teachers tried to help him, since it was obvious that he had "an attitude" in almost all of his classes. But class sizes were large, Leonard didn't create a behavior problem, and teachers weren't skilled in detecting and treating depression. So, instead of helping him directly, or getting help for him, they—in classic benign neglect—merely let him be. Like a giant weed that looks hideous but is no threat to other plants, Leonard was left alone.

- **Refugee-like absorption.**

Some depressed boys take refuge (the Latin root for refuge means "flight") in their studies, or in selected ones, or perhaps in extra-curricular activities, such as athletics. Avoiding friends, neighbors and relatives, he will absorb himself in these interests and, with a freedom reminiscent of a refugee, spend all his free time pursuing them. "Lost in his boys," "A real sports jockey," or "Eating, sleeping, breathing books/Nintendo/sports" are all apt phrases for what you may see occurring before your very eyes in your depressed son. You might think, "It could be worse; at least he's not in the streets causing trouble." And you would be totally correct. However, although work, books, and sports are all positive pursuits, your depressed son may be using whatever it is that is absorbing him as a way to distract himself from his depressed state. "Losing himself in . . ." is a phrase that might aptly describe his all-out, or even manic, pursuit of his interests to the exclusion of other hobbies or acitivites. He could be obsessed with hiding from his depression. Undoubtedly, you know adults who are workaholics and use their jobs or career interests as pathways to distract them from their depression. Leonard apparently planned his robbery in careful detail, treating it with the kind of respect he should have reserved for his homework assignments for school. He told me that it took several weeks to "get it all right." Even so, he "blew" two details: "I only saw the man in the park with a little Chinese dog. I had no idea he had this big kind of dog like it was from a Sherlock Holmes movie." And, "The guy was not supposed to be home, and I didn't have a backup plan."

- **Aggression progression**.

You may see in your depressed son the "wild child" filled to overflowing with reckless energy. And you may be baffled and outraged at how difficult he is to control. There may be increased conflicts—verbal and physical— with others. He may look for occasions to fight, injure others, or settle scores. The boys I interviewed in prison demonstrated maximum levels of aggression in their interactions with others. Likewise, you may see a violent pattern in your depressed son's behavior. Be concerned, but don't panic—yet. Just know that he is using aggressiveness as a cover for his feelings of inferiority and exposure. Despite the effects of bad, anti-social behavior, it is important not to view your boy and his behavior as one and the same. It may take some effort on your part, but as a parent you need to make maximum allowance for the possibility that the violent behavior you may see in your depressed son is his way of signaling for help. The boys who participated in my research had engaged in various ranges and degrees of violent behavior in their attempts to call for help and extricate themselves from their dire circumstances. Even their most extreme act of violence—killing another human being— was a desperate cry for help. Leonard stated that occasionally he had difficulties with other students, but his parents handled everything the same way. According to Leonard, whether he was suspended for fighting, or brought a note home from a teacher requesting a parent conference, his parents, especially his father, reacted by "cussing at me, or hitting me, or throwing things at me, or calling me names and threatening me." This was their terrible one-size-fits-all parenting approach.

- **Tears of the clown**.

To cover up and cloak his pervasive sadness, the depressed boy may engage in outrageous, comical, silly, rip-roaring and fun-inspiring hijinks. He may actually be able to gather around him, or be followed by, a group—"crew" in young peoples' parlance—of other kids who thrill to his antics and marvel at his cavorting. Clowning, the industry itself, is said to be dominated by brilliantly witty but sad people. Clowns, it has been noted, have the remarkable ability to make everybody else—but not themselves—laugh. Behind their pounds of gaudy makeup are often abysmally sad eyes that have cried rivers of tears. Since everybody loves to laugh and most people are inspired by the gift of humor expressed by another, the sadness behind the depressed boy's exhibitionist silliness makes this "sad clown" phase perhaps the most deceptive symptom of depression in boys. In other words, to family and friends, he may appear to be enjoying life. Expressing humor is an index of enjoyment. Right? Making others laugh is a rare gift. But beneath his hilarious façade is a heart quaking with fear, a mind in desperation, and a spirit in pain. Parents need to constantly talk with and be there for their children to determine whether a jocular personality is real happiness or a cover for depression. World-famous comics Lucille Ball, Charlie Chaplin, Roseanne Barr, Lenny Bruce, and Flip Wilson, besides being renowned for their comic gifts, were notable for private lives marred by extreme seriousness and utter sadness. Leonard did not say whether and when he had spots of humor in his life before he committed his crime. However, it is significant that he found humorous the final act he committed at the crime scene: "I set the man's body on fire, and I laughed about it until I left the house and rode off on my bicycle. The police later told me that witnesses told them it had to be me who set the fire because my bicycle was in the driveway, loaded with newspapers, and when I drove away I was laughing all the way down the street."

- **Chopping the rescue lines**.

Depressed boys, like all boys, want to be "manly." Thus, you may see in your depressed son an I'm-all-alone-I'll-do-it-myself syndrome that chafes at, rebuffs, ignores, or resists and refuses offers of help that would undoubtedly shore him up and assist him. "Chopping off your nose to spite your face" is a phrase that seems apt here because it may seem to you that your depressed son is, in fact, deliberately cutting the lines of support thrown out to him. His insistence on taking total charge and doing things for himself removes him from the realm of the family and the emotional and other support that await him. Isolating himself from the family in this manner could signal that he is dropping into an anti-social behavior pattern typical of depressed boys. Keep your eyes open for what he does and your ears open for what he says. Your doing so will allow you to differentiate between positive self-initiative and industry about getting a task done by himself versus an aggressive shutting out and an unrelenting withdrawal from the family and the support it provides. In Leonard's case, it would appear that the lines of support were made extremely fragile in the support *denied* him by his parents. As Leonard describes it, "they were always getting on my case." Leonard could not recall when either his father or his mother praised him. When I asked him if he knew what the psychologist meant when he described Leonard's act of homicide as "symbolically" killing his father, Leonard said, "I cried when my shrink said that, because nobody's ever understood me. And it was, like, he told me the whole story of my life."

- **Saying "yes" to alcohol and drugs**.

Generally speaking, older boys have a wider social circle and the opportunity to acquire and experiment with alcohol and drugs. While your son may have little or no involvement with alcohol or drugs, he may know or spend time with other boys whose alcohol and drug use involves drinking an occasional beer and smoking an infrequent "joint"/"weed"/"grass"/"bud"—all names for marijuana. Or, he may know or spend time with boys whose alcohol and drug use means they drink until they get drunk and regard marijuana use as the "gateway" to more serious drugs like methamphetamine, LSD, and cocaine. In 1997, a survey of teenagers revealed that almost one million eighth-graders admitted to having gotten drunk. The same survey revealed that 56 percent of youths between 12 and 17 know somebody who has used heroin, cocaine, or LSD. In contrast, in 1996, just the year before, only 17 percent of teens between ages 12 and 17 knew such persons. Saying "yes" to alcohol and drugs and experiencing their damaging effects, are behaviors that many teenagers consider "cool." An isolated, lonely boy, who sees himself a social outcast, may come to idolize alcohol and drug use as the sure "ticket" to social success. If the "in crowd" is doing them—using alcohol and drugs—and he's not in the in crowd, a depressed boy may glom onto alcohol and drug use in hopes that his life will be magically transformed and he will know happiness and inclusion. Leonard admitted that he had a "lightweight drug history." When we spoke, he was in a Twelve-Step recovery program.

- **Talking about death and suicide**.

Dylan Klebold and Eric Harris, the two desperately unhappy youths who shot to death over a dozen students before killing themselves at Columbine High School in April 1999, engaged in death-talk so much that it is sad that nobody listened to them or valued them enough as human beings to even seriously consider what they were saying. These two boys demonstrated the classic symptoms of depression and used every means they could think of to cry out for help, but they were ignored until the very end. It will perhaps forever remain a mystery as to why so many people heard the vile, mad ravings of these boys and did not even suspect that, whether they were capable of carrying out their murderous urges or not, they were certainly announcing that they weren't feeling good about themselves. Unlike Klebold and Harris, the boys I spoke to in prison had not written or videotaped stream-of-consciousness essays spewing out their wrath and pain and pronouncing death sentences upon others. Most adolescent murderers do not. Yet they exhibit other symptoms of depression that may be indicators of the further negative or worsening anti-social behaviors to come. As a parent, it is important that you look and listen very carefully. Leonard's monkish and moping behavior passed— from his parents' point of view—as his acceptance of their control. They didn't feel he was a threat. He always did what he was told, even if he did it with "attitude." So, they continued with their highly abusive form of parenting. Still water runs deep. Beneath the "stillness" of Leonard's quiet behavior, dangerous and unseen turbulence was boiling.

It would be uncommon and highly unlikely for any boy, anywhere, who is depressed to exhibit all of the above symptoms of depression. It would also be equally unlikely that he would exhibit only one of them. If you have a son who is depressed like

Leonard was, you may notice that he manifests clumps or clusters of these symptoms as most depressed boys do. Once you are on the lookout for signs of depression in your son, see it in other boys, and read literature on depression, you will learn that the range of depression can be measured in terms of "mild" and "severe." What does that mean for you? Simply this: When you see depression in any of its forms in your son, you need to act immediately to help him through the phase in which he is "stuck." It may be temporary or generalized, rather than an anvil-like weight around his neck. It may be here today and gone tomorrow. With depression, one is never sure. That's why the sooner you act, the better life will be for him and everyone else. In dealing with depression, it is better to be many days too soon and safe, than even one day too late and sorry.

The following brief case studies provide the backgrounds of three boys whose behaviors you will be able to understand as you apply the criteria in the "Symptoms Index."

### Steven

Steven, while a 6th-grader, began showing increasing glumness and escalating outbursts of anger at home after he began hanging out with kids who lived in his neighborhood but went to a different school. Steven attended the parochial school near his home and walked to it every day. Although he received excellent grades, was well regarded by his teachers, and was popular with the other students, Steven told me, "I just got more bored. I played with these kids at school but they all lived far away. The kids in my neighborhood who went to the school across town were the ones doing exciting things, and I just wanted to be with them all the time." Steven's parents, however, had a different opinion of the kids in his neighborhood and repeatedly denied his frequent requests to enroll him in the school they attended.

Steven's behavior at school began changing. His popularity started to wane as he picked more fights. His teachers began sending him to the office on "discipline referrals," for "smart-mouthing" them or not having his homework. His grades dropped. He began to withdraw from student activities and cling to himself. He even started "back-talking" his parents, something he had never done before. Usually sensitive and responsive to the needs of others—he even won a prize for raising money for a homeless shelter—he began showing a hard, cold side and an uncaring attitude. When he attacked and beat up another student and then told the principal: "I hate this place, nobody likes me anyway," the school decided to expel him.

Let's look at Steven's behavior. Several of the criteria from our symptoms index are immediately apparent: becoming angrier and disengaging from the group, unprecedented aggressiveness, problems with his teachers, identifying everyone outside himself as an enemy, and defiance toward his parents. Steven began modeling his behavior after the tough kids he hung out with after school. They were more exciting to him than the kids at his own school and were into drugs and booze. Their influence over him gradually took hold as they granted him wider access inside their group. By comparison, his school companions were boring him to death. Every time he asked his parents to let him change schools, they refused him. Feeling trapped between his parents and his boring school mates, and wanting the greener-grass-on-the-other-side picture of life that his street friends represented, he grew angrier by the day. To my mind, Steven was perhaps exhibiting symptoms representative of mild to moderate depression. Shortly after he was expelled from the parochial school, Steven was arrested for committing a misdemeanor. Steven tells me that while his mother was waiting for the police officer detaining him to finish questioning him, "I just attacked him. I lunged at him and shoved him down. My mom looked at me like she had seen a monster or something. I knew then that she was scared of me." Steven continued changing radically. His parents could not keep up with the pace of those changes. When I interviewed Steven, he was serving time for committing homicide. He had shot to death another teenager after school.

## Billy

Billy was 14 when his behavior reached a point that warranted a transfer to another school—something his principal called an "adjustment transfer." Although smart, Billy was never really a good student, primarily because he enjoyed his role as the campus prankster and clowned constantly in class. He had quite a behavioral problem, and the discipline strategies the school used ranged from suspending him for a couple of days at a time to giving him detention and putting him on the clean-up crew responsible for cleaning the entire campus.

Billy was a pleasant boy who always seemed to have a joke and a good laugh at the ready. But with reckless abandon, he pushed everybody's "button" with his nonstop capers. He did not seem to mind getting caught, and it apparently never occurred to him that his name came first to everybody's mind whenever there was a problem. Who else would risk rigging the master clock over the weekend so that on Monday, at lunch time, the bell would ring as usual but would trigger a huge power outage? That stunt drove the principal to order Billy transferred out of her school into another one in the district.

Let's look at Billy's behavior framed within the "Symptoms Index:" outrageous antics, silly pranks, cavorting in class and involving or disturbing the group, and always striving to make others laugh. Despite serving detention several times and being issued written warnings, and even having his mother billed for damage caused by some of his pranks, Billy just continued to plow ahead with his comical hijinks. As we talked, Billy, though fully responsive, was distracted by any and all activities around him. On one occasion, he stared as a representative for a tax-sheltered annuity provider talked to interested prison employees. On another occasion, he found interesting the meeting a parole agent was having with his "client" several tables away from ours. When other youths were waxing the floor for a commemoration ceremony, Billy told me why he could have done the job better.

Through discussions with Billy, I learned that his brother had been killed while attending a carnival at the local park. Though the investigating police agency determined it was a rival gang shooting, Billy's family insisted that their slain son had not been a member of a gang, but rather a senior looking forward to entering college. His grades were outstanding and he had already received several scholarships.

To my mind, Billy had been exhibiting "tears of the clown" behavior. Though seen as irrepressibly happy by his teachers and others, Billy was in fact the sad clown in hiding. What Billy's teachers and principal did not know was that he was perhaps moderately to seriously depressed because of the trauma of his brother's death. Billy tells me that he eventually got diagnosed for depression—after he began serving time for his crime. The reason he was sentenced to juvenile prison was for shooting to death another teenager who "just had to die like [his] brother did."

## Daniel

Daniel began our conversations by telling me that his mother acted more like a casual friend than a mother to him after she and his father divorced. She went out every night of the week and left him in the care of his grandmother. Whenever they were together, she seldom noticed him, except to ask his grandmother if he had been good. Then she'd say goodbye. Daniel said, "She always acted like she couldn't wait to get away from me." Daniel particularly remembered the "phony sympathy" his mother gave him when he broke his ankle during football practice. He said he just wanted her to get out of his room and leave him alone. "I mean, it was getting so I wanted her to stay away all the time, something I used to hate."

Daniel's behavior at school changed. Sometimes he would challenge his teachers and engage in arguments with them. At other times he would loudly brag about his accomplishments and claim his superiority over other students. His citizenship record reflected his worsening behavior. At home, he began leaving the room whenever his mother entered, which she took as a sign of disrespect. They had fierce arguments. When he was arrested for shoplifting, and his mother came to the police station to take him home, he asked the booking officer, "Can't I just spend the night here instead of going home with her?"

Daniel, it appears, could not accept that his mother had a life of her own that did not include him. What pained him was that she flaunted it. Each time he saw her, he was only reminded that she would soon be rushing to leave him. He began feeling her rejection early and never got over it. His behavior appears to have satisfied several of the symptomatic indices for depression:

challenging adults, exhibitionist behaviors in the classroom, emotionally rejecting his mother and pushing her out, and delinquency. When Daniel told me the crime he committed that earned him his prison cell, I became certain that he was in the throes of clinical depression at the time of his heinous deed. He stabbed his grandmother to death while both were at the kitchen sink, washing and chopping vegetables. His mother arrived home about two hours later to find him standing over her dead mother. The pool of blood in which he stood immobile, staring into space, was already beginning to congeal.

As a member of several child advocacy organizations, I am often asked by parents if their sons could turn out like Daniel, Steven, or Billy. Occasionally, a parent will venture something like: "When you were describing Steven, I was sure you had a key to our house." Our society still has this vision of its children as happy, carefree, angelic little beings. They—we have an obsessive need to believe—are not supposed to be depressed. Yet you probably know more than a modest number of children who are always unhappy. Perhaps our need to think that we adults are supposed to provide all the reasons for happiness somehow blinds us to the fact that millions of children in the country are suffering from adult-size levels of depression. Although parents are not always responsible for the depression that afflicts their children, it is parental awareness and acknowledgement of both the possibility and reality of depression and what it looks like in their children that are the critical first steps toward helping them safely through what, for many children, seems like a long, dark, lonely, endless corridor.

# Depression: What You Can Do About It

*What was I supposed to do? The man wouldn't even listen to me or let me reason with him. I had the gun pointed to his head and he still threw his beer into my face. That was his way of spitting on me. . . . I had to shoot him. I mean I couldn't walk away. Could you?—Kenny*

Kenny sat across the table from me, his back to the window. Sunlight filled the cavernous prison day room. I stared for a few moments at the elongated shadow of his body which the sun's rays spilled onto the floor. Kenny's "commitment offense" was murder in the first degree.

"The police, the judge, the attorney, and everybody else believed what the so-called witnesses said, that I was trying to rob the guy." He was clearly exasperated.

"What about Julia, your girlfriend?" I asked. "Did she testify in your defense?"

He gave me a look that said, 'get-real.' "Hell, no!" he exclaimed. "She ran out on me. As much as I did for her, and look at me now." He shook his head as though to clear away the sad picture of his life. But as he began talking, the furrow in his brow stayed.

"Hey, look out! You almost hit her!" Kenny looked on in horror as the car barreled ahead without slowing and finally

134

stopped at the far end of the parking lot of the 7-11 convenience store. In seconds, he was out of his own car and on his knees helping Julia, his girlfriend, back to her feet. "You okay, babe?" he asked anxiously.

Julia nodded weakly. "I'm all right. I didn't even see him. Maybe he didn't see me."

Kenny scowled as he stared at the car at the other end of the lot. "He saw you all right," he answered. "I mean like. . ." He eyed her scanty outfit admiringly. "What you're wearing would stop freeway traffic, so why didn't he stop?"

Julia, her composure intact, walked into the 7-11.

Kenny waited until Julia was out of sight. *That son of a b\*\*\*\*!* he thought angrily. *What is the world coming to when you can't walk across a 7-11 parking lot without almost getting killed by some clown racing his car?* He ran back to his car, looked around cautiously, got inside it and waited. Then he bent down and felt around under his seat for his gun, a .38 caliber Smith & Wesson. *This will help him remember his road manners*, he thought as he quickly checked to make sure the chamber was loaded. He put the weapon in the pocket of his baggie overalls, locked his car, and jogged the length of the parking lot to where the other car was parked. The man was inside drinking something from a paper bag.

The man lowered the window and stared at Kenny expectantly. "Yeah, what are you selling?"

"I'm selling a driving course," Kenny answered.

The man blinked. "No you ain't, 'cause I took mine years ago. Thanks anyway," he slurred.

The window started upward. Kenny jammed his gun inside the car and stopped the window. "I *said* I'm selling a driving course and you *are* buying it, okay?" The man sat and glowered. That angered Kenny. *The son of a b\*\*\*\* has got attitude. Like he's not scared or nothing. He's looking at me like he's the one with the gun!*

"Go screw yourself!" retorted the man.

"Before I shoot you," Kenny began, "You need to know that you almost hit my girlfriend head-on back there when she was walking across the parking lot."

"I didn't see no girl walking, kid. And if this is a shakedown, you don't know who you're playing with," snapped the man. He raised the paper bag to his lips and took a long pull on the bottle inside it.

"You don't even know what you almost did!" screamed Kenny. "You were driving 50 miles an hour through this lot and almost hit her, you wino!" Suddenly, Kenny felt a wet liquid splash on his cheek. Some went into his eye. "You son of a b****!" Kenny's gun roared. It would be an hour or so before the police came. But the six eyewitnesses all saw and said the same thing. They remembered perfectly that Kenny had tried to rob a man sitting in his car waiting for somebody shopping inside the 7-11. The man wasn't bothering anybody, they said. When police found him, the man's hand was inside his coat, his thumb and forefinger still squeezing the handle of a gun.

The symptoms index described in the preceding chapter will help you as a parent become more aware and skillful about identifying those occasions when your boy is depressed. Be curious and ask your son questions. You may find that he has experienced a recent disappointment or setback that he hasn't told you about. For example, my further questioning of Steven disclosed that he saw the tough kids he wanted to be a part of as moving with exciting speed but his parents moving only "to keep [him] locked down." Billy's tears began after his brother was gunned down, his grief carrying him across his own emotional stormy seas until, without direction like a ship soon to wreck, he got a gun and, blind with rage and remorse, killed another youth he did not even know. Daniel's shame and seething at being forsaken by his mother and her continuous rejecting behaviors finally drove him to kill his grandmother to whom his selfish, carefree mother always abandoned him.

Beneath the surface of Steven's glumness and angry outbursts, Billy's nonstop pranks, and Daniel's boastings and arguments with his teachers, were confused, unhappy, and lonely boys who chose the most heinous and extreme form of violence—homicide— as the final expression of their depressed states of mind? Particularly interesting is the fact that though each of these boys undoubtedly was at a different step in the cellar of depression, all of them had emotional problems that robbed them of their happiness and drove them to rob other persons of the most visible form of happiness: life.

These boys were not able to talk about their problems and were not rescued from them by perceptive adults. That is why, against today's horrifying backdrop of children killing children, it is of utmost importance that parents communicate to their sons in a variety of ways. Most of the "messages" Kenny received from his family were that he was *not* good enough. He had to work hard to get meager compliments. He described his childhood as filled with a constant pressure to "try to please everybody." Unfortunately, as he explained, "that didn't work because they didn't care."

I like the following anecdote by Milton Berle, which, through humor, speaks a child's need for parents who practice creative, understanding leadership.

> A young boy was given to profanity. His mother threatened him, "If I hear one more ugly word out of you, you can pack up and get out of this house." The boy sneaked in a good four-letter word in the next minute. His mother forced him to pack and threw him out of the house. Hours and hours passed. Mom grew a little concerned when it became dark, and decided to go look for her son. As she opened the door, she found him sitting outside. She said, "You thought it over and decided to change your ways? So you've come home." The boy said, "Sh**, where the hell could I go?"

Love and support your son so that whatever negative feelings he may be experiencing will diminish in proportion to his desire to open up and grieve and grumble. The sooner you are "there" for him, the sooner he will open up and release, through his words, those pent-up emotions and feelings of despair, doubt and disappointment. Though some boys often require professional help, the best personal help they can get can just as often be provided by aware, knowledgeable and concerned parents.

All boys who drift away from their parents do not turn into killers, and being isolated from one's parents does not precipitate an act of murder. However, all children who make the decision to kill are alienated and isolated from potentially important adults in their lives, including their parents. As a parent you do not want your son drifting from you. It is a sign that your positive influence is either not positive or is not influential. You can take steps that are progressive and will cause you and your family to avoid tragedies such as the murders and homicides in which the boys in my research study were directly involved.

As a parent, you're head of the home, so take the helm. Find out both the kind and quality of your son's relationships. Know as many friends of his as you can. Try to know which ones exercise some influence over him, and vice versa. Go directly to him for the answers to these questions. You'll find at first he may be reluctant to talk, but he will open up as you exert diplomacy and quiet persistence. Ask him what he feels about school and his teachers. Find out how he feels about his family. A strong relationship with him can prevent him from engaging in negative behaviors. Boys, despite the macho picture frame we put them in, need to feel bonded to key people who demonstrate their interest in and concern for them. From experience, they know that whatever else might happen, these people will listen. And this is a trait they prize highly. Your positive leadership in this regard will protect not only the relationship between you and your son, but also will protect him from himself, and others from him. This latter "protecting-the-social-order" benefit is invaluable, and can only result from his positive redirection of whatever violent or anti-social urges he may be experiencing.

Kenny was particularly sensitive to not being listened to or ignored entirely. He explained, "I didn't count for much in my family. What I said or felt didn't really matter much." For much of his young life, he had struggled to acquire respect and to "make sure they [other students] paid when they dissed [disrespected] me." According to Kenny's peculiar logic, the man in the car disrespected his girlfriend and himself and therefore had to "pay."

As I have already stated, the incarcerated children who participated in my study were all required to undergo tests for depression only *after* they began serving their prison sentences. One of the worst social tragedies is that their depression—as well as that of other incarcerated children nationwide—was not detected by anybody in the "free society" in which they lived and committed their crimes. Youth prison authorities suspect depression as a major emotional player in adolescents who commit homicide. That's why they order depression testing for every adolescent admitted to their institutions.

As a parent, learn to recognize the behaviors associated with depression. If you see in your son any of the behaviors we have discussed, or if you notice that he seems a little "bummed," downcast, or dispirited immediately ask him what's wrong And if he doesn't want to talk yet? That's okay, give him time. He knows you're concerned. You've asked early, and you'll have your answer earlier than if you in a state of confusion about how or where to start. Even when he's not ready to talk, stay physically close. Communicate by your presence that you are available when he's ready. Keep your errands away from home to a minimum during this time. You don't want to be across town just as he's decided he needs to talk with you.

While he's not yet ready to talk, tell him a couple of "war stories" showing that you felt the exact way when you were his age—kind of a "been-there-done-that" but with a great deal of empathy. Let him know that you know it's not easy to open up, and that you want him to know you care and you're there. End your war stories on a positive note so that he knows there's light at the end of the tunnel. Have a purpose to your war stories, though; don't use them merely to make conversation. If you don't have any stories, that's okay. Better to be silent but close than talky yet remote. Constantly tell your son that he's a good person, and tell him *why* he's a good person—who and what he is and what he's done that makes him good, other people who think the world of him, and how needed, valued and loved he is. By presenting this "evidence" to him, you don't leave him stuck wondering what "good person" means or, worse, cause him to see himself in the company of other "good" persons who are no-counts and losers. Your evidence raises this shopworn cliché to a level that is authentic and believable.

In spite of your valiant attempts to show that you care, if you try to work through your son's depression alone, you could be in for a complicated, heart-wrenching battle with so many twists and turns that will leave you not only dizzy but also depressed. No sense in helping somebody only to end up helpless yourself. So, talk to somebody else; and do this soon. With whom do you talk? A therapist. Take the first step and explain to your son later. If your son thinks you've got it in for him, simply tell him that the problem is bigger than both of you and you want solid, professional help to make his life better. If you fear going to a therapist because you think you may have misread your son's symptoms and that you are, therefore, overreacting, go see one anyway. What you learn will be valuable in any case; you will see that the time you visited with the therapist was well spent. While you are alone with the therapist, you can make a decision about whether and when to bring your son for counseling sessions. With a professional on your side, you'll sleep better at night.

Unfortunately, many boys grow up having to run through the gauntlet of shame. Far too many boys are ridiculed by parents and peers into "being tough." Boys are shamed if they cry and are told to endure the physical hurt or pain and "take it like a man." In some families, scars, bruises and disfigurations such as keloids are badges that prove the boy's toughness. Outside the family, others who see these badges may regard him as a fierce, fearless, formidable foe. Many boys yearn to be regarded this way and see the pain in acquiring these badges as being worth it. In their minds, they *are* tough when the pain they underwent for these scars produces the pleasure of reputation, of being considered, rumored, or known to be THE bad guy on campus. That, for far too many boys, is an ecstasy rivaling that of high school graduation.

When playing sports, boys are expected to be rough and tough. They quickly learn the jock's lingo of "crush," "stomp," "whip," and "waste." In college and professional sports, these words become part of the language that also includes other verbalizations like "sack," "dump," "trounce," and "rumble." Winning becomes much more than a numerical tally denoting who won and who lost.

Boys who grow up under the weight of this cultural patent carry around psychological and emotional baggage. Many would surely benefit from some form of counseling with a therapist who understands adolescents' needs, and who is keenly aware of and sensitive to the fact that boys are creatures and reproductions of a cultural code which is forced upon them. That is: Boys are fearless, tough, defenders, always right, better, winners, gods. Few can meet the standards of this code. Tragically, many boys are shamed into being strong, tough, cold and callous.

Even boys who have not been the direct brunt of this kind of parental or social conditioning, but who have observed it upon others, instantly know the boy code and are influenced and controlled by it. Chances are, their fathers were conditioned this way, too. I wish I had a nickel for every time that I've spoken to a father who has bemoaned his non-athletic son's lack of "the killer instinct."

Kenny's home life bred into him the "killer instinct," and he became a social menace. His mistreatment at home turned him into somebody obsessed about making others pay for mistreating him. He described his life at home as being so filled with ridicule, name-calling, taunting, and other emotionally threatening elements that, "at school or any place else, [he] was always angry and ready to fight about something." Years of being shamed and insulted at home "shaped" Kenny for the deadly role he played in his own life.

As you talk to a prospective therapist, try to determine whether he is inclined to shame boys or to shape them. Shaping male juvenile behavior is your prime reason for seeking therapy, whether you verbalize it that way or not. Parents who say, "I just want my son to be a good citizen and contribute to his country" are really talking about some complicated life-training that falls under the broad umbrella of "effective parenting skills." Being "good" and "contributing" are attributes that result from shaping and nurturing. They are not the growth products of a shaming environment. Determine whether your therapist supports your shaping concept of parenting. Question the therapist about and explain your ideas for nurturing, coaching, and encouraging your son. If the therapist is not in line with your goals, end the visit immediately and look elsewhere. A therapist who *shames* your son, even subtly, will never reach a satisfactory level of positively addressing your son's needs. Don't make the mistake of some parents who hear things in the therapist's language they neither like nor question, but decide to give it a chance. No! Don't take chances. Find somebody who will work *with* your son. Therapists are accustomed to parents shopping and are usually well-grounded enough not to be offended by "Excuse me, but I don't think we'd make a good match here. Good-bye."

If you decide to use a therapist and are able to find one you trust, make every painstaking effort to help your child understand that it is also his decision. At no time should it appear to your child that he is another errand to run, another job to complete, another project to get out of the way, another broken "something" to fix. One of the main reasons counseling fails is because the child senses the parent's tiredness and impatience. He internalizes this as "Mom or Dad is upset with me because I'm taking up so much of their time with all these cross-town visits to Dr. Brain Scan."

As patient and persuasive as you are when you approach your child, in your effort to start peeling back the layers of his problems, you must be equally patient every time he has an appointment with a therapist. Be uplifting. make it sound as though it's time to go shopping or out on some other favorite outing. Chances are, your child will respond with more enthusiasm than he might otherwise Be extremely patient in your expectation of positive results, either from your own valiant attempts to discover and heal the source of your child's problems, or from the efforts of a professional therapist.

It is critically important for you to ensure that your son has professional mental health resources available to him. Only you can see to it that he is provided with the best opportunity to be guided to an increasing awareness and understanding of the problems that drove him to the depths of depression. His enlightenment and understanding will also be his laser-like tool for exposing and illuminating these problems whenever they appear to be coming back to haunt him.

Kenny acknowledged knowing that he had a problem with his anger before he committed his crime in that 7-11 parking lot.

Although he had not been exposed to therapy prior to prison, he did recall Julia, his former girlfriend, as being "worried about me a lot, because I tended to go off on people and she would have to talk to me, calm me down, you know, *save* them from me. I guess she was trying to save me from myself, too."

To save your son, it is important that you *see* him in all the "worlds" that he occupies—his family, his friends, his school, his community. In your mind's eye, right now, picture your son in these settings, and in others. If you have a photograph album, go to it now and turn to pages showing your son in different scenes. Look through his own collection of photographs. The point is, your son occupies multiple worlds. Each makes an impact on him. Each demands certain things from him. Since he must respond in different ways to his different worlds, it is critical that you see—by creating the "big picture" made by the various pieces of his worlds—the multiple forces that act upon him. You must see him in this "multiple frame" context because they represent important parts of his life. That means see him for himself, as himself. Don't compare him to any other boy who you think has it all together and negotiates through his own multiple worlds just fine.

If your son is sad, find out why, through gentle, loving questioning. Don't make the mistake of blaming him or expressing your anger or disappointment in name-calling. When you talk to him, always use his given name or his nickname. Parents who feel they must call their son something *other* than his given name are—through this form of disrespect and humiliation—merely sowing the seeds for resentment and retaliation.

Phrase your questions to your son based on the "frames" in which he exists. Match questions frame for frame—athletics, academics, social, family. Try not to yield to the temptation of using a global, one-size-fits-all question. Such questions miss more issues than they hit, which could be insulting and make you look silly, and your son would only be disinclined to share anything with you. "What's wrong with you?" is a query that is hopelessly inferior to "Tell me, how's life on the soccer team/at your job/with your new friends?" and so forth. "Why can't you make it with girls, buddy?" is cruel and backward. But, "When you're ready, I've got some success secrets to share with you about boys and girls, okay?" is a more insightful key to, and promise for, profitable discussion. "Are we stuck on that issue again?" is callous and argumentative. But, "Sometimes the same problems seem to chase us over and over. Maybe we're staying in one place too long and should be changing our strategies or our thinking" acknowledges the problem and positively hints at alternative solutions.

Focusing on the frames within which your son lives will suggest problem areas. For example, if he's in the company of new friends, is he being pressured or bullied? What athletic or academic program is he struggling with? At home, what forces are threatening him, e.g., the kind and quality of your communication with him, or with your spouse, or with your other children? In his association with other boys, just where does he seem to be out of step, e.g., is he more a mediator among fighters, more into his own hobbies than into girls, or is he a bookish boy among an athlete-laden crowd? Framing your response to the multiple worlds he moves and operates in, will allow you and him to correctly identify the problem and use more appropriate strategies to solve it. Don't look at your son and view him as the problem. More often than not, he is not the problem and should not ever be made to feel that he's your target. And that's the beauty in the multiple picture frame strategy. It enables you to see the *world around* your son, and understand the various pulls and pressures upon him.

One constant pressure upon the children in my research study was their poor diet prior to their incarceration. Few had ever experienced a nutritionally-balanced food program with a variety of food choices daily. Of course, that all changed when they were incarcerated: In prison, both their diet and their eating habits changed for the better. But before they were incarcerated, many of these children were emotional and physical skeletons. I am not saying that their chronically poor nutrition led to a generalized state of poor mental health, which subsequently led to an inability to make moral, rational, or lawful choices, such as *not* picking up a gun and using it to kill somebody. However, you need to know that children whose diets and eating habits are chronically poor, simply do not have the mental energy necessary for good thinking and problem-solving. The brain needs proper food, just as the body does. Without it the brain lacks the necessary chemicals and nutrients to keep it healthy and happy. Such a brain becomes depressed. When asked about their nutrition and eating habits, most of my adolescent respondents admitted to having had poor eating habits and listed candies, sodas, and junk food as the staples in their diet. Interestingly, Kenny and Julia were at 7-11 to get a lunch that consisted of "Cheetos, soda pop, and candy bars." Kenny stated that other additions to his diet included beef jerky, corn chips and tortilla chips, and an occasional ice cream sandwich. He often missed breakfast at home and depended on the 7-11 because "[he] could go there on the way to school every morning."

Observe your son's eating habits at home, and question him about what he eats at school or other places outside the home. The mental functioning and emotional health of the adolescents whom I studied were below par when they committed homicide, but I cannot say that they committed homicide *because* of their deficient diets. There are simply too many variables to consider. Certainly, the psychological pressures and sociological forces that contributed to their depression were probably stronger than any negative mental and emotional states brought on by chronically poor diets.

Despite my reluctance to assign to faulty diet and nutrition a major role in triggering my subjects' depression, I would suggest to parents that the link between good nutrition and good emotional health is a strong one, with compelling evidence: ranging from diet-testing in rats, to noticeable improvement in patients domiciled in mental asylums, to improvement in academics and social behaviors of Head Start pre-school children served free and vitamin-fortified breakfasts.

Do not overlook diet and nutrition as you survey the areas in your son's life that could possibly be improved. A child's diet should be monitored to prevent him from succumbing to any sort of malaise that may beset them from undernourishment.

There are a number of ways that parents can involve themselves to avoid finding their children languishing under the hold of depression. The key is involvement. Enlisting the support of a therapist, becoming familiar with your child in all his social settings, and nourishing him with proper foods are three good ways to start.

# Loneliness & Alienation in Adolescents

*I can't get paroled out of here. The parole board wants me to take responsibility for my mother's death. We started having sex together when I was five. I was in kindergarten. We stopped when I was in eighth grade. I don't know what they mean, take responsibility. Yeah, I killed her but I'm not really responsible for it, know what I mean?* —Bobby

Bobby and I were sitting in the "day room," our conversation punctuated by a steady stream of tersely-uttered commands, via the public address system, for various wards to report to various places inside the huge, sprawling prison. Adding to this noisy inconvenience was the fact that the air-conditioning system was under repair; the gigantic room, this day in July, felt like a roaster.

Suddenly, Bobby blurted, "My mother and I used to have sex for a long time, for about eight years." His face was a mask of various emotions as he talked. So deep and yet so obvious were his emotional scars, that he was still seething and trembling with anger, even though his "commitment offense"—murder in the first degree—had occurred some three years prior to our meeting.

"My mother promised me, when I was 5 years old, that 'it's just me and you, my big man, against the world.' Every time we had sex, she promised me that I was her only love, 'my only man,' she told me." Bobby twisted in his chair, agony lining his face. "Well, when I turned 13, she started seeing some guy, some man she met I don't know where. Then she started bringing him over to stay the night. That was okay, if that was the way it had to be. But then this guy started bossing me around. I was the man of the house and that wasn't going to happen to me. You understand me. I was the man. My mother had already told me that. I was sleeping with her before he was." The memory filled his face with anger. His knitted brows gave his face a terrible look. His outrage was obvious. "What really p***ed me off, though, was that my lovely mother actually let her boyfriend order me around. One afternoon, the guy hits me in the back to let me know he was unhappy about me not doing something he told me to do earlier." Bobby paused a long time, looked me in the eye and said, "That's when I decided somebody had to go. But I had to punish the hell out of her first. Oh yeah! *That* had to be done. The b**** let me down, knifed me in the heart. Ugh! I'm still p***ed off. Can you believe your own mother betraying you like that? She had to pay. Do you understand? She had to pay! There was no way she could do that to me and not feel what I felt about it. I beat her until I passed out next to her. When I woke up, her body was cold, real cold." Suddenly, Bobby turned away and wearily ran both hands through his hair. "Aw, Mama, what did you do to me?"

Bobby told me he "punished the hell out of her" on an evening when her boyfriend was out of town. The Coroner's report stated that for hours after rigor mortis had set into his dead mother's body, Bobby kept beating her corpse with anything he could get his hands on—furniture, the telephone, kitchen knives, lamps. The Coroner estimated that she died almost immediately from blunt force trauma to the head, possibly from a baseball bat found at the scene. Other evidence on her body suggested that Bobby continued his assault for about three hours after she died.

As a parent, what do you think the most troubling issue is for adolescents? In survey after survey, nationwide, loneliness continually gets top billing. Teenagers are tormented by loneliness.

One of the teens who participated in my own research study put it this way: "Being lonely just blows me away. I can't handle it." Barbara Schneider, a sociologist from the University of Chicago, found that the 7,000 teenagers she studied for five years spent an average of three-and-a-half hours alone every day. Beneath the bravado of "Keep out, I want my privacy," teenagers really crave attention. Most of the incarcerated children I interviewed admitted to feeling a sense of loss and longing for adults in their lives for a long time before they committed homicide.

Poor, betrayed, depressed and murderous Bobby could undoubtedly make most kids in America look like happy, trouble-free, yearbook models. Though far less troubled than Bobby, many of today's teens—even atop the high school's honor roll—reveal, when asked candidly and confidentially, that they feel increasingly alone. Trapped by their feelings of alienation, they admit they are unable to connect with their parents, teachers or even other classmates.

Loneliness in teenagers creates emotional "hollow spaces" filled by their peers, who serve as the "stuffing" in the "package." Thus, lonely teens are spared total isolation. Since humans need other humans, some of this bonding is normal and, of course, good. However, teens are still not "connecting" as they'd like to. Their need for acceptance is quite like a biological drive. Teens hunger to be accepted just like they hunger for food.

If your child is between 12 and 14, you've probably noticed how extremely exaggerated his sense of self-consciousness is. At this age, children can be excessively "down" on themselves. Extremely self-centered, they may look to you like they spend days on end thinking about nobody but themselves and what others think about them. Targets of their own self-doubts, they think society around them has also targeted them. "Crashin' into fashion" (dressing alike) is their way of hiding in a group. This includes body piercings.

These teens are desperate for guidance, a commodity in desperately short supply at home and in school. Like birds of one feather, they flock together and engage in their own pursuits. They gravitate toward and become denizens in a world where their choices of computer games, TV, and movies define and elevate horrifically brutal dimensions of "play" that mesmerize them. In this world they become, in the phrase coined by one of my seminar participants, "baby barbarians."

Family friends of Eric Harris and Dylan Klebold report that both sets of parents said they never dreamed their sons could kill. Perhaps they never dreamed their sons suffered from loneliness either. As parents, we may not be aware of loneliness in our teens. We think that most children are too happy enjoying relatively carefree lives to meticulously write psychotic, murderous thoughts into their diaries, stockpile weapons in their garages, make scores of home-made bombs from propane tanks, and then haul this heavy arsenal to their campuses to commit the most heinous of crimes. Our national thinking is that Eric Harris and Dylan Klebold were so extreme as to be *almost* unreal. But, as we know, they were all too real. The Columbine massacre has made us look over our shoulders at our kids and fearfully wonder: *Do we really know them?*

It is difficult for most parents to understand why Harris and Klebold, both affluent kids who lived amid swarms of material possessions, felt so lonely and unhappy. "What are two white boys driving new BMW's so unhappy about?" Some folks with post-mortem cynicism offered that they would have been only too willing to trade their own unhappiness for some of Harris' and Klebold's "unhappiness." Indignation and condemnation about the heinous deeds these miserable and desperate boys did will undoubtedly rage until the next millennium. But let's try to understand these boys in the context of today's teens.

Many teens today say they feel helpless under an avalanche of pressure and responsibilities. They flip-flop back and forth from one part-time job to another, and try to squeeze good grades out of bad times for doing homework every night. Many teens head to school right after work, or visa versa, and are so exhausted they snore through early-morning classes. Look around you. How many stressed or "hyper" teens do you see trying to juggle too many responsibilities? About one-third of such teens have to work to take up the economic slack caused by their parents' divorce. Almost two-thirds of them live in households where both parents work outside the home. Many are saddled with more chores—

like looking after younger siblings—when they arrive home in the afternoon. Other teens come home to an empty house after school. Alone well into the evening, they have to fetch their own meals. Under such burdens—and the time constraints they impose—it is clear why so many teens feel alienated and lonely: there is precious little time to "connect" with anybody when a child's and parent's schedule is so full.

If you never thought you could be replaced as a parent, think again. If you and other adults surrender involvement in your teenager's life to the demands on his time or your time, your teenager will simply devise his own rules and regulations, or have none at all. Teenagers left to themselves would create a situation at home and in society akin to what happened on the farm that was suddenly besieged and taken over by the animals in George Orwell's book, *Animal Farm*.

Teens who are isolated from their parents are unsafe and insecure. They are also more susceptible to severe emotional problems. Every one of the children I interviewed admitted to suffering from unmanageable emotional problems prior to the commission of their capital crimes. The majority of these children were alienated by the splintered adult guidance and supervision arrangement—no fathers present, for example, only mothers or grandmothers—that passed for "parenting" in their home. Bobby's years-long incestuous relationship with his mother was the worst sort of "parenting." She abused and alienated him. And he, unable to rise above the tide of his jealous passions, killed her for being *unfaithful* and betraying him.

Nationally, every year, one in four high school students considers suicide. By the end of high school, many have actually attempted to fulfill this desperate act, their problems only intensifying over time. Because parents are remote and teachers are busy and aloof, often neither recognize suicide attempts for what they are: cries for "connection," friendship, attention. They simply misinterpret them. Attempted suicide is often something ambiguous like an overdose of nonprescription pills from the medicine cabinet, getting drunk or, with minds full of pre-meditated thoughts about self-destruction, deliberately crash a car.

Caring about your child is certainly admirable; this emotion clearly is a noble human trait. It was often the missing link identified to me by the incarcerated children in my study, when they cited the failures of their parents or families. But being the best, most caring parent will not protect your teenager from the universe of problems he will likely face. In order to make a positive *difference* in your teenager's life, you have to be more than simply caring—you must also be *involved.* Involvement dispels loneliness and alienation. Kids listen to involved parents. Chiefly due to parent involvement and improved education efforts, teenage drug use today is declining, and teenage pregnancy and birthrates are falling. It seems that teens are finally taking to heart what they hear from caring and involved parents. More teenagers are postponing sex. And those who are sexually active generally take more care and use contraceptives—a precaution seldom exercised by their counterparts a few years ago. You *can* have an impact and make a positive difference.

Parents commonly hear the term "teen beat." It is a natural "sound bite" used by the media and other teen-watchers. There's a national magazine that employs the term in its title. The term attempts to capture and convey the flavor and essence of teen lifestyle and culture. What most parents seem to be missing, however, is the *rhythm* of teen life. They simply are not in touch with *what* is happening with their teenage children, *when* it is happening, and *why* it is happening. Parents often find themselves missing the "beat"—the results being akin to what is implied in the ages-old parent term, "missing the boat." When this happens, the consequence is often a teenager who begins to drift, becoming increasingly lonely and alienated.

As a parent, you will want to know what attitudes and behaviors to expect from your teenager at certain times, just like you want to know what to expect from your automobile at certain mileage intervals. As your teenager puts on "mileage," his "performance" changes. As with your automobile your teenager's performance (behavior) can be adjusted and corrected by knowing and applying "tune-up" strategies.

Teenagers are dynamic organisms. They are living, breathing, changing, and growing. They are not standing still; do not expect them to do so. Slow down your own lifestyle so that you can speed up your observation of them and your ability to respond timely to their needs. How well or poorly does your teenager interact with family and peers, participate in school, and control his behavior? You should be able to answer this easily. Often, the attitude and behavior you see at home serves as a more accurate view of the existence or absence of psychiatric and psychological disorders. Traditional indicators such as school failure and contact with police usually appear only *after* problems have taken root. Although I have stated this in other parts of this book, it bears repeating that the incarcerated adolescents who participated in my research study almost never had a parent at home to observe early warning signs—attitudes and behaviors, loneliness and alienation, etc.—that might have suggested certain mental disorders. The only other adults concerned about such critical disorders were the prison officials who incarcerated them. It is no accident that Bobby repeatedly failed to get parole. His parole board wanted him to become the beneficiary of the intense regimen of mandated counseling and therapy. The parole board's view was that the benefits he could reap would be not only an enlightened capacity to accept personal responsibility for killing his mother, but an opportunity to break the down the wall of alienation and loneliness that enclosed him.

Do you know what your teenager is going through and growing through in his quest for identity and independence? Again, observe his social role: who are his friends, and what part does he play in the social group to which he belongs—leader or follower. Noting social role *dysfunction* can also assist you in determining whether your teenager's problems have their basis in emotional difficulties and will eventually be acted out as behavioral problems. Of course, if you detect no social role dysfunction, do not worry. If it is not there, it's simply not there. Your constant objective is to be on top of things, to be a *prepared* parent.

Sadly, in this country, treatments aimed at troubled teenagers are usually directed more at suppressing problem behaviors—medicating and disciplining in order to regain control—than getting teens back on the right path socially and emotionally. *When will we learn that emotion drives the behavior?* If we can change the emotion, we may possibly change, reduce, or eliminate the behavior. Behavior is emotion *in motion*. In the one case, we *feel* it (emotion); in the other, we *see* it (behavior).

What are you seeing when you look at your teenager? Let's start by looking at the way loneliness and alienation manifest differently in the separate genders.

## Male Manifestations

Be especially observant for signs of disruptive disorders. How will you know? Research from Johns Hopkins University suggests that male teenagers, in general (compared to male teens with no disruptive disorders), tend to have the worst academic performance, the poorest relationships with family and friends, and the poorest self-management skills, i.e. taking responsibility, planning, controlling anger, and being on time. Male teenagers with manifest psychiatric disorders tend to have significant academic problems, substantial troublesome bouts in their relationships with family and friends, and are markedly less accepted by peers than male teens with no psychiatric disorders. Bobby was a "classic" in this regard, for he was a loner at school, had poor grades, and almost no friends—a dominant pattern for a lonely or alienated child. He was definitely a candidate for intensive therapy. It would appear that his very personal, unsavory and unwholesome situation at home sabotaged his social and academic life at school.

## Female Manifestations

There seem to be no consistent or major differences in social functioning between teenage girls with manifest disorders and healthy girls. What does this mean? That still water runs deep? That all girls are the same, either all disordered or all healthy? Of course, neither is true. These findings merely mean that if you look at their social functioning as an indicator of the presence or absence of disorders, this particular "lens" will not reveal an accurate picture of what is going on with girls emotionally. Your teenage daughter has social skills that are markedly superior to those of your teenage son. And all the women in your family, on your job, as well as those in your neighborhood, synagogue, church, fitness club, and country club are gifted with social skills that are light-years ahead of all the males in these same social settings.

Despite the presence of loneliness and alienation and even diagnosed disorders, girls are able to function socially at high levels. It is telling that few girls, compared to boys, take up guns with which to "solve" their interpersonal problems. I have already mentioned the number of boys incarcerated in California is 33 times greater than the number of girls. Girls with disorders also tend to score higher than boys with the same disorders on every measure of social functioning except organized activities. The boys score better here because of their traditionally greater participation in team sports and events that are inherently competitive.

Girls team in more civil, more communal and less competitive ways than do boys. That is why women tend to reach decisions by consensus rather than by command or conflict. Women also use consensus as both an outcome and measure of the quality of negotiation. Women seek peaceful solutions with more zeal and perhaps more spiritual enlightenment and direction than do men.

My purpose is not merely to trumpet women's superiority over men. I want you to understand the severe implications of all of the above. Girls and women tend to get overlooked, minimalized, short-shrifted and left out. Their needs often go undetected and unaddressed because they neither exhibit the same symptoms as boys nor employ the same means or manner for exhibiting them, even though they may have the identical disorders.

If you are a parent of a teenage girl, do not be put off or dissuaded by a counselor's, psychologist's, or psychiatrist's dismissing your anxiousness about your daughter's emotional health. Simply persist and look for *non-behavioral* indicators for what you suspect are her emotional problems. What is her communication like? Does she like to originate communication, or does she speak only when spoken to? What does she think about and how does she express her thoughts? Is she given to full conversations or is she a "Janie One-Note," given to terse, one-word or one-sentence responses? To what kinds of pursuits does she

devote the majority of her time? Who are her "models"—
depressed and depressing figures such as drugged-out rock icons?
What kind and quality of literature does she let absorb her attention? What are her friends like—apathetic, depressed, critical?
These are just some of the questions that will guide you in searching
for and finding emotional problems that may be occurring in your
daughter, despite her superior social behaviors.

Most of the incarcerated girls I interviewed—with the
exception of active female gang members whose social code was
to aggress, attack and assault—had high social functioning
levels and exhibited absolutely no signs of their emotional
problems. Their behaviors were so "silent," they often went
unnoticed. It is not that they tried to conceal them; rather, it is
that we, as a society, do not look past the ways that we *expect* and
*demand* females to act.

It is society's collective "blinders" that made it difficult to
detect the still waters of hatred and resentment often spawned by
loneliness and alienation running deep within the girls I interviewed.
Intensive therapy pulled off the blinders and exposed—to prying
eyes such as mine—problems that were as deadly as they were
deep. Charity was considered the model of a perfect daughter
before she flew into a rage and knifed her older sister to death at
the kitchen table. The family had pinned its hopes on the beautiful,
outgoing and socially well-mannered Charity, after spending years
and a fortune trying to free their maladjusted eldest daughter,
Monica, of the internal demons that enslaved her. Charity's parents
never knew about *her* emotional problems. Her nice, quiet,
friendly and cooperative demeanor fooled everybody.

Gretchen—another of my case studies—recounted to me her
academic and social success at her exclusive private high school,
and her paid-in-full tuition at a large, prestigious university,
compliments of her wealthy grandparents. Gretchen, frustrated
over her family's "fake fronts, lies and deceits," finally convinced
them to pay her more attention, "like, get to know the real me,
okay?" by shooting and killing her ill-tempered boyfriend. Only
afterwards was it revealed that she had long been alienated from
her family, that she resented the isolation covered up by "social
games" and "pretense."

The very roles we traditionally assign to females—the passive domain roles of long-suffering nurturer, follower, humble servant, social bonder, our bright and pretty flowers in the garden—and their re-enactment of these roles, is what covers up and hides their psychiatric disorders whose very presence, in males, we look for in the wake of disturbing behaviors that alert us to their social malfunctioning.

## Age Related Manifestations

Now let us use age as the benchmark against which to measure our teenagers' behaviors. For across gender lines, there are common circumstances and signs that inform us of a teenager's propensity for loneliness and alienation.

### Age 12

Twelve years old, the very edge of adolescence, is a critical transition period. What happens here, and why is it such a watershed age? Kids at this age are in middle school and move—*transition*—from one teacher and one classroom to a different teacher for every subject. Does this affect them? Without question! Many kids are instantly overwhelmed. Suddenly, they've gone from relying and depending on one stable adult teaching and guiding force to having many personalities to conform to and obey. Their tasks, in terms of new teachers to know, work to be done, and subjects to learn, have been multiplied four- to six-fold. With a host of unfamiliar faces—both teachers and students—less time during the day to work and play with a fixed set of friends, and often new and foreign curriculum, they are likely to feel ever more alone.

What can you do? As you *must* do whenever your child is confronted with any kind of change, dramatic or routine, talk about it. Ask him how he feels about it. Find out through your querying how he is coping with it and where he is weak in his coping skills, as demonstrated by the varying effects his new experiences have on him. Share your experiences and a few "war stories" about the effects of middle school life on you when you were twelve years old. Especially highlight those areas where you coped exactly like he did. Share strategies that made the difference and improved things for you. Let him know that you're always there for him and will see him through to the light at the end of the tunnel.

### Ages 12-13: Transition Phase

Social bonds are strained to their limits with the arrival of puberty—typically ages 12-13. This marks the period of arguing, protesting, resisting, and fighting. As a parent it may seem to you that your pubescent child is turning against you; since you're the closest to him, you are his first line of attack. Parents often are caught by surprise here, as they realize their kids have outgrown their old fears about the discipline their parents used to hand out. Suddenly, the kids have matured, but their parents are still dishing out "kiddy stuff" threats and punishments. As effective as their repertoire of behavior modification strategies used to be during their kids' childhood years, parents are often frustrated to tears when their children enter adolescence because the old methods don't work and parents don't know why.

You may be delighted to know that from the *transition phase* (ages 12-13) to *middle adolescence* (ages 14-15), you can expect a dramatic change for the better. There are notable exceptions, however, which I will explain below. Nevertheless, be open, try to stay relaxed and get used to the rapid physical, emotional, and intellectual changes that children undergo as they develop through the transition and middle adolescence phases. A caution: Growth and development in adolescents occur at different rates. You may already know this from observing your own children or other children in your extended family or neighborhood.

The internal clock for adolescent behavior is often set at different times for every adolescent. And the emotional and behavioral "ticking" of this clock can be markedly different even among children in the same family who are close in age. Growth in each adolescent development stage occurs in about the same chronological order for most transition- and middle-phase adolescents. However, this growth does not occur at exactly the same time. That is, some adolescents get stuck or remain in certain phases longer than do their peers, or appear to have missed a growth phase altogether. Reasons for this vary, depending on the kind and quality of personal, family, emotional, and environmental (at school, for example) dimensions that influence—healthily or unhealthily—the adolescent's growth.

To illustrate how this works, let's consider the lives of the 13 incarcerated children whose stories frame this book. These children's lives had been tremendously degraded by the terrible stresses and strains of living in dysfunctional families, suffering intolerable emotional or physical abuse, and constant involvement in drugs, including alcohol.

It is difficult enough for normal adolescents and their parents to go through the transition and middle phases of adolescence successfully without disrupting or fracturing the family entirely. The children in this book, and all other children who kill, have experienced not only difficult but also insurmountable challenges. Their passage through the transition and middle phases of adolescence was radically slowed, altered from that of the normal adolescent, or stopped entirely. They became stuck in or between one phase, and their personalities dreadfully transformed because their development—or, rather, their deterioration—was driven and accelerated by family dynamics and emotional or environmental stressors and extremes that were continuously unhealthy, traumatic, corrosive, and damaging.

Children "stuck" in the transition or middle phases of adolescence often praise violence, domination, and death, as well as crow about their sexual exploits—real or imagined—and they suffer from what I call the "Zero Parent Model." Their parents or other caregivers were either absent, ignorant, indifferent, disinterested, helpless, or otherwise incapable of shepherding them successfully through these important, inevitable, and difficult psychoemotional phases. Indeed, as I stated earlier, it is the parents and the family who are *the* constant source of the traumatizing emotional events in these children's lives. Children everywhere who kill, and the currently popular crowd of violence-oriented artists—including rap, death metal, and other music forms—have one characteristic in common: They are typically victims of the Zero Parent Model. They behave just like they feel—like orphaned children who have declared war on each other.

If you can shepherd your child successfully through the transition phase, you will have your old pre-transition phase child, and your best friend, back again. Think of the transition phase as a time for bridge-building. You may find yourself reaching out (bridging) to your child so much that your arms will feel like dilapidated garden hoses, limp and dragging on the ground. Building bridges between you and your child will take time and patience. Sacrifice your bowling, golf, poker-playing, TV-watching, movie-going and hobby evenings. Develop your bridge-building skills instead. Consider it as a vital branch on your parenting tree. Spend as many evenings as you can with your child. Strive to improve and strengthen the love and communication between yourself and him. Use his interests as paths to communication. Resist the urge to tell him everything, to be the sage on the stage. Instead, listen, listen, listen. If you do this, he will tell you a world!

### Ages 14-15: Middle Adolescence

During middle adolescence (approximately the first three years in high school), teens are on their own more. School and their friends become the biggest parts of their lives. Three key growth dimensions usually happen here: a healthy sense of self, an emerging sense of identity, and the blossoming forth of their own values and beliefs.

Accomplishing tasks at home and projects at school, and receiving gratification for them, often develops positive self-esteem and a feeling of self-determination ("I did that. Wow, I'm good!"). Some teens are quietly proud and take to their growing sense of self as easily as they might grow into a new yet overly-large jacket. Other teens may be inclined to brag as they respond to their growing sense of self with enthusiasm and excitement.

An increasing level of comfort with self—for example, changing from self-criticism to speech laced with self-pride—is a characteristic of a teenager's growing sense of identity.

Teenagers in middle adolescence often verbally identify themselves with their values and beliefs. Perhaps you've observed the growth in public service advertisements employing teens who boldly speak out on issues such as unprotected sex, drugs, and driving under the influence. Likewise, advertisers have exploited the fact that teens in middle adolescence make good "voices" in pitching products where one's values are clearly seen in a range of behavioral choices, from style of dress to favorite fast-foods to faddish recreational activities. On one hand, teen voices support urgent social causes; on the other, they sell products in the billions of dollars.

During your teenager's middle adolescence, you must serve as a shepherd—guide him into being more of himself, not who you want him to be. Also, at this time, his choice of friends can completely change, so don't expect him to always pal around with the same group he hung out with two years ago. This is a time when you may hear your child defend his friendships by what they're "into." "He's a surfer." "He's into jazz music." "She's into marathon training." "She's into prepping for prep school." The "into" includes beliefs and values: "John's into Zen Buddhism because he believes an inner peace is key to success in the outer world." Part of Klebold's and Harris' tragedy was that as their groups changed at Columbine, they were left out in the cold. They felt totally defenseless and helpless—until they developed their evil, murderous plan.

As a parent, be generous in sharing what you really believe in. You ought to share what you think is important with your child. Forget SAT Math. "Moral Math"—a loaded gun pointed at a teenage peer = death and prison—is more important. Life in the teenage lane moves fast. Move with it. Don't look for that perfect opportunity to talk—"Now that we've got two hours to kill, here is what I've been wanting to talk to you about." Rather, talk "on the walk." As you're both leaving the house, say what's on your mind. Take every opportunity: in the car, at the breakfast table, even while watching television. Your kid's life may seem like a bunch of fast balls. A lot of them, he'll throw your way. Although you might think they're curves, go with the flow and work hard to get your point across. Your power as a parent comes with your ability to persist and maintain. Do so lovingly and patiently.

Teenagers appreciate and admire parents who patiently stick it out with them no matter what they "throw" at them. Parents who never give up, no matter what the emotional weather of their teen is, are highly-praised—yes, teens often praise their folks to others—highly-valued and loved parents.

I have deliberately curtailed the adolescent development model to place emphasis on its transition and middle adolescence phases. It is the 12-16 age range about which you must be critically aware. After age 16, children begin to have an amplified sense of self, increased feelings about and comfort with their sexuality, increasingly happier and more respectful times with their parents, and a growing independence in their orientation toward and philosophy about life and their choice of friends. There are markedly fewer children who kill after age 16. There are exceptions to this, however, as already defined in my previous definitions and examples of "stuck" adolescence. And, of course, there are well-publicized other exceptions: John Hinkley, who attempted to assassinate former president Ronald Reagan; convicted mass-killer Charles Manson; and Theodore Kacynski, the Unabomber. Generally speaking, however, the 15- and 16-year-old adolescent who is not at risk for killing or acting violently assumes a critically conscious level of thinking. These children grow into a level of reflection—not just *what* do I think/believe but *why* do I think/believe it—that enables them to grow toward a personal identity, moral value system, and religious or faith system.

So important are the transition and middle adolescence phases, that state legislatures around the country are examining these growth and development years and making statutory mandates to try children in court as adults who, while in this age range (12-16), commit heinous vicious and violent or capital crimes. Most of the 15- and 16-year old incarcerated children with whom I talked, though not all of their stories appear in this book, killed when they were 11 to 15 years of age.

As you observe your child in his transition and middle adolescent phases, take a hard, close look at the needs behind the behavior expressed. Try to determine the degree to which loneliness, alienation, anger, frustration, depression, self-worth, parenting, social and environmental (like school) issues are driving the behavior you witness. Your goal is to guide him safely and successfully through these phases so he will neither miss the bridge to his next phase of development nor, worse, lash out in anger or frustration—with a gun or other weapon—at whom he thinks and feels are the fundamental source of his problem: other people, of which you might be one.

# After You Recognize a Problem, What Then?

> *I lived for the day when I could kick my daddy's a\*\* for the way he beat and treated my mom and me. . . . He looked up at me and I could see the sober truth and fear in his eyes, even though he was drunk. I, battered girl, the one who always came home and did her homework and brought home good grades and prizes from school, was standing over him yelling, 'Grab your b\*\*\*s and pull yourself up on your feet like a man, you son of a b\*\*\*\*!'*—Marguerite

It was about 9:00 a.m., and Marguerite, whom I had interviewed on four previous occasions, sat across from me and confessed she had attacked her father and knocked him to the ground after she came home from school to find the drunken man beating up her mother. Battering her mother and herself was something her father had done for years. After that triumphant day, Marguerite regularly assaulted him, just for the fun of it, "just like he used to do to us." He was completely at her mercy and utterly defenseless against her hard-won fighting prowess.

Some disorganized person had left stacks of paper on the desk Marguerite and I shared and, although I had no difficulty in hearing her, I noticed that she seemed to be straining over the obtrusive mound of paper to make sure she maintained eye contact with me. Feeling the urgency with which she wanted to communicate, I quickly arose, swept up the clutter in both arms and deposited it in a couple of empty chairs along the wall. When I sat back down, Marguerite looked relieved and immediately picked up where she left off, about her plan to take control of the family from her abusive father.

"I started hanging out in the streets instead of coming home. I figured I was getting beat up all the time anyway, even though I was a good girl. I had good grades, good school attendance, everything. My teachers were happier with me than my old man was. So, since he was so unhappy, I would *really* make him unhappy. I was scared at first. I mean, home, books, and beatings was all I knew. But I was smart, and I could see right away what I needed to do to be a good fighter. My goal was to fight like I read books—all the time—then come home, or be home when my old man got there, p*** him off big time, and surprise him by beating him up like my grandfather probably used to."

Marguerite, bright as she was, soon noticed her home life changing in unexpected ways. "It took a few times for my old man to get used to me," she said. "What I really liked was the respect my mother gave me and how she began standing up to him now that she had a real protector around. Yeah, he was Mr. Macho, and he still talked crap to her for a while. As soon as I heard the dinner plates crash to the floor, I'd leave my room and just stand in the doorway of the kitchen. He and my mother would be staring each other down. Something she would never do before. She was getting bolder, stronger, and I was happy to see that. He began to sense my presence, look around and just leave the room muttering under his breath. The first few times he did that, I'd block him. 'Where do you think you're going,' I'd ask him. Oh, brother, he hated that. He'd just glare at me. 'Answer me!' I'd scream at him, and then I'd backhand him across the face. What I really enjoyed was making him clean up the mess he had made on the floor—Mama's best plates were all busted up. When he bent over to pick up the pieces, I kicked him hard in the butt. Mama would be there, watching and crying silently. I'd be laughing out loud and calling him names, you know, the kind of names the street guys I was hanging with called their rivals all the time. Words that were real crude, personal, raunchy stuff.

"I guess you could say I was stalking him, and you'd be right. He had so filled me up with hate that the only way I felt better was when I was beating him up.

"My old man began disappearing or coming home real late. I figured his and Mama's thing was, you know, all shot to hell, but I was curious to find out if he had a girlfriend. Now that I'd made home a lot better place to be, I wanted to get into his personal stuff and mess that up, too. Don't ask me why. I just had this urge to mess up his whole life. You probably think I really hated the guy. Part of me loved him, still. Surprised? Yeah, I felt guilty because I nailed his a** every time I went after him. Once I told him, 'I am Mama who won't fight back.' I don't know what I meant, really, but he looked at me with that fear in his eyes and nodded his head up and down real fast. It was funny, but it was real sad, too. If you want to get all psychological with me, you could say I beat him more than I had to, to beat out all the crap inside me that he put in there.

"Let's see. Where was I? Oh, yeah, I was curious about whether my old man had a girlfriend. Well, I asked some of my friends to watch my old man and let me know where he went at night when he didn't come home. They told me where he was and I checked it out. There was this bar he liked. I walked in there one night around 9 o'clock. He was sitting with this lady. She saw me first. I looked at her and signaled, 'get out of here' with my head. He had his glass raised to his mouth and by the time he had set the glass back on the table, she was walking out.

"He watched her butt going out the door and looked at me. He was furious. 'Look at you!' he screamed. 'You scared her away.' 'I ordered her out of here,' I said. 'What have you got on your face?' he asked me. Then I knew what he meant. I had just gotten my tattoos. He kept staring at my face, and I could tell he didn't like what he saw. And I didn't have all the ones you see on me now."

I studied her face. This young lady, who was very attractive by anybody's standards, looked like a totem pole. Her face and arms were littered with tattoos.

"So what do you think?" she asked me.

"I think I'd like to hear the rest of your story," I replied.

"Okay, so you don't like it, either. Anyway, I grabbed my old man by his shirt collar and pulled him to his feet. I slapped him back and forth across his face about ten times. 'So that's the b**** you leave Mama and me for? She's the whore who makes you come home late?' It had gotten real quiet in that place. I knew I had everybody's attention. 'Tell me how beautiful I am,' I told him. He looked at me like I was crazy. He was embarrassed and getting real stubborn on me. So, I grabbed his hair and yanked hard. 'Tell everybody here how beautiful I am,' I repeated. Finally, he said it: 'My daughter's real beautiful.' 'Say it like you mean it,' I said. I made him say it about twenty times. I didn't want to make a real bad scene and have the cops come in, so I dragged him outside where nobody could see and roughed him up. I told him, 'If you're not going to beat up your girlfriends, then don't ever lay a hand on my mama again. I know you've been good at home because I'm there. Well, if you can be good with your girlfriends here, or wherever else the hell you take the whores, you can be good at home, too. You don't need me around to *make* you be good. You get the point?' He just nodded his head up and down and collapsed in my arms.

"He was tired. I knew it, and I also knew that for some reason I didn't want to rough him up any more. With him collapsed in my arms like that, instead of being flat on his back or on his knees like every other time, well, it got to me." Marguerite looked at me for a long time before speaking again. "I just started crying right there. Can you believe that?" I held her gaze, unsure of what response to make. "I mean, how many kids inside here are telling you they were treated so bad by their parents that they had to learn to fight back and beat them up? Do you know what that does to a kid, deep down inside?" I nodded my head for her to continue. "Do you really, really know?" she asked in a louder, somewhat demanding, voice.

I decided she wanted an answer. "No, I don't, Marguerite. Please tell me."

"Do you want to know?" she asked.

I could see that, depending on my answer, she would either speak volumes or shut up and probably terminate the interview. "Yes," I said. "I really want to know."

"Beating up my old man changed me. I'm telling you the truth. I was tough, I was feared, I could knock somebody out with one punch, and on and on. My old man represented authority. Bad authority because he beat us for no reason. You won't believe what it was like. We were family. It wasn't like he was in the streets fighting enemies, or in some war fighting for his country.

"So, when I fought authority back—you know, at home—and won every time, it was like, deep down inside me, *wherever* I found authority facing me, I hated it. You know what I mean?" I nodded my head. "What I'm saying is, even the authority I really liked and respected—my teachers, counselors, the principal, the school clerks—began to look like enemies to me. They were just doing their jobs. But I had been in wars in the streets and battles at home. Stuff like that. Stuff they knew absolutely nothing about. I was coming from a different place than they were. Adults I used to get along with, adults who supported me and wanted me to win, I started disliking. Bottom line is, I dropped out of school.

"But there was something else I was going to tell you, before all this dissing authority stuff. Oh yeah. That night my old man fell into my arms, I went home and cried myself to sleep. I'm going to tell you something real weird. And what I'm about to say is probably one of the reasons one of the shrinks in here says that I've got—let's see, what is the phrase he uses—'uncommon insight into my problems and their sources.' I cried hard that night because I realized that my old, good self had died and I was, like, reborn into this new, bad self. I was making home a better place to be, but I had turned into this evil person. I didn't like myself before, as a victim of my old man, but I really didn't like the evil person I had become, either. It made me real sad to see what I had become. And with my dad there in my arms, I realized how much I still loved him. All the years he beat up on me and my mother—and it was really bad—I still loved him." Marguerite's eyes became moist. The memory brought back the emotion. I offered her a tissue from the box on the table. She took it and managed a weak smile. "I beat him up so much, I evened the score. But that night, it was like the love I still had for him was beating up on me. Weird, right?"

Marguerite might have claimed the victory at home, but the streets claimed the victory over her life. Her parents divorced, her dad moved out, and her mother found a job. But Marguerite didn't change. She became a victim of the street's vices and its excesses. Because of her enormous power and respect, she was able, through her gang, to move large quantities of drugs and guns.

One night, after spending hours engaged in raucous partying with her gangbangers, Marguerite was on her way home when a male member of a rival gang cornered her and raped her at gunpoint. He was brutal, and she spent several days recovering in the hospital. "It was a real head trip, I went through some bad changes in the hospital. That guy hurt me bad and my mind wouldn't let me forget, you know?" she said.

Marguerite hated being disrespected—"that's the part of my old man's beatings that got to me the most, his total disrespect"— and when she was pronounced healed by her doctors, she went back onto the streets with a singular thought in mind: To track down and find the man who had brutalized and raped her. "I was willing to give my life for what he did to me—go to prison, the graveyard—my life, you know what I mean?" In summarizing her eventual finding and assaulting him—an event that actually did send her to prison—she said, "I stood over him and smiled. I could see the life leaving him. The blood that flowed from where I knifed him pooled under his head and looked like a shiny, wet, red pillow. I told him how he had taken advantage of me, dissed me big time, and put me in the hospital; how a nice girl like me wasn't supposed to get revenge; and how good it felt to be able to pay back bastards—all men—who loved to hurt other people. When I said that, his eyes opened real wide. It was weird, like that's the last place his spirit went—into his eyes. I knew in my heart, then, that he understood. He closed his eyes and that was it. He died right there."

Marguerite abruptly ended our interview with, "Inside this prison, nobody screws with me."

We all know that something is wrong with a child whose social behaviors include bullying, threatening, beating up innocent people, poor academic performance, putting herself at personal risk, and committing crimes. Our traditional approach—suppressing these behaviors by medicating them or disciplining their "owners"—has never worked effectively. By failing to search for the deeper causes of the behaviors, we leave them untreated and they worsen until, as in the case of Mr. and Mrs. Kinkel's son, their "owners" victimize others.

Preventative measures against children victimizing other children ought to be established rigorously in our schools. For example, in the case of Marguerite, her teachers and counselors might have been more aggressive and called the department of children and family services to suggest that Marguerite's innumerable bruises indicated a pattern of abuse within the home. If her dad had been arrested and Marguerite taken out of the home and placed in protective custody, perhaps her life may have turned out differently.

But what happens when the schools don't recognize the telltale signs, or a child exhibits none of the behavioral dysfunctions educators are familiar with? Earlier in this book, I mention my interview with Mr. Larry Bentz, Principal of Thurston High School in Springfield, Oregon, where in May 1998 a 15 year-old Kip Kinkel shot and killed his schoolteacher parents as they ate breakfast. Before the day that Kip killed his parents and then threw his gun into his backpack, hauling it and the rest of his troubles to school, Principal Bentz was convinced Kip was a "normal" boy. Unfortunately, at school, Kip showed everybody just how troubled he really was, beneath his casual manner and smiling veneer, by shooting 24 students—two of which died.

Just the day before the shooting, Kip had been suspended by Mr. Bentz for a day because he had brought a gun with him to school. So, that next fateful day marked the second time he had brought a gun to the campus. Given that he (1) may have been seething because of the embarrassment of being "busted" with a firearm in front of his classmates; (2) may have resented being hustled off the campus by the sheriff; or (3) may have been obsessed about getting even with Principal Bentz for discovering the gun and suspending him, why, if Kip Kinkel wasn't troubled, did he even bring a gun to school *the first time*?

This unanswered question may plague us forever. According to Larry Bentz, Kip Kinkel did not exhibit any warning signs. Even his possession of a gun the day before did not sufficiently alarm school authorities to expel him— something most schools in the country do under a policy known as "Zero Tolerance." So, school administrators suspended him for one day, because, as one administrator said, "We acted according to our policy and its stipulations for first-time possession of a firearm." Springfield police did not even make an official report of Kinkel's possession of the weapon; he was merely escorted back home. Perhaps because his parents were both teachers who worked in Springfield, he was accorded something less than a slap on the wrist. While not the most popular student on campus—that is, he wasn't a star athlete, the king clown on campus, or student body president—he was nevertheless trusted, respected and viewed as a "normal boy, whom his parents loved, somebody who knew everybody here and somebody we all liked," according to Principal Bentz. Although the media has learned and reported that Kinkel had an ugly fetish for trapping and stabbing small animals, Mr. Bentz tells me this inhumane, vile streak is not true. "I don't know where the press came up with that story," he says. "Kip did not make a game of tormenting and stabbing rabbits and cats to death." Thus it seems unlikely that Kip or his parents would have been recommended to any counseling programs based on the observations of his school support system.

If, on the other hand, a school or even you as a parent recognizes a behavioral dysfunction, is merely *knowing* that a problem exists, that a child is exhibiting behaviors commonly accepted as wrong, enough? Of course not. The tragic life stories of the incarcerated children I interviewed and share with you throughout this book, the carnage Kip Kinkel created in Springfield, Oregon, and the massacre that Eric Harris and Dylan Klebold unleashed in Littleton, Colorado serve as a hellish and horrific backdrop warning of your need to do more than pick up the telltale signs of dangerously aggressive behavior in your child. You also need to be willing to make it a full-time job and get past all the people who will try to tell you that everything's fine. There is no question that professional help is what parents in these kinds of difficult circumstances need. But that professional help is not always easy to access or an immediate remedy, as Kip Kinkel's parents, who *did* identify problems in their son, apparently found.

For 15 years, Kip's parents seemed to know their son in ways his principal did not, and in ways that Eric Harris' and Dylan Klebold's parents should have. Kinkel's parents tried desperately to get help for grave problems they spotted in Kip years earlier. Since elementary school, he had been fighting with classmates. Numerous parent conferences with his teachers failed to solve the problem. Next, the Kinkels sought medical and psychological help for Kip. The answer seemed to be in placing him on Ritalin and, after that, Prozac. But Kip's behavior continued to worsen. Ever resourceful, Mr. and Mrs. Kinkel pulled him out of seventh grade and arranged to have him home-schooled. Perhaps being around so many people constantly during the day is what continued to incite him. But Kip's eruptions continued at home, as though his environment had never changed. And after he stashed a fully loaded .32 in his locker at school, the Kinkel's begged a juvenile detention center to lock Kip up—something that never happened.

When Kip's high school suspended him for just one day for the gun possession, and the sheriff didn't even write an incident report, the Kinkels felt they had no other options left. They had put up the good fight to get help for their son and had lost. But why? Perhaps there may be numerous reasons, perhaps none. The Kinkel family saga, in many ways, is worse than the Harris's and Klebolds' of Littleton, Colorado. For unlike them, the Kinkels knew for a very long time that something was desperately wrong with their son. The Harrises and Klebolds never seemed to know their sons were in dire need of professional help, even when obvious evidence of highly dangerous behaviors was erupting all around them. Could it be that, although the Kinkels knew *something* was wrong with Kip, their not knowing precisely *what* was wrong is what killed them? The Harrises and Klebolds apparently felt *nothing* was wrong with their sons. As we now know, the *something* they didn't know is what led to the killing of 15 children, including their sons.

Kip Kinkel's problems started early, as do most kids. Unfortunately, Kip's parents, as aware as they apparently were about his troubles, and despite trying to move mountains and convince others, ultimately failed to get him the help he so desperately needed. Knowing there is a problem by attentive observation is a good start, but finding the necessary and *effective* resources to assist you in addressing your child's behavioral problems is the key.

Since 1981, researchers have had a fairly good idea of effective ways to help these kids. One such avenue is based on adult role-modeling, called "Multisystemic Therapy." It is a novel at-home program based on a therapist's entering the home to teach parents how to enforce rules, keep their child from bad influences, and help the child find and take advantage of a support network. Doubtless, such a program will help many parents and children, especially where mandated by the courts or district attorney for parents under court supervision for some offense. But there exist no programs to find those parents who, because of their affluence or "public face" remain undetected as being in severe need of parent education, therapy or counseling? Because these kinds of parents have committed no crime, the court or district attorney can't demand they enroll in court-approved Parent Education classes as a condition of their court supervision and probation. Developing a program designed to attract parents who need help may offer preventative solutions to the kinds of tragedies orchestrated by Kip Kinkel, Eric Harris, and Dylan Klebold.

It was also in 1981 that 49 states contracted with the "Parents as Teachers" program. The goal of the program is to teach mothers and fathers to help their child emotionally and socially through simple games, reading, talking and loving. Unfortunately, "Parents as Teachers" reaches only 500,000 of the estimated 19 million children under age five; that's less than three percent. It would be prudent to financially assist such worthy efforts as "Parents as Teachers"—preventative programs geared to foster healthy emotional and social skills—but the monetary commitment necessary is large, and as yet, our society has not caught the vision of these critical programs.

Another effective program called "First Step to Success" also ran aground of financial barriers. This Oregon-based program screens kindergartners for antisocial behavior and then spends three months turning around bullies-in-development by rewarding good behavior at school and showing parents, inside their own homes, how to teach their problem child to cooperate, make friends and develop confidence. "First Steps to Success" costs only $400 per child; however, it is available in schools in only 10 states.

Where such programs are not available or utilized, schools tend to wait and see which kids develop serious problems in sixth grade before they summon help for them. This backward and haphazard approach on the part of schools is a blindness that weakens their attempts at instituting prevention programs and causes parents to wonder whether our school's "walk" (actions) matches their "talk" (intent). Unfortunately, a school's size is one of the culprits that breeds this approach, both because of funding concerns and the logistical difficulties in administering large student populations.

The advantage of a smaller school may be greater control over financial resources and a more hand's on administration; a smaller school may actually reduce the need for the kinds of programs I've mentioned—though, certainly, they should always be available. The larger a school is, the more scarce help seems to be. The ideal school size, say education researchers, is 600 to 900 kids. Smaller schools leave fewer students marginalized, that is, suffering assaults to their identities and egos which can warp personalities. These students have a better chance to develop and blossom healthily. Their personalities are less apt to be forged by inhumane treatment from those who *intend* to hurt them, or by the unresponsiveness and indifference of those who were supposed to help them. Also, smaller schools make it possible for more kids to be core members of an extracurricular activity and follow an adult role model. Further, administrators have a better chance of getting to know each student.

Large schools typically are able to deal with only two kinds of students: the class president or the kid who is trying to burn the school down. In such schools, parents are often rebuffed in their attempts to get help for their anti-social, overly-aggressive child or are placated with meaningless phrases such as, "She's going through your garden-variety angst." Many parents are even ordered to shape up their bad-performing offspring or the school may expel him. Such institutional insensitivity runs counter to the philosophies and purposes of schools, and suggests that, like all of us, school administrators have had it up to their eyeballs with resistant, anti-social, poor-behaving, dangerous and violent children.

Parents see such schools as part of the problem and resent the implications that they, somehow, have failed in their roles as parents and are unleashing their virulent children—like so many deadly bacteria—upon society. Marguerite's case, however, justifies the implication of parental culpability. In contrast to the loving guidance advocated by the above mentioned programs, or even a structured, regulated school environment, her father abused his authority in the home, and her mother abdicated her responsibility in family affairs. Their failures created in Marguerite a classic "at risk" profile. With no supporting guidance, Marguerite shows how schools, and by extension all society, are only as safe as the homes they serve.

# Hearing Your Child's "Voice"

*My mother just whimped out and took Daddy's side, like she forgot what it was like to be young and want to stay with friends you've met. I really felt outnumbered and, man, oh man, that night I really got the picture. It was real clear I didn't count for much in my family. . . . I don't really know what I would have done if they had walked in and seen me on the stairs looking over at Floyd's dead body. If it took holding a gun on them, too, to make them understand . . . well, maybe I should have waited up for them and forced them against a wall to listen to me.*—Lorraine

L orraine responded to each interview in an identical way: "By the time I started 9th grade, I had already been in almost 30 different schools." Our third interview was no exception. I let her continue, knowing that after she got past a certain point, she would undoubtedly give me new or better information than before. I had to be patient with all my adolescent research participants. But with Lorraine, I had to be especially patient. The most important men in her life had let her down. *Let her repeat herself; one day she won't feel obsessed to do so*, my mind kept telling me. Lorraine liked to stand up and pace during our interviews. That was fine with me; she wore sneakers and her pacing never got into the tape.

In the huge day room, she only paced within a radius of five feet, if that.

"My daddy was a dog and horse trainer," she said with a sigh of resignation and a shrug. "We always had to follow wherever he went because that's where the job was; and wherever the job was, the money was right there. It was tough making friends. Sometimes we'd drive all night until we reached whatever state the job was in. We'd sleep in the truck and the next morning, no matter how little sleep I had gotten, my mom would be running around town with me, trying to check me into a school. When she got me in, I'd only be there a few weeks or months before they'd pull me right back out and have me criss-crossing the country with them to the next job. I can't tell you how lonely I got and how bad I felt. It was miserable. Sometimes when we'd stop for gas and groceries, and they'd go inside, but I'd stay in the car and scream out my frustrations.

"Pretty soon I began to envy the dogs and horses Daddy trained. Sometimes it was fun seeing strange animals run from him or look like they wanted to jump on him and attack him. But, like magic, he'd have horses eating sugar cubes out of his hand and dogs sitting on their haunches taking jerky strips from him. Wherever he went, they'd follow him like little children. He had the gift. But then, I started hating them. He seemed to love them more than he loved me. I could tell by the way he looked at them, how much time he spent with them, stuff like that. Some dumb animals were running our life. And I hated that."

Lorraine met a boy she really liked at school. His name was Floyd. They started dating, and soon they became inseparable. Her parents liked Floyd and allowed Lorraine to see him in their home even when they were not there. A few months after Lorraine and Floyd started dating, Lorraine's father received a telephone call from a horse owner who wanted him to drop whatever he was doing to travel some 4,000 miles to his stables. The man promised to pay Lorraine's father a handsome salary, a "loss fee," for interrupting his current job, and a bonus on top of that. At dinner that night, Lorraine's father announced the opportunity he had been offered. Lorraine immediately said she didn't want to go. Her father told her she didn't have a choice; the decision was already made—her father was going to accept the job. They argued and argued about it and, according to Lorraine, "My mother just wimped out and took Daddy's side, like she forgot what it was like to be young and want to stay with friends you've met. I really felt outnumbered and, man, oh man, that night, I really got the picture. It was real clear that I didn't count for much in my family. I ran from the dinner table and went straight to bed. I think I cried all night."

The next day, Lorraine's father and mother left so that he could take a three-day job, something he referred to as an "easy-money-quick-turnaround-job." It was Thursday, and although the job was out of state by about 600 miles, Lorraine's parents assured her they'd be back by the time the "60 Minutes" newsmagazine came on television, the forthcoming Sunday evening. "At first, I started getting angry," Lorraine said. "The nerve of them to just suddenly decide to leave me so Daddy could take an easy-money job somewhere a couple of states away. I mean, like they couldn't see the need to spend more time with me, especially since he was going to take that big offer from that rich stable owner, anyway."

Lorraine had an idea. "After my parents left, I called Floyd and invited him over. He didn't sound too happy; in fact, he sounded kind of faraway, you know, in his mind, like he was unsure about something. I thought maybe it was that he wasn't sure how he was supposed to react to what I told him about my parents. I mean I told him some things I really should have told them, like how they were always abandoning me for their own selfish needs, and stuff like that. Anyway, he said he'd come over."

Floyd, true to his word, did come over. His visit, however, did not have the pleasant effect on Lorraine that his presence usually did. "The minute I opened the door and looked into his eyes, I knew something was wrong," she explained. "I told him, 'You look so guilty, Floyd. But you're the perfect angel, so it must be me. Remind me to get my eyes checked.' We sat down and then he told me. He had met somebody else, but he promised we could still be friends. The more he talked, the more it felt like all those times my parents promised me, as we walked into whatever my latest school was, that I would have even more friends there. I hated promises. Before I knew it, I was crying. And when Floyd started trying to hug me, to try to quiet me down, I felt even more hurt. I couldn't take it. I pushed him away and ran upstairs."

When Lorraine returned downstairs, Floyd "was still sitting there, fidgeting with that guilty look on his face," she said. "I called him. I was on the second or third step of the stairs and his back was to me. He turned around. I will never forget the look on his face when I pulled the trigger." A single shot from the rifle that Lorraine's father owned killed Floyd instantly.

As Lorraine and I talked, it was clear to me that she simply could not get over the anger and hurt of being pushed aside, pushed around, and pushed back by her parents' busy and complicated lifestyle. Despite her position as the only child, she was consistently side-stepped and ignored. Although her parents didn't really act as if Lorraine didn't matter, they often acted as if she weren't there. Seemingly born to their passion for dogs and horses, they were blind to what their lifestyle was doing to her. She was forced to suppress her emotional needs and get tough as she got older. Her former snits and whimpering and whining gave way to long, cold, stony silences. Long accustomed to her parents abandoning her for their celebrity animal training and grooming business, she was nonetheless vulnerable to Floyd, whom she desperately loved.

As Lorraine and Floyd grew to know each other, he began to fill the emotional chasm inside her. They grew closer and when her parents were not there, Floyd usually was. He became her emotional center. Although she had shot and killed Floyd in cold blood, Lorraine told me, "I loved him. I know you think I'm crazy, like, you only kill somebody you hate, right? But not me. I really, really loved Floyd." Floyd, represented for Lorraine, and to the world, the last person who would abandon her. In a sense, he was the sacrificial lamb, an unwitting symbol of the intolerable and constant desertion of her parents.

What Lorraine said about her parents, with respect to that night, reveals the real objects of her fury. "They were supposed to be home at about the same time Floyd came over. But they had a last-minute call to see about training somebody's horse. I don't really know what I would have done if they had walked in and seen me on the stairs looking over at Floyd's dead body. I really think I would have shot both of them, too. You see, I was so p***ed off at them. They never seemed to understand. And I think they would have only cared if they had looked up and seen the rifle pointed at one of their heads. And I wouldn't have wanted that. I wouldn't want to kill somebody to make them love me. Feeling abandoned and mostly left alone really tore me up inside, more than my mother and father will ever know—even now. If it took holding a gun on them to make them understand that, well, maybe I should have waited up for them and forced them against a wall to listen to me."

How and what parents and their children talk about are measures of (1) the parents' value of the child's "voice" (opinion and view); (2) the importance of the topic to them; (3) the value of communication to the family; (4) the psychoemotional needs of the child; and (5) the strength of the love within the family.

As your children grow older, it is important that you hear their "voices." From infancy to toddler-hood, they need to hear your voice to thrive, learn the language and get to know you. As they develop, however, it is critical for them to recognize that you value and respect their voices as well. They are members and stakeholders in the family and your acknowledgment and acceptance of their voices and views will enable you to give them increasing responsibilities. Some parents are "control freaks" and neither want to hear their children's opinions nor give them meaningful responsibilities within the family. Thus they make them "social misfits," unable to really communicate with anyone on a meaningful level, and hinder their ability to achieve. Don't fear, disregard or suppress your child's voice. Instead, encourage, respect and amplify it.

Allow me to adopt the child's voice and put words to what our youth are trying to communicate to us. The following "Commandments" are written to honor and amplify the child's voice.

## Commandments
*You shall have no other jobs before me. Working for me but*

*not being with me is not right. While I respect your labors, I need your love. Only love, not work, will nourish my spirit and feed my soul.*

*Tell me you love me so I will know. Those words are the music for my soul.*

*You shall not abandon nor forsake me, nor make for yourself any exception to me, but you will always love, protect, defend and care for me, so that I will grow wise, strong, and loving, and ready to do my part for the world of the future.*

*You shall not replace me with other pursuits or pleasures, for I the child of you, am a jealous child.*

*I am you, even as you are your father or mother. Remember this, and all the days of our lives will be good. If you love yourself, you must love me.*

*You must always speak to me in kindness, touch me with love, teach me with gentleness.*

*Hold back your anger, hold forth your love, and I will stretch forth my wings and fly.*

*You shall not be arrogant and vain, for you are to bless me with the gifts of love, laughter, and health.*

*I require your honesty and faithfulness. I am you. If you defile, defraud and defame me, you do so to yourself.*

*I need your patience and longsuffering. Though I am you, I am the stripling while you are the oak itself. If I am to grow aright, it will be through your patience and kindness.*

*My mind, body and spirit are precious. Take care of me, for I will not pass this way again.*

*I am the brightest light in your life, the best thing that you have to offer the world. I will get better as will you, if you so desire.*

A child without a voice is a lost child who is primed for depression and negative self-esteem. Go find your child by "finding"—listening to and acknowledging—her voice. Thus you will have what most parents need: A constant thermometer to "read" the temperature of your child's feelings and emotions.

Equally important as reading your child's emotions, is knowing that the *way* you talk and *how* you say what you have to say, influence the relationship between you and your child. Be especially careful how you react to topics discussed. Be *open*, so that you get as much information as possible. If you close out or shut down, your child feels judged and rejected. Just as you would be hurt or offended if somebody discounted your views, do not *invalidate* your child or what she tells you. Do not *revise* what your child says. Instead, accept what she says at face value. Changing what she has told you only communicates back to the child that she, as well as what she says, is somehow defective and needs fixing. Do not *criticize* your child for being open and candid with you, or for whatever she tells you. Never, ever use profanity or obscenities with your child. Doing so is simply not okay. It is a disgusting practice and will only drive the child away from you, as will outbursts of anger. Use only your child's given name or special term of endearment (we call our second son "Sweetie") when you address her. Do not call her by something other than those names you use when you are not angry. It is disrespectful, shameful and offensive to her. One morning, I called a child's home to find out why he wasn't in school yet. I heard his father in the background yell, "Hey, stupid, how come you didn't go to school today?" When I heard that, I knew instantly that the boy's school attendance was only part of that family's problem.

The behavior of Lorraine's parents played a decisive role in shaping her development and how she acted and reacted within and outside the family. The critical failure her parents committed was failing to hear Lorraine's "voice"—her opinions and needs in the ways she was capable of expressing them. From early on, she was constantly denied the psychological and emotional support that is usually attached to the actions and presence of concerned, loving parents. Were her parents loving and concerned? This is a difficult question to answer. Lorraine's story of her life, however, suggests that there was a chronic void and longing deep inside her. She yearned to be emotionally bonded to her parents, to feel rooted in their love. Every time they left for a job, though, she was stripped of the chance to bond, and her hopes were dashed. The resultant void inside her was an emotional desert, a wasteland.

The eminent psychiatrist, Rene Spitz, conducted the most well-known study of such extreme psychological deprivation. His focus was on what occurs in children when early parental attachment is prevented from forming altogether or disrupted once it has begun. During the 1930's and 1940's, Spitz entered the institutions for unwed mothers in Mexico. The differing policies of the institutions actually provided him with the life-and-death determinants of attachment prevention and disruption. Some of the institutions he visited required a mother to leave her baby six months after the baby's birth, so as to free the baby for adoption. Other institutions forced the mothers to depart within days after their child's birth. In both cases, the babies without mothers were well taken care of, that is, their *physical* needs were met. They were bathed, fed, clothed, and given medical attention, as appropriate. However, they were not loved. No adult played with them, talked "baby talk" to them, sat with them, or went near them. Not only were they motherless, but they were also "un-mothered."

Spitz's first group of surveyed babies had opportunities to form attachments to their mothers for about six months prior to being psychologically abandoned. It must be noted that many of these babies died, in spite of receiving good medical care and wholesome, nutritious diets. The babies who died, expired because they starved to death emotionally. The second group of babies never formed attachments to their natural mothers, thus the psychological bond never existed. Equally important, these babies never connected with anybody else.

Rene Spitz demonstrated that a child who is removed from his attachment figure (usually the mother) goes into a state of deep bereavement. There is little or no documentation by other researchers replicating Spitz's work, but perhaps the scarcity of this kind of research can be explained. This particular kind of research, while yielding stunning and surprising data, is highly controversial. It is seen by some—because it can produce severe harm or death for its participants—as "social experimentation," dehumanization, human manipulation, and even barbarism. Others see this research akin to vivisection of animals and other stress-inducing animal laboratory experiments. But if we use Spitz's work as a frame, it would appear that Lorraine was in constant resentment and perhaps periodic bereavement. Lorraine's case illustrates that despite her being markedly older than Spitz's study group (all infants), emotional and psychological desertion can drastically affect and harm anybody, regardless of his or her age.

Parents should realize that children's emotions are dynamic and, like electrical currents, they flare and flame all the time. Lorraine's emotions flared up every time her parents had to relocate to the next big job. And after a while, the emotional effect on Lorraine was as though her parents were ridding themselves of her—a form of punishment. The empty feeling and constant hollowness she experienced depressed and devastated her. She quickly transferred to Floyd her obsession to form attachments. She made him the object of her affections. For a while, he fulfilled her needs. Then, when his own needs changed, he wanted to withdraw from the emotional part of the relationship (their intimacy) and reconstruct it on a purely friendship level. To Lorraine, this was intolerable. After all, she had "friends" in the form of her parents. Perhaps in her desperation to fill her emotional needs, she actually began driving Floyd away. In her mind, though, Floyd was the one responsible for the separation. And she could not take that. Desertion and disconnection are threatening, especially if one has been their repeated victim and has been left depressed in their wake. Lorraine had been through all of this before and could not tolerate even the thought of being abandoned again.

Rene Spitz's research perhaps suggests that, just as human babies can die of psychological abandonment, it can cause heartache and emotional desolation in older children as well. This emotional starvation-by-degrees is undoubtedly what Lorraine was experiencing with respect to her parents, and which was painfully repeated in Floyd's confession that he had met somebody else.

The theme that constantly surfaced over the months that I spoke with Lorraine, was that her parents seldom listened to her. Her characterization of her mother as a "wimp" suggests that only her father made the critical family decisions, stifling or rejecting any input from Lorraine or her mother. As Lorraine grew older and her emotional needs increased, her mother "was not around, even when she was there." Lorraine explained: "She was tied so much into what my daddy wanted to do, and jumped at everything he said, that, like, hello, Mom? Why don't you look at how some of the other ladies are real mothers to their daughters since you don't have a clue!"

In the presence of her parents, Lorraine was strangling emotionally; in their absence, she felt deserted. As she grew older, it seemed to her that their absences were more frequent. Indeed, after she turned 13, they usually left her at home by herself. In constant torment because she was "never listened to" and did not have the mother-daughter bond she craved, Lorraine saw her father as somebody distant and selfish. She told me: "He was easy to p*** off, oh brother! All you had to say was something like, 'But I thought you said you'd take me shopping today,' and he'd start shouting about some job that came up." Lorraine's parents suppressed her voice and thus were never really in touch with her needs. As they seldom listened to her, they only infrequently connected to her emotionally.

You might have been shocked and saddened, as I was, if you had heard the overwhelming number of incarcerated children I interviewed tell me how strained their relationships with their parents were; how poor their communication was; how verbally abusive their parents were to them or to each other; how their views, needs and wants never seemed to matter at all, and thus never got resolved; and how low were the value and priority placed

---

on communication by their parents. Most of these children had parents who chose to originate communication by criticizing them, bossing them around, or calling them names. Their young lives were literally dogged by failed communication. It was tragically inevitable that when they experienced communication problems with their peers, they responded by choosing guns to represent their voices and bullets to represent their words. Six of the 103 children I interviewed killed a member of their own family.

The topics your child brings to you for discussion should be received in a non-judgmental way by you. They represent what your child is thinking about. It follows that your child should feel that being with you provides her a communication "safety zone." She should always feel welcome to discuss anything with you. Saying or showing (by your behaviors) that "I'll discuss anything from A through D with you, but you'll never get me to talk about E through Z, is that clear?" sends a warning signal that could come back to haunt you. If teenagers are not allowed by their parents to discuss certain topics with them, then where do they go for the answers to their questions about those topics? Usually, to other teenagers. Do you trust your child's teenage friends to provide the answers and right kind of advice on certain topics that only you can? I doubt that you do.

For years research has shown that pregnant teen mothers admit knowing next to nothing about sex. Equally sad is that a shocking number of teen fathers confess that they simply did not believe their girlfriends would get pregnant from having sexual relations with them. Sex is a taboo subject in many households in America. Yet ignorance is neither bliss nor blessing. It can be a curse, as the millions of teenage pregnancies in the country continue to prove. If you refuse or resist talking to your child about sensitive issues and concerns such as sex, then you leave her ignorant. There is no other way to say it. You, not some teenage friend of hers, are the world's best person to inform her and guide her understanding about sensitive issues. Refusing to discuss those issues with her is nothing short of abandoning her. If you know a parent who has or had a pregnant teenage daughter, but who never provided any instruction, advice, or knowledge about sex to the daughter, then you know what I mean. Not talking about sex could result in a crisis. According to the American Social Health Association (ASHA), one fourth, or three million of the estimated 12 million new STD (sexually transmitted disease) cases each year occur in teenagers. ASHA publishes a booklet, *Becoming an Askable Parent: How to Talk With Your Child About Sexuality*. This booklet helps prepare parents for the stages of sexual development and offers some help by answering the tough questions kids always have. For a copy of the 18-page guide, send $2 to ASHA, Dept. PR66, P.O. Box 13827, Research Triangle Park, NC 27709. The fee covers printing, postage, and handling.

The psychoemotional benefits that result from a healthy, ongoing, positive communication relationship between you and your child are invaluable and innumerable. A child instinctively looks to her parents as the founts of wisdom. She seeks their approval, and wants their guidance. As she grows and develops, her needs increase. As a parent, you have already "been-there-done-that," in certain senses, and are the most qualified person, she instinctively knows, who can help her. The point is: do *you* also know that? Children who communicate the most with their parents tend to feel better about themselves, get better grades, form friendships easily, and have fewer discipline problems at home and school than do other children who are estranged from their parents even while living with them.

Consider your child a "vessel" to be filled up with your love, a plant to be "watered" with your words of wisdom and caring, and a "house" under construction, whose foundation is solid and structure is strong because they are built on love, kindness, understanding, and the free-flowing, *expected and respected* exchange of words, ideas, and opinions. Such was not the case in Lorraine's home. Despite her outspokenness, her parents neither expected her views and opinions nor respected them. When she expressed them, her mother "wimped out and took Daddy's side."

Some parents seem to think that communication needs in the home can be fulfilled by the media—nonstop television, video and radio in every room of the house. Such outside communication will never substitute for heart-to-heart talks with your child. Your child needs to hear your own voice. So, turn the television/video/radio off more often, and talk about school, current events, your job, the kind of people with whom you work, your child's interests, her school friends, her goals and dreams, family projects, and so forth. Make communication around the breakfast/dinner table interesting: inviting, new, terrific, enthusiastic, rewarding, eventful, surprising, topical, inspiring, nonstop, and genuine. Not: critical, judgmental, argumentative, boring, hurtful, or depressing. Yet, in many families that's exactly how communication is. If you limit the amount of time the family spends watching television and increase the amount of time talking to each other, laughing, and shareing, you will see a recognizable, positive difference in how the family members relate to each other and to you. A family that communicates constantly is a constantly powerful family. The above communication formula is yours for the taking. Choose it, and use it.

# To Parent Your Child, Know Yourself

*My dad liked to do drugs and get high. When he got out of prison, he promised me he loved me so much that, to prove his love, he wanted to o.d.—you know, overdose—with me. That was weird. Why should we die together, like kill ourselves on drugs, to prove he loved me? Still, I went to my mother and asked her, 'How come you never tell me that? Don't you love me?'* —Josi

Unlike most of my other research participants, Josi was blunt from the first, and remained forthright and candid over the years and through several more interviews. She always seemed to be "warmed up" to the topic. Despite the parade of people walking past us in the day room today, she spoke loudly and bluntly as though we were alone. Frankly, I was not used to such candor and found my forehead wet with perspiration as I nervously wondered how many people walking past us were *hearing* Josi as I was. I had to steel my nerves and concentrate on getting her "message."

During our first interview, Josi stated, "The sight of my own blood relaxes me." Josi still had her first teeth when she began to suffer physical abuse from a menagerie of adult drug addicts in her family. Life at home was more hazardous than happiness. As Josi described it: "Most everybody in my family was on drugs. I had uncles, aunts on drugs. And they were hitters all the time. The teachers were tripped out. They would see bruises on me, and I had to lie for my family. And I got tired of getting beat up. So I told the teacher what was going on."

Josi's parents may hold some kind of record for giving up the most children to foster placement: under court order they surrendered Josi and her seventeen brothers and sisters. The parents were arraigned for reckless endangerment of children and judged as being unfit and negligent. It seems that both parents and other adult family members spent all their time getting high on heroin, cocaine, and booze. As a result, they spent almost as much time in jail as they did at home.

The love and caring her family should have given her, she found instead among her teachers who were "tripped out" by the bruises she brought to school. It was clear to Josi that her family had little love or wholesome regard for her. To them, she was expendable, merely an accessory for their convenience. Curiously, lying to protect them left her defenseless. Her parents and other relatives battered her as though she were just another feared and hated denizen of their drug underworld or an otherwise threatening presence. Their neglecting to love and protect her and treat her like their daughter, certainly must have caused her as much psychological distress as the physical pain to which they regularly subjected her.

Embarrassed to go to school and be seen with welts and bruises on her tiny frame, and constantly reeking of body odor, Josi became truant. She explained: "We were ditching and stuff. And we were coming dirty; we had lice in our hair." Although her teachers were concerned, caring, and intervened to stop the constant beatings she received from her family, it was her consistently dirty and disheveled appearance that pained Josi. She did not wish to be seen among her teachers—rescuers—looking bad and smelling worse. In their presence, Josi felt that she was not good enough. Her uncleanliness was extremely embarrassing to her, a permanent physical problem that was always in evidence, even more than the bruises from the abuse she endured. She recalls that even at the early age of eleven, she noticed differences between her life and those of other kids her age. "Every time I would see a little girl walk up to their mother, I would get jealous, because my mother never came like that to me. She was never there for me, my mom. Nobody was there for me when I needed them." Indeed, everybody in Josi's family seemed to make it a point to castigate her for any reason, real or imagined. Even their failure to keep her clean appears to have been some kind of punishment dealt her. The family demonstrated a profound unwillingness to love her and an extreme disregard for her emotional needs.

Josi's life among adults was a caldron of pain, disappointment, and disillusionment. It is adults from whom she sought love and whom she tried to love, only to be physically brutalized. And it was caring adults—teachers—who came to her rescue, but from whom she fled because she felt unclean and undeserving and, perhaps, not really wanted. Desperate for some real family around her, after years of bouncing in and out of foster homes, Josi became pregnant.

Seven weeks after the baby was born, Josi, having been repeatedly awakened by the infant's fitful crying all night, placed her pillow over the newborn's face and smothered her to death. Josi spends part of each day, every day, writing letters to her daughter "in heaven," begging her forgiveness. Josi told me, "What I did was wrong. I know it was wrong. I should not have done it. My baby was seven weeks old—almost two months— when she died. I remember the date: September 10. In court, they tried me for manslaughter, involuntary manslaughter. I killed my baby. It was like an accident. I am a person that can't hurt some- body else. I hurt myself. I have to see my own blood to be able to feel relaxed. I always felt that way."

I looked at Josi and swallowed hard. A chill crept up my spine and I shuddered involuntarily. "Why do you have to see your own blood?" I asked. She explained that when various members of her family would beat her, the only way she had an inkling as to when the beatings would come to an end was when she started to bleed. "My mom, dad, or whoever would stop when they saw the blood." Years after the beatings ceased, Josi told me that she still needs to see her own blood before she allows herself to feel comfortable, relieved, and relaxed. That's when I noticed the scars

191

and scratches that cover both her arms. Little acts of self-butchery, they deliver the message her abusive family instilled into her years ago: "You are no good, nothing, until we beat you." Her masochistic nature having been literally beaten into her, Josi's own blood serves two purposes: to assure her that she is good (cleansed) and to signal the end, for now, of the pain.

Aside from the obvious biological answer, *why* is it that you are a parent? The question is designed to provoke some thought and analysis. What is it that you want to accomplish with, through, for and by your child? What is your life's mission that only being a parent will fulfill? What is the purpose and mission of your family? If given a choice of being a parent versus a non-parent, what are the reasons for the particular choices you might make?

Most parents, even dysfunctional ones, yearn to bestow upon their children abundant happiness and emotional and spiritual fulfillment throughout their lives. But life can sometimes be one huge, complicated and fast moving expressway with lane changes and detours are often made "on the fly." Often parenting ends up being more supervising than supporting, more nagging than nurturing. One parent once offered, during a seminar I was conducting, this sobering view of parenting: "Being a parent felt like I had built a new road with no exits!"

What are some of the things that complicate your parenting? Are you up against the wall trying to make a living? Are the stresses and strains of daily life sometimes too overwhelming, too unmanageable? Is there some emotional "tonnage" you're carrying from your own childhood? Are you living with a spouse whose parenting inadequacies are themselves a problem? Are you often the receiver of bad advice? Are you a good parent with bad children? Are you just "there" and doing the best you can, alone, with no help, advice, direction?

The aim of this chapter is to provide you with ways to get in touch with yourself and your loving inclinations, and create the time you need to effectively parent your child. It's probably safe to say that no two people respond identically to parenting. Many parents spend the better part of their children's growth years adjusting to the myriad attitudes and behaviors the children express and exhibit as they develop. Some parents are thoroughly and sincerely pleased to be parents and rise, with alacrity, to every challenge and occasion. Other parents feel locked in, trapped by the very children they helped to create. What you think, your child may never know—but they often do know what you feel. For they feel the same tensions, anger, resentment, or love and affection that you feel. Children "read" feelings by seeing your attitude. You are the "motion picture" they watch most of the time. But they do more than watch, they *feed* on the feelings you display.

What are your parenting goals? Your intention to respond to your child's growth and development needs is what defines your parenting goals. Before you can make an appropriate response, however, you must be with your child physically, observe her, talk and play together and, in short, do everything you can to establish and enhance the bonds of trust between you and your child. This will allow you to know your child so well that, when she's "down" and preoccupied with a problem, you can read the signs and step in to help. A child's inner happiness is derived by the parent's response to her need for love and attention. In many ways, it is the parent who is being trained by the child. Even in the beginning, it is you who gets up in the middle of the night, stirred awake by her "wet" or "hungry" cries.

How much time and positive attention do you actually give your child? If you had to account for this, say, in a log book, what would the daily and weekly totals look like? Giving adequate time to a growing child requires a commitment. This commitment more than likely is an investment in time, and will pay you rich dividends in a loving lifetime relationship with your child.

Children whose needs are not met manifest disturbing symptoms of anxiety, depression, and anger which disrupt their sleeping, eating, learning, and social life. A child who sleeps fitfully may be depressed, as might be one who overeats or undereats. The child whose good grades plummet for no apparent reason may be hiding behind a mask of depression. And the child who withdraws from the group and hermetically seals herself off by loitering in the deep recesses of campus, holing up in the restroom, or hiding behind closed doors at home, could well be in the throes of depression. If you are wrapped up in your own needs or driven by your own unhappiness, you may miss the signs of depression in your child. There is a Chinese saying that goes, "He (or she) who is wrapped up in themselves makes a small bundle." It is possible to be so wrapped up in oneself that your eyes are blind and your ears deaf to the sounds and symptoms of depression, anxiety or other forms of unhappiness exhibited and expressed by your child. And if you are afflicted with an addiction—whether in the form of substance abuse or lifestyle and behavioral excesses—you are so overwhelmed that your knowledge and awareness of the symptoms of your child's depression is all but nonexistent.

The reports of the incarcerated children I included descriptions of parents who were too overwhelmed by their own inner unhappiness or by outside pressures to be aware of, or even interested in, their children's problems. Many parents were simply unwilling to subordinate their personal desires to the goal of helping their children become happy and functional. Indeed, most parents did not have this or any other family goal. I was often struck, as I spoke to these children, by how their parents seemed just as immature and unsophisticated as they. The "blind leading the blind" is an apt expression for these dysfunctional families and for all the families of children who kill. To the extent that parents emerge from the shell of their own problems, they have greater insight, vision, energy and desire to lead their children. Moreover, they will be impressed by the strength of the love they feel for their children and by their general unwillingness to crawl back into that shell of unhappiness or protection.

Children are with parents for but a second, figuratively speaking. The problems and challenges parents face, however, often seem permanent, even though they are usually temporary. Parents need to reorder their priorities and put their children permanently in their hearts and minds, in their lives, and at the center of their attention. The love you have for your child will always motivate you to address her needs instantly and constantly. Then you will be more apt to find ways and resources to resolve your own problems. Save your child first; saving yourself will be the result.

Your energy, attention, and time will always be the most important gifts you can give your child. Material things are a poor substitute for and run a distant second to the positive energy, attention and time so desperately needed by your child. To bask in the comfort of your love and to receive support and wisdom to address and resolve the plethora of challenges she meets are what she wants most. Giving of yourself provides a spiritual dimension to your relationship with your child that nothing else can. The soul of your child will feel and respond to your love. It is instinctive; it is automatic. In Littleton, Colorado, following the disaster at Columbine High School, police officers found Eric Harris' automobile parked in the student parking lot. Only weeks old, the shiny, new black BMW his parents had given him still had the new-car smell. As the officers closed in on the car, they realized it was completely wired with explosives! Children do not want toys, they want their parents' love. Remember that.

Lorraine, from the previous chapter, didn't even want her parents' toys—the dogs and horses that overfilled their lives. She only wished they'd given her the love they exhibited in countless ways for their beloved animals. And Josi seemed to recognize the strings attached to receiving her father's love. He could not free himself of his toys of heroin and cocaine; so, in a perverse twist, decided he could prove his love to her if she agreed to overdose together. Again, children merely want good, pure, unattached, unconditional, freely-given, abundant love! In spite of how it seems sometimes, *love* is the only "demand" they make of us.

As a parent you know that satisfying the emotional needs of children is taxing and time-consuming. There is no shortcut, nor is there any reasonable alternative. From one acorn a mighty oak grows. Plant that "acorn," nourish it, love it, praise it, help it back to an upright position when it stumbles, be there when it needs you, and watch that acorn—your child—become a mighty oak, able to pass on the love she received from you, and able to bless and enrich the lives of others. If you fail to satisfy your child's emotional needs, then teachers and other professionals or agencies—social workers, psychologists, probation officers, courts—might eventually take up the slack and try to fill the "holes" that began at home.

The energy, attention and time you spend fully and completely satisfying your child's constellation of needs must be driven by your love in order to be a joyful and successful parenting experience. Without love, the result is a chronically upset, unhappy, difficult and perplexing kid who seems deliberately to do everything he can to make life a beast for you. If you don't want a problem kid, don't be a problem parent. Do it with love.

Sometimes parents feel suffocated by their child's over-whelming needs. "Life is passing me by and I can hardly take care of my own needs," said one parent at a workshop I conducted. Effective parenting will not leave you feeling robbed and cheated, if your parenting goals and your personal needs and desires are not in conflict. That is, they can be integrated together. With some resourcefulness, you can usually find ways of handling your personal responsibilities and needs in ways that do not impede your ability to "be there" for your child or otherwise compromise the quality of energy, attention, and time you give her. Your resourcefulness will bring you results.

My wife and I have three sons aged eight, five and three. The two oldest are in AYSO (American Youth Soccer Organization). Their practice schedules are not only on different days but also at different times. My oldest son's coach used to schedule practices on Tuesdays and Thursdays at 5:00 p.m. Later, he kept the same days but changed the time to 5:30 p.m. My second son's coach insisted on practice at 4:00 p.m. on Fridays.

At first, the prospect of getting my second son to the soccer field at 4:00 p.m. looked highly doubtful. When the coach called to give me the information about the time and place, I informed her that, "Many parents are going to find it hard to make a four o'clock practice time. In my case, I have to drive an hour to be there, because I come from work, and then I pick up my soccer-playing five-year-old and his little brother from primary and pre-school located in a different city. Is five o'clock a possibility? I think that will be a much better time for not only me but also for other parents." The coach argued that "four o'clock was better for most parents, and I've already changed the schedule forty million times to satisfy everybody." I told her I would try my best to get my son there, but it really looked doubtful. I asked her if she really wanted to break the heart of a five-year-old boy who had been waiting months for the soccer season to start and was noticeably more frustrated when his older brother's practice schedule began three weeks earlier. She held firm on 4:00 p.m.

My wife and I had to be resourceful to solve this problem. She is a physician at a large medical center specializing in patient rehabilitation, and it is just about impossible for her to leave work early to accommodate the children's soccer practice schedule. As a director of child welfare and attendance for a school district, I have District Guidance hearings for expelled and transferred middle school students on Thursday afternoons. Also, I preside over the District Guidance hearings all day on Tuesdays for high school students.

We asked our sons' grandparents, my wife's parents, if they could help us out. Fortunately for us, they could. They drive our oldest son to his soccer practices on Tuesdays and Thursdays. On the same day as my second son's first soccer practice, my first son had a 1:00 p.m. appointment at his orthodontist. On Fridays, I do not conduct hearings in court or at the school district head-quarters, so, I took a half-day vacation that particular Friday, picked up my second and third sons from their primary and pre-school, then picked up my eldest son from public school, and arrived at the dentist's office with three boys, only one of whom was a dental patient.

The orthodontist was finished by 2:00 p.m., and with two hours to spare, we easily made the 4:00 p.m. soccer practice for my second son. His first game was the very next day and his team won 3-0. Right after the game, one of the parents said, "Can we schedule practice next week for five, because four is just too hard to make." Other parents began to agree and champion the idea. I didn't say anything, but decided to listen to see how the second flight of the very idea I had already broached was going to turn out. The coach turned around to all of us and said, "See, I've got a childcare problem. That's why four works better for me." I said, "Since we all come to soccer practice, as parents maybe we can help you out with your childcare. I have no problem with bringing my son to practice, and while you coach, I can babysit your son." Instantly, other parents offered to sit for her little toddler and, just as instantly, we realized that the solution was ready-made. The coach agreed on a 5:00 p.m. practice time, and we all agreed, "Everybody wins here. She gets good babysitters and we get a more reasonable practice time."

In this story the theme that stands out—expressed by my son's soccer coach—was her steadfast commitment to *her* child. The 4:00 p.m. soccer practice schedule was arranged because she had a childcare problem, not because "40 million" parents wanted a 4:00 p.m. practice time. As a parent, you have to be just as selfish—stubborn even—and make a full commitment to your child. And having made that commitment to her own child, my son's soccer coach would not or could not consider other resources. We, as parents of other soccer tots, had to be resourceful and negotiate. Thus, we honored our commitment to our own children as well, by being willing to help the coach solve her babysitting problem. Undoubtedly, it hadn't occurred to her to ask other soccer dads and moms to help her out by babysitting.

Your children need you every year of their lives. Of course, as they grow older, you will have more time to begin or resume activities and events you put on hold because your child required most of your time. Those activities—exercising, reading, picking up the violin, hiking, traveling—you will again have time for and can begin anew. But remember, you are still a parent; your child is older but she is still growing emotionally. Enjoy yourself as you "dust off" your past pursuits and pleasures; don't forget, though, you have to be "on call" for your child, too. The E.A.T. Formula (energy, attention, time) works best when your child's developmental needs are the critical mass around which your own rotates. So, keep in mind that her needs define the balance between your personal objectives and your parenting desires. It could turn out that your teenager demands an inordinate amount of time and makes you wonder, "Why don't you just grow up!" You may find it hard to "shift gears," as in prior years, but your child is not out of line. She is merely expressing an age-appropriate need for your attention. By responding, you fortify her emotional growth. Far from being out of line, Josi's very strange question to her mother (demanding why she never offered to prove her love in the "weird" manner suggested by her father) was her signal to the woman that she needed her attention.

As you might imagine, the children in my research study had shattered and ugly lives. Like unguided missiles, they were destined to crash. But they were other peoples' children. You have your own child with her own needs. It is key critical that you understand the root-causes of your child's internal unhappiness. If you understand the inner environment, the outward behavior will become clear. The expression "no pain, no gain" actually began with an older generation of parents who felt that a few scrapes and bruises and disappointments along the way never hurt any child but actually toughened her up.

The generation of parents that spawned the "Baby Boomers" were generally advocates of that archaic philosophy, "Spare the rod and spoil the child." For that generation, it wasn't as prevalent to encourage a child to express his feelings in words. It was often considered "unmanly" for a father to let his son cry for a prolonged time or to pick up the bawling boy and hug and talk to him to console him. The Baby Boom generation ushered in the era of "Mr. Mom"—a father who loves to parent his children, bathe them, change their diapers, and even rearrange his work schedule to spend more time at home with them. Equally important, the Baby Boom generation was responsible for the view that male children ought to use their vocabularies to express their feelings. Baby Boomers also championed the philosophy: "If it makes your child unhappy, ask yourself if it is truly necessary."

Young children are saplings unable to reach the heights of the towering oaks of mature judgment. Simply stated, children lack sound and mature judgment; after all, they are just children. And children whose special emotional needs delay or prevent their healthy development often misidentify the abuse and mistreatment they suffer at the hands of their misdirected, uninformed parents, as an ideal state in which to be. Thus, children who are habitually made to feel sad move not only toward the expectation of sadness but also seek sadness as a way to feel totally loved.

When parents can stand outside the dark den of their own problems and shine a light on their child's needs, then that child has a much better chance of finding fulfillment and thriving in the love of those parents than when they stumbling around, dazed, confused, angry, and depressed—as dysfunctional as the child. Your daily life as a parent is filled with choices. Problems too. But it is the choices you make that increase your skill and effectiveness at accommodating your child's needs. Whatever you have to do to rearrange your life, to make more space in it for your child, then you should do that. Take special care in choosing, however. If you make a bad choice, unexpected harm might result. It's like the old adage, "Practice makes perfect." That's not quite true. *Perfect practice makes perfect.* If you're making bad choices (practicing *imperfectly*), then your goal is to recognize that problem and evaluate your criteria for making choices. Then change the one criterion, or even all the criteria, as necessary. You will find that the outcome will change as a result.

# Do More Than Say 'I Love You,' Show It

*We dug the hole and Henry poured gasoline over him and set him on fire so he couldn't be identified.*—Pamela

Pamela and I sat in the dining room. Empty, except for the two of us, it was huge and felt like an arena. It was clean and the ancient, off-white linoleum floor gleamed. Indelible scuff-marks from thousands of shoes scattered in veined patterns across the floor, and made a peculiar graffiti beneath the morning sun. She sat motionless at my table, directly across from me, and watched intently. Something about her manner, or a certain lack of it, told me that she was accustomed to waiting. A wistful smile played across her face as I checked the battery light on one tape recorder, then turned to check the volume control on the other. Her eyes followed my motions, tracking my hands as they glided from the one machine to the next. Satisfied, I looked up. She smiled.

Pamela said she wanted to tell me the whole story of her life, her home and family, her school and friends, all the personal details, and the march of events that led up to her *commitment offense*—the Department of the Youth Authority's soft euphemism for the hard crime of homicide. We both took a deep breath, smelling the heavy odor of stale, greasy food and Pine-Sol.

201

"I am an example of a kid who comes from a 'loser' family and beat the odds for a long time, before they started beating me back," Pamela explained. I asked her what she meant by "loser family." "My mother's best friend died suddenly," she begins. "She lived with us for years and suddenly she was gone. I missed her, too, but not as bad as my mother did. For me, she was like a dad: she took me places, played ball with me, and got me into soccer." She paused and inhaled deeply. "But for my mother, she was really a close, personal friend. My mother cried for a long time, longer than when her mother died. Then she went to being angry or real moody all the time. You'd never know from day to day. It wasn't until when I got older that I realized that, uh, Helen, uh, you know, served as the man in my mother's life. She was her friend and lover." I asked her why she thought that. "Well, after Helen died, I began to put two and two together. For one thing, my mother used to always tell me my father was dead. One day I was walking past her bedroom and I heard her on the telephone. She was very angry and telling somebody that he better send the check for my support or she'd have him arrested."

Pamela's awakening continued for many months following her mother's best friend's death. "I realized that the little oddities about my mother were because of her own personal conflicts. I don't think she knew who or what she really was or wanted to be. She always seemed tense or afraid. She'd have men come over, and I've got a brother and two sisters—by the way, we all had different fathers—but it was like she was putting on an act. And besides, it seemed like she was the angriest around men. And most of them stopped coming around. They were attracted to her, but once they got inside the house, I think her attitude and behavior really insulted them. When I saw the elaborate arrangements she made for Helen's funeral and the weekly visits to the gravesite to trim the grass and plant flowers around Helen's headstone, I figured that Helen must have been her lover."

Whatever the relationship between Pamela's mother and her best friend Helen, it seemed clear that Helen's death had a greater impact on Pamela than she realizes or cares to admit. Perhaps the impact was only indirect, but it was traumatic nonetheless; the supportive relationship provided Pamela as a result of the bond between her mother and Helen suddenly vanished. Pamela's mother grew more distant yet more demanding. When Pamela ran into some extreme difficulties, each time her mother was unforgiving. "I got raped by a guy who saw me walking and pulled his truck over to ask directions. When I gave them to him, he offered me a ride. I took it since his destination was on the way to where I was going. Well, he raped me right there in his truck. I ran all the way to my mother's job. She came out because they told her it was a family emergency. Well, right there on the spot, she told me never to interrupt her on her job for anything. I left feeling dirtier than ever. I mean, she treated me like I was pulling a holdup or something."

Pamela's childhood was further marred by continuous fights she had with her younger brothers and sisters. "They'd beat me up constantly, because they thought I was the favorite. I'd arrive at school with bruises all the time. Finally, the teachers called the social services department. I was taken to the principal's office where all these important-looking people were, and I had to answer questions about the bruises on me. Well, my mother and her sisters really got mad and told me that what's in the family stays in the family, and that I was really doing something bad by cooperating with the social services people."

Pamela just couldn't seem to do anything right at home. "When I got 95's, my mother wanted to know why I couldn't get 100's on the tests at school," she recalled. "And when I got 100's, she blamed the school for making things too easy for me. That lady—I mean my mother—just refused to be satisfied. Yet she never even met the wonderful teachers who desperately wanted me to succeed." Pamela said she just seemed to be the object for "everybody to use and push around." When her sister became pregnant, Pamela's mother forced her to take care of her sister's child. "That right there really threatened my schooling," she said. "But I loved the little baby, Oliver, so I decided if I had to stay up all night, I'd get my studying done." Pamela said her mother thought her sister needed to finish her high school education, a difficult feat when one has a child. "I took care of Oliver so much that I knew him perfectly. During recess, I'd call home and my sister would be all in a panic about him crying and being irritable.

So, I'd say, 'Does he have gas? Uh, check for how you're burping him. Is he coming down with a cold?' and stuff like that, because I knew if I was there he would be okay. His own mother was dumber than he was."

Pamela said that instead of life getting better for her, it got worse. "My sister got pregnant again. So now I had two kids to take care of. My grades were still 'A's' but I was weak all the time, couldn't try out for sports because something was always going on at home. One day, a male cousin came over to visit. When the babies were taking a nap, he tried, you know, to, well, force himself on me. I fought him off and he really got mad. I kept fighting and told him I was going to tell my mother. He ran off, angry. The thing is, I wouldn't tell my mother because I couldn't. He didn't know that, though."

Pamela, although very intelligent (from memory she quoted to me passages from Virgil, Shakespeare, and Homer) and on her way to a prestigious college, allowed herself to be coaxed into being an accessory to murder: Her ex-boyfriend persuaded her to help destroy the evidence—the body itself. He told Pamela that the slain man had sexually abused his girlfriend, who was Pamela's age. Pamela told me, "He really twisted my arm and kept telling me over and over about the guy who raped me and other guys who hurt and used me, and even mentioned my brother and sister who loved to beat up on me. Finally, I agreed when he told me that this was my chance to get even with every man who had ever done something bad to me." Pamela said she actually liked the person whose body she helped to ignite. She and others had spent a very pleasant afternoon with him just hours before his death.

Always when I met and interviewed her, Pamela described her passion for writing essays and entering short story contests. "I just got a reply from the sponsors of one contest," she eagerly told me. "I missed the deadline. The mail goes out so slowly from prison, I guess. But they told me they liked my story," she beamed. What she was especially proud of was the insight into herself that the required counseling was affording her. "Every-body was using me all my life, it seems," she announced. "My ex-boyfriend was a smooth one. He was actually telling me I was more *qualified*—because of all the bad things in my life—than I realized to help him and his new girlfriend kill her father, the poor man. He brainwashed me, pushed me over the edge, but I let him. I didn't have to do that. I also had a few people who were working to turn things around for me. Slowly but surely I was on my way to a prestigious college, thanks to some incredible teachers who went miles out of their way, so to speak, for me. And then, I blew everything in one afternoon of letting myself be used to do something illegal and immoral. I didn't kill that man. I helped set his body on fire. But in court my ex-boyfriend and his new girlfriend blamed everything on me."

It is difficult to say what exact combination of elements provides the sure "recipe" for a child to commit homicide. Obviously, bad conditions at home are risk factors that develop the temperament and personality of the child murderer or student terrorist. But what about the children who are abused who never commit any crime at all, much less murder? And the children who live their whole lives in dysfunctional families, and emerge from them as law-abiding persons with successful families? And the children who have siblings on their way to prison but who themselves are headed for the university? The variety and complexity of cases are confounding. But there are things you can do to both reduce the risk to your children and demonstrate your love.

First among these must be your commitment to your child. Undoubtedly, you love your child dearly. But in the same manner that I adopted the child's "voice" in the "commandments" of chapter 10, may I suggest the following vow as a guide to the commitment of demonstrating parental love for a child.

### My Child, My Life: My Vow to Always Love You

*I am your parent, you are my child, and I vow, as of this moment and until time is no more, to love you. You are the best part of me. I hold you, hug you, touch you, teach you, and shine my eyes upon you in love.*

*With patience, I joyfully share my strength with you. With kindness and praise, I show you right from wrong, good from bad. When you fall, I gently pick you up and the feather of my kiss brushes your tears away. The rhythm of our hearts is the beat of our love. It is with pride that I am your model of gentleness, your mirror of sensitivity. I am the grownup you will become. You are my joy and it is with total love that I touch and teach you, guide and lead you.*

*My life is complete happiness because you are in it, at the center of it. It makes me sad to leave you, and I rejoice when we reunite. For you I must, and will always be, the sum of patience, the temple of goodness, the soft winds and silent springs of compassion. Your life makes mine meaningful.*

*We are one with this gift called Life, and heirs to the blessings of our grand and glorious Universe, which is filled with abundance. I will teach you to desire only good from the Universe and give only good back to it. You will learn the importance of sharing the blessings the Universe pours upon you. I will teach you to never look back upon yesterday, nor pine away for tomorrow. You will learn that virtue comes from being thankful for the nowness that is today, for it is the gift we call The Present.*

*I promise you a home in which your spirits will lift you to newer and greater heights and where you are free to dream and express the full palette of your talents on the canvas of your personality. I will show you how your desire gives you the energy of angels, and you will learn to soar with your enthusiasm. I will show you how to live well—with hope and vision, the confidence to climb any mountain, the trust to reach out and touch. You will learn to help others with a heart that heals.*

*I will teach you to love life fully, give to others generously and let your light shine. Perfect love replaces fear, and you will learn how to greet each day with love, salute the Universe with joy and thanksgiving, and to let the quiet night comfort your soul.*

*I will teach you to see and to focus upon your goals with a single-mindedness. You will learn how to gain strength from obstacles. You will know how to dream and live in the theater of your mind and act on the stage of your imagination.*

*You will gladly and graciously meet others and find that they, too, are to be respected, valued, cherished and loved. You will learn not to judge.*

*You will learn that the mind is a great source of strength, that love is the root of your character, and that life is filled with goodness. I promise to let your talents guide, cheer and support you, for that which you love is where your heart is, and where your heart is, there you will thrive. Through peace, you will learn to negotiate; through love, to communicate; and through respect, to articulate. For by giving to others what they need, you thus build the bridge to what you need. Thinking of others is a virtue you will always value. You will learn that laughter is often the best medicine. I promise you days filled with laughter and learning so that your sleep will be filled with dreams of joy. Life is not a lullaby, but you will know that your humor is a music that gives life flavor.*

*You are an important, vital member of our family, a very necessary member of the human race. You help to make family and community strong. From this moment on, until time is no more, I promise to love you.*

*Thank you for helping to show me what the truest treasure in life really is.*

There are clear and definable things that parents can do to show their love once they have made an earnest and steadfast commitment to their child. Diligence in teaching and maintaining these principles will go far in reducing your child's risk.

**Teach Independence**

In Pamela's case, it could well be that, on her own, she might have never been involved in anything close to homicide. However, under the unrelenting influence of another person, anything became possible. As you reflect on Pamela, one lesson to learn is that your child must not only be taught to be a good, peaceful, nonviolent, law-abiding, caring, and a contributing member of society, she must also be taught to be *independent* and *free from the influences of others.* Your goal is to "build" a healthy, happy, generous, caring, and loving individual who, whether by herself or in the presence of others, knows the right thing to do *and* does it—at all times! You can never over-emphasize to your child the safety of learning to set her own sails, think with her own brain, and march to the beat of her own drum. This does not mean she will turn into a selfish, isolated, eccentric human being. It merely means that she will be learning and practicing the elements of *responsibility,* as well as common sense. An essential component of her learning responsibility is how you yourself model your beliefs and behaviors at home. Your very actions become part of the "stage" on which your child tries out and finds her own voice. If the stage is strong, she will find all the support she needs. That support will make her a knowledge-able and competent leader, instead of an ignorant, incompetent follower.

**Embrace a System of Moral Beliefs**

The process of building good children with leadership qualities can be compared to cultivating good soil for a garden. Soil preparation is based on knowledge and beliefs about soil health and vitality. Likewise, cultivating a successful family must be based on your knowledge and beliefs, whether they be spiritual or philosophical (non-religious/secular). A healthy, high-yield garden is energized and achieved by the additives that are used to grow it. A healthy, productive family is energized, enriched, and realized only by your carefully selecting the right "additives" to "grow" such a family.

Is there only *one* system of beliefs that always produces the right "additives?" No, there are families that are hugely successful but have neither an avowed religious belief nor affiliation with any house of worship. Conversely, there are families that profess a religious belief but are troubled, alienated, confused, unproduc-tive, and anything but law-abiding. Some raise the point that many of the wars in history were "holy wars"—an oxymoron for the bloodbaths orchestrated by the religious leaders of the day. Accordingly, this fact seems clear: One need not be religious or profess a belief in a supreme being to be a good, wholesome, moral, ethical, unselfish, caring, and enlightened person.

There are many routes, and people take many different roads to the "mountain" of Truth. After they arrive, the view from the top is the same for all of them. In other words, there are a variety of beliefs that have the right "additives" for producing the view necessary for growing a healthy, happy, productive family. The destination can be arrived at from either religious or non-religious roads. Perhaps to clear up any confusion about what *is* the "best" religion for imparting ethical or moral beliefs, the answer may lie in this commentary by world-renowned singer and pastor, the Reverend O.C. Smith: "The best religion is the one you practice."

Considering that this nation originated as a country of deeply-held religious convictions and a nation that encouraged the pursuit and embrace of spiritual ideals, Reverend O.C. Smith's statement is truly compelling. It is understandable, then, that there are those who caution that it is the absence of practicing religious, philosophical, ethical, moral convictions which has produced killer-kids (*made in the USA*) and has rendered this nation especially vulnerable to its youngest inhabitants. It may serve us well to be reminded that the absence of vital additives in your garden will inevitably produce killer weeds which overpopulate and choke off the healthy life struggling to emerge.

Some people believe that the healthy life of a child is more a byproduct of her being guided by her internal "moral compass" and less a result of their (or their family's) practice of religion. Others insist that morality has nothing to do with rearing healthy, caring, peace-loving children, but rather, it is a child's awareness and acceptance of the virtues of respecting others and treating them as she herself would like to be treated that makes the difference between a child's success or failure, her living or dying. Still, there are others who argue that it is one's belief in and respect for the laws of the land that compel one to conform to socially-accepted norms of behavior. For those of you who choose to align yourself with an organized religious body, or pursue a spiritual quest, you may find certain advantages in these goals. For those of you for whom a supreme being is not a reality, and religion is not the answer, you may also find certain advantages in your adherence to this point of view.

So, you may consider yourself a religious person and your next-door neighbor a non-religious person, but there may be little significance in this when it come to behavior. What *is* significant is that your *and* your neighbor's actions be the same. You must both teach your child respect and reverence for life, a passion for treating others as she would like to be treated herself, and the virtues of doing good social works.

It does not matter whether one's successful family and their good works are the products of a belief in a supreme being, the chanting of mantras, or the daily repetition of affirmations. What matters is the kind and quality of child produced by that family and the good he is prepared to render to society. For as its children go, so goes society. At this particular time in our nation's history, the gun death rate among U.S. children 14 and younger is nearly 12 times higher than the combined rate in 25 other industrial nations. Such statistics give an entirely new meaning to the saying: "And a little child shall lead them." And as far as what religion or other belief system to instill in children, it is, arguably, less important to pass along the mantle of religion than it is to show your child she is consistently and unconditionally loved. For among youth 10 to 19 years old, there were 1,308 suicides with guns—more than three a day. For adolescents, suicide is the highest form of self-criticism. *Only a loveless child can take the one-way route that leads her to achieve her own destruction by her own hand.*

**Play & Exercise as a Family**
Taking an active hand in getting in shape and keeping fit as a family will produce dividends for you. Whether you go out for evening walks, bike rides, or stumble and fall from your in-line skates (rollerblades), the time you're spending together is golden. It allows you to talk, laugh, play and create memories as you go. And you're creating your own fun, not having it served up to you by any entertainment medium. Moreover, everybody in the family is getting some exercise, and that's a health benefit. The *key* benefit, here, is that you're being a good role model. Children do as they see their parents do. Your interest in and desire for exercising as a family, and having fun at the same time, will mean a lot to your child. They will regard exercise and fitness as a natural part of life. The National Association for Sport and Physical Education (NASPE) publishes a free pamphlet entitled, "99 Tips for Family Fitness Fun." It is filled with informative

and innovative suggestions. To obtain it, send a legal-size, self-addressed envelope with .55 cents postage to NASPE, 1900 Association Drive, Reston, VA 20191.

The younger the child is when she becomes involved in physical activity, the more likely she will continue it as an important activity in her everyday life. A ride in the jogging stroller, a "baby ducks" swim program, or a mommy-and-me gymnastics program are all great ways to begin. As your child gets older and begins school, the family activities you do together do not have to be pegged to a rigid framework for the whole family to gain benefits. Simple activities like gardening, bowling, biking, family photo album organizing, or an occasional picnic are fine. The key is family togetherness. There is a special dimension at work here, as well. Whatever you call it—"down time," "free time," or "kickin' back"—time spent and enjoyed together as a family engaged in physical activity provides the family a chance to release tension. As we saw, Pamela did not have this kind of family. She was essentially a slave to the various and sundry wishes of others in her family. Thus "conditioned," she became easily manipulated by those outside it.

### Support & Encourage Your Child's Exracurrilcular Activities

In the modern world of the two-income family, attending games and other school-related activities may be difficult for many parents. But more and more parents are making the effort to be on the sidelines to cheer their child on to victory. When you're there at your child's event, your presence tells her that she is important to you, that she is the most essential item on your busy schedule. Leaving your own world for a few hours to spend some time in the world of your child produces a great bonus: it opens an avenue for better communication. If you ask your child, "How was your day today?" she may seldom answer, or answer ambiguously (my oldest son used to always say, "I forgot"). But when you attend your teenager's athletic event, music recital, or a drama presentation, then you have something real to talk about. And you will get feedback from your child, instead of some hurriedly mumbled, "I don't know."

If your child is not involved in any sports or extra-curricular activities, persuade her to become involved. Research shows that teenage girls who volunteer in community-service projects or who are involved in athletics are less likely to become pregnant than girls who are not involved in athletics or social service projects that help others. Experts say that involvement in social service and athletics raises self-esteem, something that aids girls in making choices that are essential to long-range planning. Pamela—though there were certainly many contributing factors to her commitment offense—was clearly not the beneficiary of involvement in community service activities that encouraged her to *reach out* and help others. Since she was neither active in community services nor involved in athletic activities, she missed out on learning the right kind of teamwork and experiencing the joys of individual and group achievement—a lost opportunity that might have tempered her otherwise fractured psyche.

**Assign Achievable Tasks**

As a parent, you will constantly revise and refine your relationship with your child to achieve the kind of teamwork to which provides healthy companionship and honest communication. Build your relationship with your child on trust and respect. Yes, you must deliberately do it or it simply won't happen. That means that you must require your child to earn your trust, to deserve your respect. Give her special projects at home. When she completes them to your satisfaction, let her know she did a good job and that you are pleased. And whenever these projects are not completed satisfactorily, tell her where the "holes" are. In this way, she will learn one of life's most valuable lessons: how to do a job right. Chores around the house can be divided into smaller tasks that lend themselves to teaching responsibility. Whether it's folding clothes, setting the table for meals, learning to cook, gardening, or preparing the grocery list, these provide wonderful opportunities for your child not only to earn your trust but also to respect the fact that tasks assigned to her must be completed according to your standards.

Tasks are especially effective tools for teaching responsibility. "Responsible" means being *able to respond*. That can only occur if your child (1) knows how to do the task, and (2) understands toward what standards her efforts must be directed. Thus, she is able to respond; for you have identified the task, shown her how to do it, and informed her of the standard she must meet in completing the task. If you set no standards, then do not be surprised if the completed work is sloppy, late, or only partially done. The standards you set, then, must include quality (how *well* the job must be done), time (*when* the job must be completed), and totality (how *much* or *little* of the job you will accept). Soon, your child will have enough proficiency and skill to acquire part-time or summer jobs and earn her own money. Her resultant sense of accomplishment—that began from her first jobs around the house—is the truest form of self-esteem. She has demonstrated that she can do *real* work, earn *real* trust, and make *real* money.

When your child begins to date, drive a car, or leaves for college or university, you can rest assured that the lessons in trust and respect, which began with small tasks at home, will guide her in her social encounters and life challenges. You will not need to worry. Her sense of ethics and responsibility will prevent and protect her from disappointing you or, as many teens today say, "letting mom and dad down." Children appreciate parents teaching them the values associated with right and wrong behavior. As they mature, they begin to realize that while they are behaving "right" for you they are the ones who reap the benefits. Eventually they understand that responsible behavior coupled with right choices gives them personal power and control over life situations that many of their peers lack. Teach your child personal responsibility and she will be an effective problem-solver in later life.

If your child has demonstrated continuous success in completing her tasks according to your standards, use her work habits as "capital" with which she can acquire the latest fashion accessories that seem to be so mandatory for the young set. It's easy to run up a bill of two hundred dollars for the latest fashion items. Not to worry. Simply buy her a couple of items she wants and get her agreement to help you with the tile-setting or windows or laundry for the next several weeks. Such bartering is an effective "win-win" for both of you. She gets the clothes she wants, and you get some valuable assistance with the household chores.

How much "response" is your child "able" to make? You'll have to experiment by trial and error to arrive at a good sense of how much responsibility to give her. If you give your teen too much responsibility and it doesn't work—she "flaked out" or you weren't around enough to shepherd her to success—that doesn't mean you failed. It merely means that the timing was not right. Maybe a few months down the road, she will be perfectly ready to assume that much responsibility. In the meantime, "baby step" your way to success with this one. That means break down each task or project into manageable "taskettes" so that a phase of the task can be done and a sense of accomplishment can still be attained by your child.

My oldest son (8 years old) knows that he has to read 25 pages of new material every evening. He can pick the book, or my wife and I can choose it. He began reading the Paul Bunyan series but "flaked out" a couple of evenings in a row. My wife astutely observed that the book itself contained over 200 pages, and perhaps its sheer volume was "psyching" him out and discouraging him. So, she bought him a half-dozen chapter-books. These are books with no more than 25 pages. The stories they contain are complete, with a beginning, middle, and end, as well as plot and theme. As you might have guessed, he took to these chapter books instantly. He achieved the standard of 25 pages a night, which for him is an *entire* book! His renewed joy in reading is equaled only by his increased self-esteem. He eagerly chows down an entire book every evening.

If, on the other hand, your child deliberately does not meet the standard that you have set and to which she has agreed, apply the consequences but in a non-emotional way. Emotion driven punishment may make you feel good and righteous, but the only thing your child will remember is the guilt. If your child breaks her curfew by a couple of hours, give her a couple of hours of tasks the following day. Explain that you lost hours of sleep worrying about her the night before. Remove the emotion from the punishment and delete power from the issue. It's not about who has the most power. It's about your child learning to be responsible. Your teen is less likely to resent you if the punishment (consequences) is framed in a logical manner. "I lost two hours of sleep last night staying up and worrying about you. The clothes still have to be washed, and I don't have the time, so I'd like you to spend a couple of hours doing it" sounds so much better than "You gave me your word! Doesn't that mean anything to you and your crowd anymore? I'm really disappointed in you. It's like you just said you'd be home by twelve just to get rid of me! Who's the boss here anyway?!"

You can also serve your child by helping her set clear, attainable objectives. Thus, she will develop the habit of seeing into the future. Once she has attained an objective, the child learns she can achieve and acquire more confidence in making new objectives. The future need not be bleak, confusing, or something to fear. The key is to have clear-cut, easily defined objectives for charting the future.

Part of both the wonder and weirdness of life is that it is so competitive. Darwin believed that only the strongest survive. Today, however, the *smartest* thrive. Teach your child to think about her objectives, set them, and then go after them. Practice in setting and attaining objectives will give your child a head start. Getting good grades should be a primary objective for your child. Show her various ways to achieve this objective. Let her know that you are as interested in *how* she meets the objective as you are in *whether* she meets it.

For example, in helping your child attain and maintain good grades, you may wish to discuss a range of options she may chose from and then make up a "contract" to incorporate her choices. The contract could cover, but not be restricted to, limitations on television watching, visiting the local library regularly each week, investing in and using a computer, tutoring and practicing tests at home, consistent homework help from mom or dad, rewards and treats for maintaining good study habits at home, allowing you to inspect the quantity and quality of homework, and purchasing supplemental books and other materials. Maintain a checklist of the options used or completed. Tell your child she is on her own honor for signing this checklist and checking off the option completed. Honestly completed checklists should later lead to improved academic performance and ultimately to proper behavior.

Despite Paul's harsh views—a sampling of which we saw in Chapter 2—this former high school dropout completed both high school *and* the requirements for a Baccalaureate degree from LaVerne University. How? He followed a contract that required him to "sign-off"—write his name on the checklist every time he completed an agreed-upon objective necessary to achieve his educational dream.

## Spirituality: Lighting the Flame

Responsibility may also have potential roots in other relationships besides the one you create with your child. A highly significant number of effective teenagers apparently have a strong commitment to and relationship with their Creator. A remarkable *New York Times*/CBS News poll surveyed 1,048 teenagers. Ninety-four percent of the respondents said they believe in God. Michael O'Donnell, Ph.D., president of the International Family Life Institute in Rochester Hills, Michigan, surveyed 4,000 teenagers across the nation and found that the effective and high-achieving teens in his survey credited a higher power for their strength and peace of mind. Further, families who attended church, in more cases, had children who demonstrated higher levels of emotional wellness than did children who came from families who did not attend church together.

As a parent, only you can light that spiritual flame which will keep your child on solid ground. You must decide how you will nurture your child spiritually. An advantage of selecting a house of worship is echoed in the old adage: "It takes a village to raise a child." An organized spiritual group creates a network for your child of like-minded people who share your views, live your values. However, if you were to choose not to align yourself with a house of worship, be vigilant in seeing to the specific spiritual nature and character of your child. Nurturing these creates a child capable of empathy and compassion.

Of the 103 children I interviewed, 70 were attending church in prison or seeking spiritual counseling. These 70 professed a complete transformation in their lives as a result of attending church regularly and having a spiritual leader on whom they could call and seek counsel. Most of my 103 respondents claimed to have had no real religious background at the time they committed homicide. Despite frequent complaints about the juvenile prison system nationwide, these institutions excel in at least one area: recognizing a marked lack of spiritual and moral direction in these children's lives. That individual pastoral and spiritual counseling are available and that the prisons have places of worship on their grounds, is a tribute both to the juvenile prison system itself and to the children who told me their lives have changed for the better as a result. Charity, whom we met in Chapter 3, told me, "I have learned so much about love and giving; and I even think my parents are seeing a different me. They are still very much hurt by what I did, but at least they are *both* coming to visit me, something they didn't do before. I know I can still have a good life. I never believed that before."

**Family Governance**

I grew up in a family that made and enforced inflexible rules. How I chafed under that regime. There is a place for rules, and rules for a particular place. I do not believe that running a family ought to be a military affair. Unbending, tight, and overly-restrictive rules will not work with teenagers. The obedient "yes, mommy" and "yes, daddy" that parents think they hear only when they angrily declare martial law, can still be had if mommy and daddy would relax and realize that home is not occupied territory inside a military zone. All the rules parents make up still will not shelter children from the real world. Indeed, harsh and overly-restrictive rules can have the effect of making the taboo behavior more tantalizing.

As a parent of a teen, you don't have a lot of control over your child. However, you do have influence. So, take off your parent-as-manager hat and put on your parent-as-consultant hat. Give your teenager guidelines for her behavior and be willing to negotiate. Make a bigger deal about the decision-making skills you want to teach her than about vague, desperate rules like: "And don't drink any alcohol at all unless it comes from your own refrigerator in your dorm room." (A rule intended to keep your child from accepting drinks—advances—from strangers in swanky bars.) But what if she buys the alcoholic drink herself at the bar? Since the drink didn't come directly from her own refrigerator at home, has she broken your rule? It is questions like this that mandate negotiation between you and your child. A solution could very well be that she buy her own drinks at the bar or restaurant, rather than agree to a new male acquaintance shouting, "I'll be back; going to get us a couple of brewskis." The brewski could be laced with a controlled substance, such as Rohypnol, which is known as the "date rape" drug. So, be less passionate about the rule and more zealous about your child having the knowledge and social skills that will serve her like loyal foot soldiers each and every time.

## The Honest Child Has a Honed Mind

The honest child's honor produces a honed mind. This is as true as the law of gravity. As early as middle school, children are confronted with various choices that are as dizzying as they are numerous. It is impossible for parents to always be there to shelter their children. How will your child survive in such an environment? She can survive very well, indeed. To the extent that she knows what her values are, and if she has been taught since her toddler days that it is okay to stand up for her values, she won't succumb to peer pressure as easily as kids who have no values. I'm reminded of Louis Carroll's *Alice in Wonderland*, in which Alice is asked, "Where do you want to go?" She answers, "I don't know." The response to this is, "Then anywhere will do." As a parent, you know that anywhere will *not* do. Therefore, you must teach your child honesty and integrity. These values will guide the direction of her life. She will know precisely where she wants to go. And—unlike Alice in Wonderland—she *will* get there.

Begin teaching the values of honesty and integrity at home by asking your child to name some people she knows who are honest and have integrity. Tell your child about a time when you upheld a moral principle even though nobody agreed with you and it was tough to do, but you believed it was the right thing to do and you did it. Be your child's model of honesty and integrity.

Say what you mean and mean what you say. Treat others fairly, properly, and graciously. The cliché is true: "Example is the greatest teacher."

## Talking & Listening to Your Child

It cannot be overstated or too often mentioned that one of the critical keys is talking and listening to your child. Develop the habit of taking a few minutes daily to ask your child about her school day. To spark the conversation, notice something about her—a new pair of shoes, a new haircut, a new book, a new friend. Teenagers whose parents "check in" with them this way tend to talk to their parents more. They appreciate that their parents are "there" all the time. Even if you are not interested in discussing your child's day, do so anyway. Act like you are interested instead of tired, upset or bored. The interest you give your child will pay you both handsome dividends: She will turn to you as a matter of habit when tough issues occur and she needs a true friend and caring listener. Who better than you? And you win because your countless "check-ins" will have produced a conditioned response—you won't have to worry about whether she will turn to you in her time of need.

Approach every conversation with your child as though it is a concert. Listen to the "music" flow from your child and you will be informed, eventually, of what her problems are. Stifle any urge to "tell her a thing or two." Timing is everything, and this is the time to let her talk. Once she gets used to your letting her, your child will tell you much that you did not know. Eventually, she will come to you first and disclose her problems. There is no set time for any of this to occur. Spend some time every day talking with your child; that much you owe her. Let her see a different side of you other than the parenting side of giving orders, expressing anger or disappointment, or setting limits. When you talk to your child, that is the time for you to learn.

The key to showing interest is in how well you listen. Be the most interested parent and the best listener that you know how to be. Without a doubt, your child will soon know it, too.

In conclusion, I am grateful and I feel privileged to have been allowed by the State of California to repeatedly interview, for a period of four years, children incarcerated in state juvenile prisons for committing homicide. These kids told me precisely the reasons why they killed. They tracked the trail for me from their life at home to life in prison. What they told me about their tattered life histories corresponds to what other researchers know about kids who kill—the seeds of their destructive and heinous acts are usually sown right at home. It is at home where many of them saw brutality, torture and abuse inflicted on their mothers and sisters and themselves by fathers, brothers, boyfriends, and lovers.

These children also witnessed assaults on people in their neighborhoods. It was as though they had been rocked and cradled in a culture of violence. When these kids resorted to violence, this response had been so inbred in them that they became, indeed, accidents waiting to happen and bombs waiting to explode: Natural-born killers. The reasons behind their capital crimes also apply to Kip Kinkel, Eric Harris, Dylan Klebold and to scores of other children whose killing sprees have instantly disgraced their schools and made famous their communities. Ultimately, whether by overt abuse or emotional neglect, youth aggression and violence branch out from root causes found in these "soils:" loneliness, isolation, alienation, parental indifference, low self-worth, depression, and anger.

Like it or not, we must face the fact that when children kill, that act is their desperate reaction and response to what is going on at home. Children kill because one or more adults in their lives at home has killed their souls through a variety of harmful acts, be it physical, sexual, or verbal abuse, the inability or unwillingness to change harmful home atmospheres or environments, or chronic and painful indifference to their plights. Suppressive, knee-jerk reactions in the wake of a campus shooting often lead to cosmetic improvements in school safety. Indeed, it would be difficult for a school to explain why it chose *not* to install metal detectors, a spate of video cameras, or increase the size of its school security force after a campus killing. But in most cases, these are merely hurriedly adopted strategies-after-the-fact. But even these must be matched by safety measures instigated in homes.

Indeed, the ultimate strategy for saving children's lives is to find out what is happening in their homes which causes them to be depressed, alienated, isolated, lonely, angry, aggressive, anti-social, and violent. Increasing the number of Parent Education programs must be given high-priority status as well as the marketing of those programs to parents in dire need of them. Parent Education programs must be marketed like the World War II War Bond campaigns, the national cry for small pox, typhus and rubella immunization, and the country's various anti-drug and safe-sex crusades. Affluent homes in America's tranquil-appearing suburbs are as much in desperate need of Parent Education programs as are poor homes in America's impoverished, police-packed inner cities. When we have safer homes, we will have safer schools. Like inhaling and exhaling, one will happen only *after* the other takes place. Only safer homes will provide the foundation for safer schools to build a safer society.

Of course, parents can grow ragged trying to figure out a child, and sometimes feel like giving up in disgust. Parents, in a constant search of answers, have often spent unrecoverable hours, days, weeks, months, and years trying various and sundry approaches to help their child "get well." Yet researchers continue to emphasize the importance of the healing quality of the parent's *own* voice in helping the child through personal crises and challenges. My recommendation is that you, as a parent, get in touch and in tune with your child and share your love through your voice, its inflection, your vocabulary, your words of love, and speech that is drenched in patience.

And once you have gotten in tune with your child through your words and voice, listen carefully, letting your child know, through your "uh-hmms" and other non-verbal responses that you are listening and understanding. Bite your tongue whenever you feel the need to edit, evaluate, interpret, or invalidate what your child is telling you. If you do any of that, you effectively stifle the flow of communication; it's just as if you placed your foot over a small gusher in your grass. The "return flow"—back pressure—is felt through the plumbing and, if you had a stethoscope, you would be able to hear the pipe vibrate. Whether you like what you are hearing or the way your child is saying it, do not indicate, through your facial expression or critical comments, your *dislike* or non-acceptance. Children who are listened to eventually come out of their shells, face their demons and conquer them, overcoming their neuroses. In other words, they heal themselves. Their problems vanish in the flow of communication much in the same way dirt and debris vanish in the river that cleanses even as it moves.

If you can communicate with your child, and dedicate yourself to doing so regularly, you will never have thoughts of "My Child, My Enemy," nor will your child have thoughts of "My Parent, My Foe."

But what more can you do as a parent? One positive way to begin would be to recognize that adolescentcide (the killing of children by children) is the most deadly and threatening national phenomenon to have occurred since the horrid and hated child labor exploitation that existed at the turn of the 19th century. It is a social virus that puts all kids at risk. Dr. Deborah Prothrow-Stith, from the Harvard Medical School of Public Health, calls adolescentcide and other acts of juvenile violence a "public health problem." As a nation, we are ailing; we are not whole.

Every day seven teenagers and ten young adults are the victims of homicide. Homicide is the third leading cause of death for children ages 5 to 14 and is the second leading cause of death for adolescents and young people ages14 to 24. In a recent survey, 270,000 of the nation's 13-year olds stressed that a gun is their preferred "companion" for school every day. Adolescentcide is the national cancer killing our children today and imperiling our future like our war-time enemies of a bygone era never could.

With the nation's hourly death toll for youth homicide ringing at 0.54 homicides every 60 minutes, how many children would you estimate have died from acts of homicide in the time it has taken you to read this book? Although you have finished reading this book, the clock on juvenile homicide ticks on.

How can you, as a parent, do your part, fulfill your role to help heal this cancer of adolescent alienation, frustration, anger, depression, and hate? Because it is paramount, allow me to reiterate the critical fist step: Start by analyzing your own parenting behavior. Change what you're doing that's unproductive, negative, harmful, and simply ineffective. Revisit any part of this book—and other books you are hopefully studying on the topic—that caused you to think about your ways of parenting. It is imperative that we fix ourselves first. You might join a group dedicated to wiping out adolescentcide—like M.A.D.D. (Mothers Against Drunk Driving). Sometimes a group can be extremely effective and powerful on a national scale. But remember: The enemy is often within! Uniting with a support group is fine, but uniting with your child and family is the top priority. Children who kill are home-grown. They grow up among us, in our houses, sleep in our beds, eat food from our table, spend money from our purses. They age and develop right before our very eyes.

There is no way to keep your child from knowing about weapons, violence, and war. It's tragic to realize that even though we are a nation that is not currently at war with any foreign power, our own children have declared war on each other. In the words of William J. Bennett who served under Presidents Bush and Reagan as director of the Office of National Drug Control Policy and Secretary of Education, it is only early, twenty-first century America that can legitimately be called "history's most violent 'civilized' nation."

As a nation, we expended large amounts of time, money and effort preparing to meet the twenty-first century by immunizing our ubiquitous computerized technology systems against the notorious "Y2K Bug." However necessary that crusade might have been, the larger issue remains: How much time, money and effort are we—you and I, as parents—prepared to pour into the real Y2K's-Year 2000 Kids, who possess the power to change the course of American history forever in a devastating way we used to attribute only to THE BOMB? Only you can answer that question by the active role you play and the actions you take to stop adolescentcide.

It is the parents of this nation who have the only real power—through a renewal of their parental love—to refresh and rebuild the spirits of children too long alienated, isolated, abused, neglected, frustrated, sad, and very, very angry. These children are the little lambs whose final acts are to break their silence with deafening roars of gunfire in school shootings heard around the country.

Act now and save our children for, since they are at war, they cannot save themselves. Take a personal role and do your part in the nation's greatest rescue effort. Help rescue our children from the age we have helped them to create: The Age of Violence. In lending your heart and hands to the effort of saving our children, you do nothing less than work to recreate a kinder, gentler, more loving community, one where dreams may be realized, hope encouraged, and a generation of children will *live* to honor and love you for the peace you helped to ensure.

# End Notes

## Communication

1. Include your child in even sensitive, problematic or otherwise important family situations. Excluding him may breed feelings of resentment, distrust, and alienation. Ask your child how and what he feels. Honor and accept, don't "re-arrange," his feelings. Children who have constant, positive communication with their parents have better self-esteem than children who do not. You can talk so your child will listen to you and listen so you child will talk to you.
2. Let your child know that he can discuss anything with you. Strike a balance between the hours of watching television and the minutes of having a genuine conversation. Try reversing that: converse for hours, watch television for minutes. Listening to your child, rather than watching television, is one of the best ways to learn what is going on with him. Patiently and quietly talk your child "through" any changes he encounters, dramatic or routine.
3. Your child is exposed to you but a fraction of the time, in contrast with his exposure to ideas, people and events *outside* the family. Try to make each of your interactive moments

with him joyful, meaningful, rewarding, and loving experiences. Parents who are in touch with themselves and their loving attitudes and inclinations are more effective parents.

4. Parenting is a balancing act between the stresses of making a living and providing for your child and the "growing pains" of your child's attitudes, emotions, and experiences. Your child needs you every day of his life.

5. *ALL* children who make the decision to kill somebody else are alienated and isolated from important adults in their lives.

6. As a parent, you must serve a "multi-purpose function" for your child. Accept it and commit yourself to operating on a variety of levels for your child. Physical exercise with your child (jogging, biking, tennis, softball, bowling, and so forth), as a family project, is a marvelous way to keep the lines of communication going and get in shape at the same time.

## Your Child's Feelings

7. Emotion often drives behavior. Always consult your child's feelings; how he feels will tell you how he is coping. Children's emotions are dynamic and their flare-ups illuminate their feelings. Addressing the emotional needs of your child should be a constant priority. Teenagers appreciate and admire parents who patiently stick it out with them , no matter what they "throw" at their parents, in terms of behavior. Parents who never give up, no matter the emotional "weathers" of their teen, are highly-praised (yes, teens often praise their folks to others), highly-valued and -loved parents.

8. Children who are ignored, never listened to, and constantly abandoned in favor of their parents' "more important" pursuits, will often become hurt, depressed, enraged, frustrated, resentful, and obsessed about striking back.

9. How your child thinks and what he thinks about should be of vital interest to you.

10. Emotions are the hot irons of the soul. A furnace stoked with too many hot irons will become overheated. The point here is: take pains to *know* your child's emotional "furnace" and

lovingly guide her to safer, cooler, calmer attitudes. Realize that your child is a bundle of emergent energy and emotions. She is never too young to experience or understand the pain of illness, separation, and death. She may not always know *why* these phenomena occur, but she *always* knows her *feelings* are involved. The point is, you must also know that.

11. You *can* rear a happy, emotionally healthy child who will turn *to* you for help instead of *against* you, in anger, confusion, and frustration. Your home must be deliberately and carefully structured (or re-structured) as a *safe* place for your child. A child's suppressed feelings can burrow deep within him and explode later in acts of violence. Your positive parenting methods, practiced repeatedly, will show obvious results. As a parent, you need to know what is going on with your child *all* the time. React and respond to your child's fears and problems with love, support, comfort, and patience.

## Moral Education at Home

12. Instill principles of honesty and integrity in your child. Children appreciate knowing what the standard is and reaching it. Knowing right from wrong clears up their thinking. Help your child set clear and attainable objectives and thus have the satisfaction of controlling his future: that is what really produces genuine self-esteem. Children who lack the capacity for self-love and self-esteem can never realize their full possibilities. One of the most important gifts you can give your child is to teach him to be responsible ("response-able"); that is, *able to respond*. Consequences for not meeting the standard should always be applied in a non-emotional way.

13. Teach your child to seek and become aligned with a spiritual purpose. You may find that a church or house of worship can help you to do this in an organized, efficient, and consistent way. You are the ultimate model for your child, whether you know it or not: you were his first teacher. From you, it is important that he learns there are more good people than bad

people and more reasons to be happy and optimistic than sad and sullen.

14. Children lacking in moral intelligence do not have the capacity to make moral decisions. If no moral teaching has been instilled in them, there exists a void that will be constantly filled with anti-social thoughts and actions. There is a connection between a child's ignorance of, or disregard for, right and wrong moral behavior and his decision to kill another child.

15. Teach your child nonviolent communication strategies and peace-building skills. Teach your child that a gun or other weapon is never, ever an acceptable alternative to nonviolent interaction and positive communication.

## One View of Your Child: Wee Against the World

16. Boys who become a menace to the larger society do so because they feel menaced in their smaller society: inside their own home and family. As a society, the behavior of our boys gives us *one* picture of our collective selves. As parents, we must train our sons, early on, to verbalize their feelings. How we treat our sons is how they will treat others.

17. Check your son's "surroundings." Is he surrounded by friends, toys, TV shows and movies that encourage "macho," tough-rough-and-ready behavior? You *can* rear a caring, considerate, compassionate, and *feeling* son, strong in his own identity and secure in the love that has shaped him.

## Depression

18. Boys tend to express their depression in a variety of ways— all of which are driven by a hidden yet hot anger. Depressed boys seldom exhibit only one symptom; they usually show several symptoms. Boys who appear bored and drained of energy, seem reclusive, yet occasionally act rashly, are probably suffering from some form of depression, but watch for the non-traditional signs of depression I've listed, as well.

19. In our social culture, many boys grow up having to run through a gauntlet of shame. Depression is like a tight mask that covers all sorts of feelings and emotional currents and, at the same time, sparks new behaviors and puts on them a false face that is misleading and upsetting. Parents who persevere and gently and lovingly question their depressed son and remain "there" for him, have the greatest chance for helping him through depression. It is better for parents to seek professional support in working through their son's depression.

20. Angry boys tend to disengage from the group. Depression is often inverted anger, so look for depression's root causes. Anger is often depression's outward "picture." "Ice water veins" describes a young boy who is struggling with his depression yet appears to be stoic and even cold-blooded. Comforting and embracing him when he is in pain will not make him a "sissy." You're merely giving him humane, caring, nurturing and loving treatment. Leaving him hurt and in pain does not make him tougher—it's only cruel, inhumane treatment.

21. Look for outward signs of disruptive disorders in your male child's behavior.

22. Girls in early adolescence are forced to face overwhelming growth-changes that threaten their identities and sense of self. Adolescent girls victimized by their erupting and confusing ego and identity needs survive this difficult period when parents care, share, comfort, listen, and understand. See your children as yourself (in miniature). Don't use her as an *object* to garner selfish attention and flattery. Respect her as you wish to be respected. If it's flattery and attention you need, find these through other pursuits and endeavors.

23. Look for *non-behavioral* inner signs of emotional disorders in your female child.

### School and Your Child

24. Constantly reassure your child that he is beautiful and talented and that he has a very special place in your heart and a birthright position in the world even if he is not on the

athletic team, in the student orchestra, or in the drama production.

25. Intergroup understanding and respect are extremely important and necessary in our highly diverse country—we must choose between being either a country in peace or a country in pieces.

26. Be an active parent-participant in your child's school life. Find out what's going on and voice your opinions and concerns.

27. Schools are only as safe as the households they serve. Just one emotionally-wounded/alienated/lonely/depressed/angry/frustrated/self-hating ARMED child can turn a schoolyard into a graveyard.

28. Some of the resources that states expend in testing children for depression *after* they are incarcerated for committing a capital crime (murder and homicide) should be available to depressed school children *before* they commit such terrible acts. As a parent, you may wish to exert your efforts in "re-purposing" some of your school's budget so that monies are set aside to help depressed or otherwise emotionally-troubled children.

29. Children who kill at school or elsewhere have reasons—*always*. Although you may not have seen the warning signs, they were there. The *Ostrich Posture*: ignoring or failing to see the need to diagnose the real, deeper causes of social behavior dysfunction and, instead, superficially treating the anti-social behavior by suppressing it through medication or discipline until the behavior "detonates" and victimizes others. In this age of adolescent violence, teachers and parents should refer for counseling any student who rhapsodizes about violence in his writings.

30. As a parent, you need to do more than pick up the warning signs of dangerously aggressive behavior your child exhibits. You may need to prepare to work almost full time to get the "system"—schools, social and psychological service agencies, law enforcement—to work for, instead of against, you, as you race against time.

31. Just as a tuned-up auto performs better, your teenager's performance (behavior) changes can be adjusted and corrected by your knowing and applying "tune up" strategies.
32. Teach your child early on not to be a bully and how to steer clear of bullies. Teach your child to be assertive and not to address bullying with violent behavior but to walk away and get help from a teacher or other adult.
33. These symptoms may tell you that your child is being bullied: sudden loss of interest in school, a drop in grades, withdrawal, or signs of physical abuse. If your child is a victim of bullying at school, tell school officials immediately. Keep a record of names, dates, times, and circumstances of bullying incidents. Give a copy of this "incident report" to the school principal.
34. Be open in your communication with your child and encourage him to share with you information about the events at school. Most parents, even dysfunctional ones, desperately want to do everything they can to make their children happy.

### HANDS ARE FOR . . .
James E. Shaw, Ph.D.


Hands are for BANDING and linking together
Hands are for SHARING to make life better

Hands are for HOLDING, to show we are friends
Hands are for HIGH FIVES even if we don't win

Hands are for embracing people and pets
And HUGGING to make life its very best

James E. Shaw


Hands held together are a story that tells
Of friendships not found on grocery shelves

Hands comes in all shapes, sizes, and colors
They even TALK and work special wonders

Hands can fly through the sky
Hands can scratch bugs out of the eye

Hands are for waving to folks near and far
And for scraping peanut butter from the jar

Hands show pleasure, of course
Hands can measure the height of a horse

Hands are for pizza and everything gooey
Hands are for squeezing cookie dough, oh, so chewy

Hands are for LOVING and SHARING
The whole world gets better when hands are CARING

(Winner of the *"Editor's Choice"* award from the National
Library of Poetry Contest)

# Bibliography

American Social Health Association (1999). *Becoming an Askable Parent: How to Talk With Your Child About Sexuality*. Research Triangle Park, NC: ASHA

Bennett, William, & DiIulio, John, & Walters, John (1996). *Body Count: Moral Poverty...And How to Win America's War Against Crime and Drugs*. New York: Simon & Schuster

Berle, Milton (1989). *Milton Berle's Private Joke File*. New York: Crown

Children's Defense Fund (1999). *The Adolescent and Young Adult Fact Book*. New York: The Children's Defense Fund.

De Becker, Gavin (1999). *Protecting the Gift: Keeping Children and Teenagers Safe (And Parents Sane)*. New York: The Dial Press

Faber, Adele & Mazlish, Elaine (1980). *How to Talk So Kids Will Listen & Listen So Kids Will Talk*. New York: Avon Books

Garbarino, James (1999). *Lost Boys: Why Our Sons Turn Violent and How We Can Save Them*. New York: The Free Press

233

Goleman, Daniel (1997). *Emotional Intelligence.* New York: Bantam Books

Gottman, John, & DeClaire, Joan (1997). *Raising an Emotionally Intelligent Child.* New York: Fireside Books

Grossman, David, & Kloske, G. (1996). *On Killing: The Psychological Cost of Learning to Kill in War and Society.* New York: Little Brown & Co.

Kindlon, Dan, & Thompson, Michael (1999). *Raising Cain: Protecting the Emotional Life of Boys.* New York: Ballantine Books

National Education Association (1999). *Safe Schools.* Washington, D.C.: National Education Association

National Institute of Mental Health (1999). *Plain Talk About . . . Dealing With the Angry Child.* Washington, D.C.: National Institute of Mental Health

O'Donnell, Michael (1999). *Survey: 4,000 Teens.* Rochester Hills, MI: International Family Life Institute

Pieper, William, & Heineman-Pieper, Martha (1999). *Smart Love.* Boston: The Harvard Common Press

Pipher, Mary (1994). *Reviving Ophelia.* New York: Ballantine Books

Pollack, William (1998), *Real Boys.* New York: Henry Holt and Company

Prothrow-Stith, Deborah, & Weissman, Michaele (1993). *Deadly Consequences: How Violence is Destroying Our Teenage Population and a Plan to Begin Solving the Problem.* New York: Harperperennial Library